8th May 1945 — VE Day — was Anneliese Wiemer's twenty-second birthday. Although she did not know it then, it marked the end of her flight to the West, and the start of a new life in England.

These illustrated memoirs, based on a diary kept during the Third Reich and letters rediscovered many decades later, depict the momentous changes occurring in Europe against a backcloth of everyday farm life in East Prussia (now the north-western corner of Russia, sandwiched between Lithuania and Poland).

The political developments of the 1930s (including the Hitler Youth, 'Kristallnacht', political education, labour service, war service, and interrogation) are all the more poignant for being told from the viewpoint of a romantic young girl. In lighter moments she also describes student life in Vienna and Prague, and her friendship with Belgian and Soviet prisoners of war. Finally, however, the approach of the Red Army forces her to abandon her home and flee, encountering en route a cross-section of society ranging from a 'lady of the manor', worried about her family silver, to some concentration camp inmates.

Anneli Jones

REFLECTIONS IN AN OVAL MIRROR

Memories of East Prussia
1923 – 1945

Reflections in an Oval Mirror
Memories of East Prussia
1923 – 1945

by Anneli Jones
edited by Adam Jones

Text & photographs © Anneli Jones, 2008
Maps & diagrams © Gisela Wittner, 1989

Published by Ōzaru Books, an imprint of BJ Translations Ltd
Street Acre, Shuart Lane, St Nicholas-at-Wade,
BIRCHINGTON, CT7 0NG, U.K.
www.ozaru.net

First edition published 8 May 2008, reprinted 1 November 2011
Printed by Lightning Source
ISBN: 978-0-9559219-0-2

CONTENTS

ILLUSTRATIONS

MAPS AND DIAGRAMS

FOREWORD

"You should write all this down" was a phrase I kept hearing after the war. I heard it so frequently, I can no longer remember how frequently and from whom I heard it.

But I do remember that I felt extremely inhibited concerning writing anything when I felt that I had no language to write in: the more my English improved, the less capable I felt to write in *any* language.

I had written articles for the News Guardian, a British army newspaper, and there were fewer and fewer corrections from the assistant editor. Later I also wrote the occasional article for The Observer news service and had my reports printed, mainly in Australian papers.

But I still did not believe that I could write.

Mr E.F. Schumacher, a German-born economist who had lived in the UK for many years and who had been invited by the Berlin Press Club to give a lecture at one of our functions, almost convinced me that it was not necessary to be totally absorbed in one language in order to write; that even he himself, though he had written many books and was giving many lectures, would still count in German up to 20 before he switched into English! So I made a few rather feeble attempts to write some of my experiences on paper.

Robert Stephens and his wife Taqui greatly encouraged me. Taqui herself wrote – and published – her childhood memories in a book called "In Aleppo Once" and thought that I should do the same.

But it was not until I felt the need to give some understanding of their roots to my own 5 children, and, moreover, when I discovered that my mother had kept all the letters I ever wrote to her (even though I had urged her to burn the lot) and began to read those, that I seriously began to write all I could recall from memory, from my old letters, from old photo albums and mostly from my own diary which my grandmother had given to me… and which had a little lock with a key to stop other people discovering my secrets!

So here it is, mainly as a source of information for my children, but also for myself to indulge in nostalgia. I hope that other people will enjoy meeting my East Prussian family, my animals, my forests.

Die Krähen schrei'n
Und ziehen schwirren Flugs zur Stadt:
Bald wird es schnei'n –
Wohl dem, der jetzt noch Heimat hat!

Whirring to the town,
Crows screech as they roam:
Soon snow will fall down –
Happy are those with a home!

Nietzsche

Dates of Birth of Relatives Mentioned in the Text

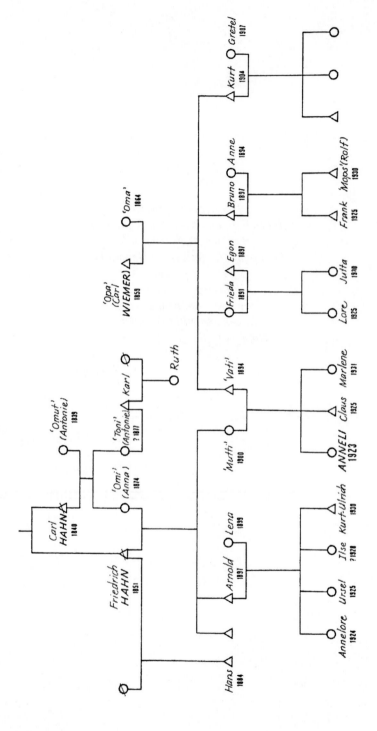

Ø ◭ — died before 1923

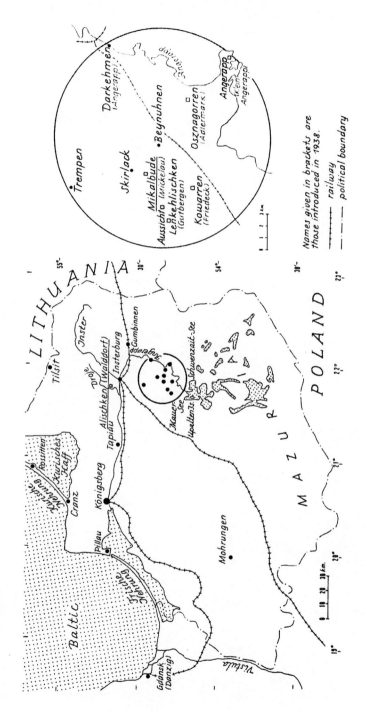

East Prussia

Names given in brackets are
those introduced in 1938.

—+—+— railway
—·—·— political boundary

5

YEARS OF CAREFREE INNOCENCE: 1923–1933

My first clear memory is of the full-length mirror in my mother's dressing room. From its ornate oval frame a girl aged two-and-a-half stared back at me in admiration, not for my thin blond curls or my large blue eyes, nor even for the lovely bright tartan dress with a big white collar and red bow, shop-bought by my grandmother Omi, who believed in the quality brand *Bleyle* rather than the home-grown-spun-woven-knitted garments my father[*] insisted on. What I admired in my reflection was the tray I held ever so carefully with a glass of very hot lemon juice on it. Thereby my newly-acquired status as the big child in the family was confirmed.

Behind me, in my parents' bedroom, stood a basket on a stand with a canopy of white curtains sprayed by tiny forget-me-nots which reached all the way down to the floor. The same soft material lined the inside of the cot where my baby brother slept or grunted. Since he had come home from hospital, Mutti, my mother[†], had often made me stand on tip-toe to look at him, and I quite liked doing so. I had probably seen him at Christmas, but I have only a very vague memory of rustling starched nurses, of a large, polished, chestnut-coloured table next to Mutti's bed and a Christmas tree seen through the door of the adjoining room.

Mutti had shown me a photo of when I was as little as my brother Claus now was and a starched nurse lived in the house to look after me. After her I had a nanny whom I called 'Blum-Blum' because of the floral patterns on all her clothes. I still remembered her dresses, but had forgotten her face. I no longer needed a nursemaid: I was a big girl now.

The steam from the lemon juice began to blur the better half of my reflection. Below were crinkled stockings and lace-up boots; these had no part in my moment of bliss, but were a constant and constantly irritating image for many winters to come, winters of itchy legs, of vain attempts to pull the stockings tight and, worse, of growing frustration with manoeuvring laces through eyelets, worst of all when the metal bits at the ends of the laces had come off. Why, oh why, I wondered angrily, did girls' fashion dictate eyelets when boys' boots had simple hooks? And why indeed should my dear mother and Omi, my grandmother, conform to fashion for children?

But footwear apart, my Omi was wonderful, and I was very proud to serve her with hot lemon juice. She had overcome her usual reluctance to leave her own farm only because she wanted to help Mutti with the baby; and now Omi found herself confined to the spare bed in the dressing room with 'flu. Small as I was, I could feel her depression and homesickness, because I thought of her Alischken as paradise.

Alischken, where my mother had grown up, was smaller than our farm in Mikalbude. It was attached to a village of the same name. Omi lived there with her mother, my great-grandmother Omut and, until his wife inherited a farm of her own, my uncle Arnold and his family. When he left, Omi ran the farm with the

---

[*] I usually called my father 'Väti' using the East Prussian dialect
[†] I addressed her using the Russian word 'Mamushka' much of the time

aid of an 'Inspector', a farmer's son who, as a paid overseer on someone else's farm, underwent several years of practical training.

She was only in her forties when I was born, though she always looked very, very old to me. Both Omut and Omi were widows and wore their former husbands' wedding rings soldered to their own. Both wore mourning clothes, black dresses, black aprons, black stockings, black shoes. Only on Sundays and at birthday parties was the black relieved by white lace *fichus* pinned to the neckline, Omut's being the more frilly and elaborately embroidered of the two, while Omi wore a more decorative gold brooch to hold hers in place.

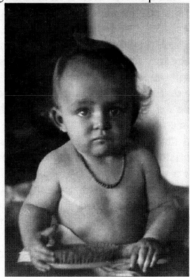

A few months old

Mutti always thought this showed my "Eve-like" nature. I myself felt it was closer to the Hamlet misquote "Vanity, thy name is woman!"

My great-grandfather had died from a sudden heart attack in 1885 after a bankruptcy shock. At that time Omi was not yet eleven and her sister Antonie only eight years old. The latter, whom I knew as Aunt Toni and greatly loved, later married the widower Karl Krumm, who had a daughter called Ruth, whom I hated. Not that I was particularly fond of Uncle Karl either; he was an intelligent civil servant at the Ministry of Finance in Gumbinnen and an ardent Social Democrat, which made him unpopular with our adult relations; his equally ardent belief that children must be seen but not heard made the younger generation fearful of him. I resented the way he allowed his stupid yellow canary to jabber incessantly while prohibiting children's comments on adult conversation.

Omi herself had also married a widower, whose son, our pleasant Uncle Hans, lived on a farm called Gendrinnen with his wife and two boys. A framed photograph of my grandfather hung above Omi's bed, below an embroidered picture of Christ, which had the words "ECCE HOMO" written in gold thread. I felt sad never to have seen the gorgeous bushy beard and the kind, smiling eyes of Mutti's father in real life. He had died in 1918, a few weeks before the War ended, quite

8

suddenly and unexpectedly. The postman had brought news in the morning that their elder son Kurt had been killed in what turned out to have been the last battle of that war. My grandfather rode to the fields as usual, talked to his workmen and fell dead from his horse.

Omut, Mutti, Anneli and Omi

Sometimes, when we took flowers to his grave on the hill above the farm, I wondered what he would have said to me, and how warm and deep his voice might have sounded.

Omi stayed on in Alischken with her two remaining children and her mother Omut. Neither woman would ever have contemplated re-marriage, though Omi had many attractive suitors even in my lifetime. Both women were full of fun, music, poetry and stories, but they were of very different character. Omi played a limited range of semi-educational games of the 'I Spy' kind. She loved to recite long ballads in song or words, which she had taught herself after her formal education had come to an abrupt end through her father's bankruptcy. I enjoyed learning poetry by heart, which pleased my grandmother very much. Goethe's *Erlkönig* and Schiller's *Glocke*, long as these were, became part of my repertoire even before I started school. "Learning is the most beautiful thing on earth," Omi impressed upon me: "I missed my chance to become a teacher, but maybe you will be one, if you work hard." She also taught me the three phrases which she had learnt in her only two English lessons: "Good morning, Mr Teacher", "Take the slate pencil" and "Go to the blackboard".

At night Omi read fairy tales from a book or told in her own words those Bible stories that she loved best. After we had said prayers she would kiss me good-night and sing a song before she closed the door: "Do You Know the Land Where the Lemons Blossom?" (with words by Goethe), or the folksong "Do You Know How Many Stars There are in Heaven?" More than any other, it is Schubert's 'Lindenbaum' that will always remind me of her, perhaps because there was a lime tree with a big stem in front of her house, among the chestnut trees.

Omut too recited verses, but I could never learn them by heart, because she did not manage to repeat them word for word. I soon realised that she was making them up as she went along. They were always funny and sometimes quite naughty. The stories she told were of her own life, a Cinderella story in reverse. They began with glittering balls and princelings who had turned from royal Prussian to imperial German in Omut's youth. There were chandeliers and crinolines "in silks so soft that they billowed like balloons when they turned to the music". There were also landowners who wore penguin suits instead of braided uniforms. It was one of the latter who became Omut's husband, but not without strong opposition from her family on account of his not being a Salzburger, or, as Omut expressed it, "not one of those mountain tribes who gathered annually in Gumbinnen to celebrate the fact that their ancestors could yodel".

The Prussian king Frederick William the First had offered asylum and land for colonization to Protestants who were persecuted and expelled from the Salzburg region in the early 18th Century. 20,000 of them settled beyond the Vistula. Huguenots had come there before, after the revocation of the Edict of Nantes in 1685; other persecuted groups followed – Mennonites, Scottish Presbyterians and others, not to speak of adventurers and religious crusaders who had been summoned to colonize the land by a Polish archbishop in the Middle Ages. Many had died from the plague before the Salzburger immigration. Most upheld their ethnic identities with fierce, and frequently absurd, pride. Almost 200 years after the arrival of their forefathers authentic Salzburgers were recognised by the '-er' endings of their surnames. When my grandmother Antonie Schneller married a Hahn, she greatly offended the sense of propriety of her social circle; but after a few years she was forgiven. By the time my father's cousin married a man with the very un-German nasal-sounding name of Jean Guerlin, the family hardly whimpered.

The Hahns had many children and were comfortably well off, but not rich, Omut told me. Dancing was and always had been her great passion, and a large ballroom with three French windows leading to a wide garden terrace had been her most cherished dream. The dream came true when the Prussian government planned the construction of a railway to East Prussia and my great-grandfather was given the contract for the supply of gravel. On the strength of this promise he borrowed a large sum of money and built the dream mansion. But alas, when it was discovered that he was a Liberal, the government withdrew the contract.

Omut referred to these people in terms I could well understand, calling government officials "the townies", which was the worst term of abuse known to me. They were more contemptible still for coming from Berlin, a place of stone and cement in a country called the Reich, somewhere beyond a dangerous place called the Polish Corridor. I felt hot with indignation when Omut came to that part of her story. How could they do such a thing to a Liberal of all people! Omut had explained that the term 'Liberal' described a person who wanted all human beings to have equal chances to live happy lives.

When the money-lender called in the debts immediately, my great-grandfather suffered his heart attack, and after his death Omut and all her children were taken into care by various relatives, who treated some of them hardly better than cheap young servants. But Omut went on dancing, the lady in black among all the colourful silks. She was often the caller for a dance called Contre, and had to say "*Messieurs à gauche, les dames à droite.*" I loved to repeat those strange words, but *'carnet de bal'* with all it implied was quite my favourite. My uncles and aunts thought it was "absolutely delightful" when I mouthed the strange sounds, and that gave Omut an idea for a wonderful game. She, Cousins Annelore and Ursel, Aunt Toni and I sat on the purple plush sofa and purple plush rococo chairs in the Middle Room, round a table with a purple plush table-cloth and a smaller lace cloth on top of that. We had to hold imaginary coffee cups very daintily, with our little finger outstretched, like Omi's friend Frau Becker. And then we had to engage in small talk, repeatedly using two names which Omut had invented: "This is very good coffee, Frau Itzenplitz"; "You must give me the recipe for this cake, Frau Kribbelbibbelbimski"; and "The asparagus is growing well, Frau Itzenplitz" – a particularly adult remark, because children disliked asparagus; and so on, until our tongues would not go round Kribbelbibbelbimski any longer.

Omut's Contre calls

A Birthday Party

I well remember Omut's ninetieth birthday party. It was the 8th of November 1929, a day before Uncle Arnold's birthday, and the two anniversaries were celebrated together. As always in winter, the swing hung indoors, suspended from hooks between dining room and Middle Room; and Omut thoroughly enjoyed swinging with us on her lap, making a nuisance of herself in the eyes of the maids, who had to dodge us with their plates and cutlery when they were preparing the table for the midday meal.

Our lunch was like all birthday lunches in Alischken, starting with almond soup, a kind of thin white sauce, sweet, and flavoured with chopped almonds which had been simmered in the milk and decorated with 'icebergs', an uncooked meringue mix floating on top and sometimes sprinkled with cinnamon. I cannot remember exactly how this was on Omut's birthday, as the same soup was served on similar occasions for many years. This was followed by roast turkey stuffed

11

with a concoction of liver, herbs and breadcrumbs and accompanied by potatoes, carrots-and-peas, pickled gherkins and pickled pears. The dessert was a lemon mousse, but with cream instead of whites of egg, as the latter had been used for the icebergs. Omi's bottled strawberries and more whipped cream were served with the lemon mousse. Adults drank wine; children had home-made red currant juice.

By the time the guests from the neighbourhood arrived for coffee it was already dusk and the electric lights had been switched on. We children liked to go round the house with a maid to close the dark green shutters of the ground floor windows. They were released from clamps in the wall – left shutter first, then the right one, which had an extra board that overlapped for a tight fit. We pressed firmly until we heard the click and knew that they could now only be opened by releasing a spring on the indoor side of the window frame. Carriages stopped at the front door, coats and hats were hung in the hall, windowsills began to overflow with azaleas and cyclamen, and the sewing table in the drawing room was piled with bottles of eau-de-cologne and boxes of chocolates.

Only Annelore and I managed to count all the different cakes on the dining table. Omi was always proudest of her yeast cakes and puff pastries, but I preferred the squashy, creamy ones, and Omut liked poppy seed gateaux best, the kind that were made of shortbread crust filled with a thick layer of ground poppy seed, chopped almonds, sugar, and of course eggs to set the mixture during baking – as I found out when I grew up.

Later, at dinner, we children had champagne like the grown-ups, so that we too could clink our glasses with Omut's and wish her all the best. It was never done to take a sip before bowing to at least one other person at the table, saying *"Zum Wohle!"* This rule applied on all occasions, not just birthdays. The Inspector continually filled up glasses all through the meal.

As a ninetieth birthday was a special occasion, we all had a copy of an anniversary magazine, about eight or ten pages long – such pamphlets were often produced to mark celebrations such as weddings, baptisms, confirmations, the end of a school term, or later the end of a period of war service. Karl Krumm's frequent contributions were very witty, but perhaps too sarcastic and overly long. Uncle Arnold gave an impromptu speech at the start of the meal, after which he and others read aloud verses from the paper, some serious, but most of them funny, with allusions to events of the past 90 years. Several were headed: "To be sung to the tune of…" – well-known songs in which everybody could join in, such as the Lorelei, "Eine Seefahrt, die ist lustig", "Horch, was kommt von draußen rein", or "Muß i' denn".

The roast at dinner was venison, accompanied by bottled pears which were cut in half and stuffed with cranberries. The traditional vegetable to go with game was hot red cabbage, stewed for a long time with apples, onions and a little vinegar flavoured with caraway seeds. Home-made ice-cream of the *Fürst Pückler* type[*] was the last course before pumpernickel and cheese. Mocha was served in the Middle Room for the ladies and in the drawing room for the men, who drank stronger liqueurs with this than their wives.

---

[*] containing chunks of fruit or nuts

Omut with four of her seven great-grandchildren

Apart from the joys of the swing, my most vivid memory of Omut's last birthday was the way she danced and swirled to the tunes of Strauss waltzes.

A few months later she died. Uncle Arnold said that she died dancing. The pastor could not make an impact with the last rites, as she kept telling him to go "*à gauche*" and let the ladies go "*à droite*". Omi insisted that she had heard her whisper more pious sentences at the very end, but I hoped that Uncle Arnold was right.

Mutti would have liked me to see Omut in her coffin, but we arrived too late, when the lid had already been nailed down. I could not believe that she was really in that small wooden box which the men carried so easily uphill to the cemetery. They had left space for Omi's future grave between my grandfather's and the hole they had dug for Omut.

When all the people had coffee and cakes in the dining room, I went to the Middle Room by myself. There was a golden horse on a low ledge that held the big rococo mirror. It was such a heavy horse that even Omut had not managed to lift it without help from the Inspector or a maid. But this time I managed to pull it down by myself and drag it along to Omut's chair. Then I sat on the horse as I had done so many times and pretended that Omut was telling me how her *carnet-de-bal* was so full of names that the orchestra had to add extra dances.

Alischken

In addition to Mikalbude, the farmstead to which my parents had moved upon their marriage, my early life centred around two places: Alischken, where my mother was born, and Angerapp, my father's home.

I was the eldest among the steadily growing number of cousins and must have been to all their christenings, but I remember only Ilse's and Kurt-Ulrich's. That was because of the geese. They marched in single file right into the arbour of Linden trees, just when the pastor was sprinkling water on Ilse's little head. I

13

thought it sweet, because there were fluffy goslings waddling between the legs of the guests, but Omi said it had disturbed the pastor. Consequently the geese were kept shut in at Kurt-Ulrich's christening – but not shut up! We could hear the shrieks of the imprisoned birds all the way from the poultry shed to the big arbour on the lawn. Annelore felt so sorry for the birds that she added to the disturbance by loud sobs, and Aunt Lena had to balance the new baby on one arm while comforting her eldest daughter with the other.

Alischken estate

"If you shut up the geese for my wedding, I will never get married," Annelore threatened her grandmother later.

"You could always choose to marry in a church," Omi smiled.

The very thought of it! To have the most important ceremony of one's life imprisoned in a building? I thought the *pakrausch* would be even better than arbours and began to test its feasibility with my cousins. One of the attractions of the place was its strange name, unlike any other we knew. It had been called the *pakrausch* for as long as I could remember. Some people thought it might have been a corruption of a Lithuanian or Polish name, but failed to find even remotely similar words in either language.

This etymological mystery was by no means the only appeal of the *pakrausch*, which was the steep and wild right bank of the River Droje where it looped round the Alischken Park. In winter it was a dangerous place, inaccessible from the garden, because the footbridge had either been dismantled and stored in time or swept away by torrents of fast-rising waters.

In summer the Droje Bend was a shallow river-bed with calm, transparent pools, narrow creeks and bubbling streamlets winding their passage between and across stones under which crayfish hid. Uncle Arnold caught these creatures with his bare hands while we anxiously side-stepped their claws when we waded to the other side with bare feet.

Then we scrambled upwards in the undergrowth of ferns, hazel bushes, wild raspberries, some brambles, pausing for breath when we could hold on to a bigger tree, or when we came to a patch of ground that we had levelled with our spades. We built houses by wattling bushes into walls and holding them fast with string. The prettiest pieces of broken glass or china from the farm rubbish dump served as dishes for raspberries or mud pies. We were honeymoon couples, or mothers and fathers, or Kribbelbibbelbimskis, or just plain us. Sometimes we were all the people necessary for a wedding, and this included Anna, who was a few years older than myself. She lived "up top", as we referred to the farm cottages, because they were built on a hill above the farm, along a road on the other side of the Droje. Her father was the foreman; her mother often helped Omi in the kitchen at such occasions as slaughter-time, including goose-plucking, or with baking and washing up at birthdays.

The important thing about Anna was that she knew what pastors had to do at weddings. Draped in a dark curtain from one of the boxes in Omi's attic, she led the procession, which began, like all weddings and christenings, from the terrace along the broad gravel path between the lawns. I always remember Alischken for the heavy scent of phlox and stocks and Sweet Williams. Omi grew flowers mainly for their perfume in a herbaceous border that was like a long, wide field separating the lawns from the vegetable area.

Alischken house

Ursel and Ilse followed our 'pastor', wearing ordinary summer dresses and with crowns of daisy-chains round their heads. They carried little baskets which we normally used for Easter egg hunts and scattered flower petals from them. Annelore wore a nightgown and a lace curtain pinned to her dark hair, and I wore my navy track-suit with my plaits hidden under an old top hat.

We did not turn towards the arbour on the left, but walked straight on, into the formal park. The trees stood in neat rows like pillars of a church, much vaster than our village church, which I knew from harvest festivals. Where a shaft of sunlight dropped through the fir roof, the trunks reflected an auburn glow. We processed in stately magnificence until we reached the footbridge, where the bridesmaids asked the pastor to stop. They wanted to throw petals upstream and see them race under the planks. We all shouted encouragement to our favourite colours and groaned when they sank. When the baskets were empty, we reluctantly moved into the *pakrausch* to have the ceremony over and done with.

Annelore and I wore metal finger-rings taken from the mouths of pink chewing-gum snakes which we bought at two for ten pfennigs every time Omi paid us

15

for currant picking. The grocery-shop-inn was at the other end of Alischken village, just opposite the mill. We wore these rings on our left hand, the engagement hand, with the sparkling glass stones hidden inside our palm. When we had both said "Yes" to whatever our pastor was mumbling, Anna changed the rings to our right hand and pronounced us man and wife.

When the farm dinner-bell rang from the turret, we always dropped promptly whatever we were playing and ran to the house, so that Omi and the Inspector would not have to wait: we loved them both and everybody loved punctuality. Torn clothes, bloody knees or tangled hair did not matter, but we had to wash our hands before a meal. It was easy in Alischken, because Omi had a tap with running water and the maids did not have to carry jugs to washstands. We waited behind our chairs until Omi said *"Mahlzeit"*; we all replied with the same word, meaning literally "mealtime", which seemed an absurd thing to say until I discovered that it was an abbreviation for "Blessed be our mealtime".

We often had lunch in the hall, because it was next to the kitchen and, with the front door wide open to the drive and the midday sun, it was a bright, warm room. During the meal Herr Puffhahn, the Inspector, told funny stories; afterwards he reported to Omi on farm matters while we waited for our meringues. These were the by-product of *koggel-moggel*, egg-yolks beaten up with sugar, which Omi brought to our beds every morning. Mutti called it "sugar-egg", the German equivalent of the original, much jollier-sounding Polish name. The meringues were kept in tall cylindrical tins in the cupboard under the stairs, next to the entrance to the domestic cellar.

A larger cellar for root vegetables lay in the middle of the farmyard and was covered above ground by a long, rounded roof with thick layers of turf. This was 'home' for games of catch, which we called Wild Knave and Angels'. Ilse, who always wanted to know the precise meaning of words, asked what a knave was. I told her it was an old word for a boy.

"Then why don't we just call it Boy?" she enquired.

"Because it does not go with angels." The explanation satisfied her.

Caesar, the St Bernard, was tied to a chain under a chestnut tree of the drive, so that he could not trip us up when we played wild games in the yard. Omi sat close to him on a bench, knitting woollen petticoats on a circular needle. Sometimes Aunt Toni was also there, likewise knitting petticoats.

We greeted visits from Mutti's cousin Annchen with mixed feelings. She was very clever at building sandcastles with elaborate serpentine roads leading to the top; and up there, on a sand tower, was a nest of moss, in which stood a stork. This bird was made from the blossom of Bleeding Heart by detaching one half carefully, so that the stamens could be pulled out to look like legs while the pistil was inserted into the slender tip of the heart to produce the effect of a beak. Similarly she manipulated delphinium blossom to look like coaches driving along the road. But all this imaginative skill was totally offset by the way she insisted on talking to us in baby language, as no other adult in the family or among the farm workers ever spoke even to real babies.

"We all know that cows say 'moo', so why does she have to call them moo-cows?" I complained to Mutti.

"You really are unfair," my mother defended her kind cousin. "Annchen is a trained nursery teacher, in charge of a nursery school at Count von Finkenstein's estate, as well as being governess to his own children. You don't imagine they would keep someone who was not excellent?"

"Heaven help those kiddilies, and most of all the countessalas," I mocked.

The kindness of this aunt was most insufferable at Omi's birthday in February, when sandcastles could not be built and Annchen's strength was not up to igloos. We suspected that she even worried about our health if we played a slow game outdoors in freezing temperatures. She tried to tempt us to watch quietly from the drawing-room window how "sweet little reindeerlies" (they looked like perfectly grown-up reindeer to us) came from the snow-covered forest to feed on the hay that had been put out for them.

Fortunately there was much else to be enjoyed during that birthday week in Alischken, and in any case Aunt Annchen never stayed for longer than a day.

Angerapp

My father's parents lived only 20 km. from our farm, and we could visit them without having to spend the night at their house. We called them Opa and Oma. They were worthy people from a long, pure line of Salzburgers who had slowly, conscientiously, thriftily and undramatically worked their way up from the status of country pastors and peasants-in-liege to that of feudal lords, or at least of tenant farmers on feudal estates. Opa was the first in his immediate family to rent an independent large farm of his own; he provided an even larger estate for his eldest son, my father.

Several of my father's brothers had died before I was born, some in the War, one by drowning in the River Angerapp, which flowed through the park of their estate of the same name. His death was probably the reason for all those fences, walls, locked gates and general prohibitions which prevented us from exploring what might have been a place as exciting as Alischken.

Aunt Frieda was the only girl in the family and a very good pianist. Boys were not allowed to learn what my grandfather Opa termed 'superfluous nonsense', however much my father pleaded for the chance. Many years later, when Opa died, we discovered that he himself had indulged in private Latin lessons and kept his glowing tutor's reports in a suitcase under his bed, together with billions of Marks in paper money from the time of the great German inflation.

Aunt Frieda was a member of the *Luisenbund*, a women's organization named after the Prussian queen who had charmed Napoleon on a raft in the River Memel. The queen's favourite flower was said to have been the cornflower, and I recall bright blue dresses walking among white statues of the park in Beynuhnen where the Luisenbund had its annual meetings. I can remember one such occasion, because it was the only time I have ever seen people faint. I did not understand that this was not abnormal on very hot days – and summer temperatures could rise to above 40 degrees Celsius just as they sank to 40 degrees below zero in winter.

Aunt Frieda married a dashing young insurance agent called Egon Kowalewski, who was himself a very good musician. They had two daughters – Lore, whom I disliked, and Jutta, a good friend of my little sister Marlene.

17

Väti's brother Bruno was an engineer in Königsberg. He and his wife Anne had two sons – Frank, half-way between myself and Claus in age, and Rolf, nicknamed Mops, a year older than Marlene. They were often sent to our farm for holidays in the country.

Claus and I were always suspicious at the arrival of town cousins and ran to hide on top of a straw stack. Since this was standard procedure, the cousins knew the place and fought us verbally from below while we pelted them with bullets made of twisted strands of straw. Usually Mops succeeded long before his brother in making friends with us.

In Angerapp, 1925

Opa & Oma with Adolf, Bruno and Frieda and their spouses & one child each

Uncle Kurt was the youngest of Väti's surviving brothers, a lively, cheerful Jack-of-all-trades. In terms of worldly success he was the black sheep of the family. But he married a beautiful girl with a lovely soft voice, an innkeeper's daughter. Lore and I were their bridesmaids, scattering flower petals all the way from the inn to the church. We felt so important that it was not too difficult to keep awake until midnight, when the dancing took a new turn. The groom had to dance away his buttonhole carnation, blindfold, dancing on his own in the midst of bachelor solo dancers until the music stopped suddenly and he – still blindfold – grabbed the man nearest to him in order to put the flower into his buttonhole. After that it was the bride's turn to dance her veil away in the same manner, "because the veil is a symbol of virginity, about to become redundant", my father explained.

The chosen couple was expected to marry before another year had passed – though they seldom lived up to this expectation. However, they danced while Un-

18

cle Kurt and my new aunt Gretel watched for a few moments. Then the newly-weds were suddenly surrounded by their guests and chased with pretended threats and laughter until they ran upstairs and were locked in a bedroom. We all waited near the door until we heard screams of disgust and giggles. "Now their feet have touched the pig's stomach filled with water," Väti said, "and that means bed-time for you." In later years we often copied the pig's stomach idea to frighten our visitors when they spent the night at Mikalbude.

As a child I was not impressed by the stiff upper lips with which my Angerapp grandparents hid personal grief; nor did I admire their material success. I saw nothing but boring frugality, morality, strictures concerning our manners, prohibitions, locked doors.

Angerapp, the 'meadow of Rapp', had only two things which I liked: one was a glass spoon, around which sticky, fresh honey glistened like liquid amber; the other was Ida, the chambermaid. She had seen the 500-year-old ghost of the robber knight von Rapp, whose ancient, crumbling castle now housed the mangle room and various stores. The doors were locked to keep children out of danger from structurally unsound walls. But Ida once took me to the mangle room and pointed to the trap door through which the knight was said to have dispatched his unsuspecting guests à la Sweeney Todd, bed and all. Ida also promised to let me see the ghost if I ever spent the night in Angerapp. It was a tempting offer, but she probably knew that I would be able to resist such a temptation. Even after birthday parties which lasted well into the early hours of the morning we still drove home.

The parties themselves were probably good fun for adults. The food was not fancy, but very good and possibly expensive. The central item of the birthday coffee was a *Baumkuchen*, a tall cake in the shape of a tree trunk. It had to be specially ordered from a town baker, because normal ovens were not suited to the complicated process of adding layer after layer of a rum-flavoured Madeira-type cake mix around a centre, so that the tree grew in rings. There was one ring for every year of the celebrant's life, which created a considerable diameter for Oma, although eventually she allowed some cheating. The final layer had knobs, knots and a caramel glaze. Like the adults, I admired the appearance of the cross-sections (the cake was always cut in horizontal slices); but I much preferred the taste of cream, fresh fruit and nuts in other cakes.

One part of Angerapp seemed totally out of character with my grandparents' normal pragmatism. My grandfather had built a summer-house, only a few yards from the long, glass-roofed veranda of the house proper. The garden building was completely round with benches all along the walls and an enormous round table in the centre. Oma herself had crocheted and embroidered bench cushions and a tablecloth, and Opa was always arranging plants in the flower beds facing the summer house so that they created a visual display. Perhaps all this was genuinely aesthetic; but since I had made up my mind that Opa and Oma were stodgy, I could not see the beauty.

Our Farm: Mikalbude

Alischken – Angerapp – Mikalbude, our own farm: these and hundreds like them, varying in size from a thousand to ten thousand acres, were the microcosms of the only world we knew; other worlds, towns, the Reich, the moon and the stars were dim ideas on the periphery of life.

Our farm stood almost in the centre of our land. The nearest village lay 2 kilometres away, invisible behind the trees. The farmhouse and yard were built on a low hill with orchards on the northern slope down to the farm cottages. The carpenter's workshop, the mangle room and the forge were on the southern slope. In front of the forge a horse walked in circles round a well, forcing water uphill to one pump in the yard and another in our kitchen.

View from Mikalbude to neighbouring Aussicht

We loved to join the washerwomen in the mangle room – though with hind-sight it seems to have been a rather masochistic love. There was a sturdy wooden box, about the size of a bed, but loaded with heavy stones instead of eiderdowns. It ran on rollers, one at each end, on a table of about the same size as the box. When the box was tipped at one end, the woman at the other end could fold a pile of sheets under her roller. We liked to add our weight to the tipped-down side, so that the heavy box would not suddenly fall on the hands that were arranging the washing. But most of all we liked to be rolled along after both ends had been loaded, to and fro, bumpety, bumpety, on hard stones.

The granary at the western end and the big barn on the other bounded the southern side of the farm yard proper. In summer tar dropped from the long, hot roof of the barn in lumps which solidified on the ground, but could be moulded into artistic shapes before they had grown cold.

Opposite the barn a partially whitewashed stone building housed poultry, horses and the dairy herd. Oxen, heifers, sheep and farm labourers' cows occupied a red brick building along the eastern boundary; along the western side of the yard stood our house.

A wooden veranda built on stilts of stone was our main entrance. At the other end the buildings extended beyond the kitchen entrance at a lower height and half the width: here lay the bakehouse, the swill kitchen, the wood-and-peat shed and the pigsties. Behind the entire length of these buildings were the terraced lawns, herbaceous borders, lilac hedges and arbours of our main garden, extending into vegetable grounds to the level of the forge.

Mikalbude barn at threshing time

On the lowest lawn stood a frame with spiralled iron hooks for our swing, which could be used with a seat, a bar, or leather-covered rings and be adapted to whatever height we liked. But these elaborate contraptions, which could even be moved to a door frame of our dining room in winter, were dull in comparison to the ordinary swings made of stout rope tied to the highest beam in the barn, where the boldest could perform trapeze acts and land softly on straw.

Our playgrounds did not require toys bought in shops. Although I could not understand why so many well-meaning relatives presented me with beautiful dolls of the Käte Kruse make, after reading a book called '*Puppe Wunderhold*' I did at least take care never to ill-treat a doll, just in case she might be able to write about me like the doll in the story. But dolls' prams and dolls' bathtubs were of much more use for playing with live St Bernard puppies.

View from my window over the main farmyard at Mikalbude

Fields and forests offered endless scope for exercise and imagination. The forester's cottage, deep inside the woods, was the witch's house from Hänsel and Gretel, we told our town cousins. Not until they began to cry in fear did we take them into the house to meet Lisa, Hubert and their friendly mother, who gave us black bread and honey instead of gingerbread.

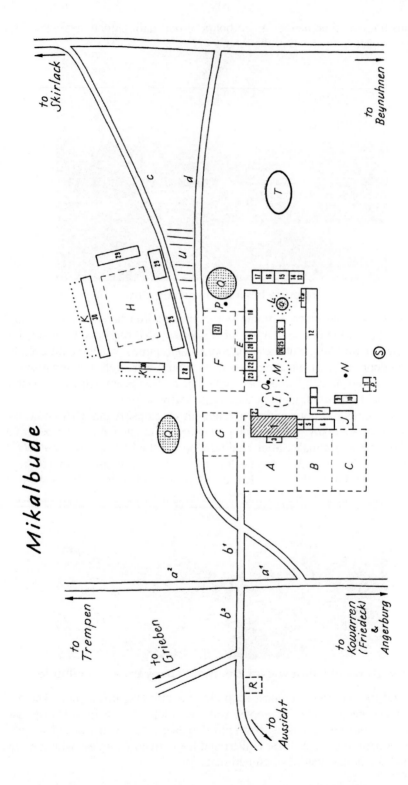

Mikalbude

to Skirlack
to Beynuhnen
to Trempen
to Grieben
to Aussicht
to Kowarren
(Friedeck)
&
Angerburg

Note: not drawn to scale

ROADS

a   main road from Trempen to Angerburg via Kowarren. In the early 1930s this road was partially surfaced with asphalt and hence referred to as the *chaussée*, but in kindness to horses half of the width remained a plain earth track.

b   birch avenue leading from the farm to the farm cemetery; at the place where it crossed the *chaussée* a bus shelter was built for me

c   unsurfaced road to Skirlack (the village school, the post office, a shop-cum-inn and the dairy)

d   unsurfaced road to Beynuhnen, the main railway station and the von Fahrenheid estate; it crossed the main road to Darkehmen, but the postal bus to Darkehmen went via Kowarren along the *chaussée*

BUILDINGS

1   main farm house

2   courtyard veranda

3   garden veranda

4   entrance to the room where pigs' swill was cooked; from here stairs on the right led up to the kitchen, other stairs went straight on down to the cellar, and a door on the left led to the bakehouse and later the prisoners' dining room.

5   wood and peat shed; living quarters for the farm cats

6   pigsty (sows and piglets)

7   pigsty (boar, weaners and porkers)

8   granary

9   carpenter's workshop, also containing the mangle

10 store-room for farm implements, wheels and vehicles requiring repair

11 forge with adjoining bedroom

12 barn with separate dog-kennel at western end

12a chaff shed with chaff cutter

13 ox-shed

14 large beef cattle (same as ox-shed, partitioned)

15 young beef cattle

16 sheep-shed

17 labourers' dairy cows' shed (same as sheep-shed, partitioned)

18 main dairy shed; bulls in partitioned stands

19 shed for work-horses (four foursomes)

20 shed for two foursomes and partitioned boxes for mares with foals

21 coach horses and riding horses

22 yearlings and two-year-olds

23 poultry house; later a separate poultry house was built and young horses were stabled here

24 young calves

25 coach house

26 stand for farm vehicles (open except for west and east walls); on the floor above 24, 25 and 26 stood another granary

27 shed for storing blocks of ice covered in peat (for refrigeration in summer)

28 oldest farm cottages; later they served as cottages for a displaced Lithuanian family and as prisoners' camps

29 farm cottages

30 pigsties, poultry houses and latrines for farm cottages

OUTDOOR FEATURES

A   upper lawns with herbaceous borders, roses etc.

B   lower lawn with swings etc., also used to dry washing

C   garden for vegetables and cut flowers

D   small garden for early vegetables under glass (protected by a solid wooden fence)

E   vegetables, soft fruit, bee-hives

F   main orchard

G   rambling orchard and wilderness of raspberries

H   labourers' gardens (vegetables and flowers)

I   small, oval-shaped garden with four cypresses, a central bed for annuals and some rose-beds

J   pigs' run

K   labourers' pigs' runs

L   fenced-in garden and pond for goslings and ducklings

M   enclosure for exercising and breaking in horses

N   tread-mill for pumping water up to the farmyard and kitchen pumps

O   farmyard pump

P   farm cottages' pump

Q   ponds

R   farm cemetery

S   gravel pit

T   peat bog

U   dug-outs in which root vegetables were protected from frost by mounds of peat, straw and earth

Half our land consisted of pasture for about two hundred cattle and fifty horses. The breeding bulls were kept tied in their shed and only taken for daily exercise on a long pole attached to a ring in their nose. The other animals were harmless, albeit slightly disconcerting in their habit of following us when we crossed their field. It made no impression on them if we shouted "Boo!" Only when we turned round to face them did they stand still. I am sure there is something in the idea of a cow being stupid, because horses and sheep did not behave in such a manner. They did react to human voices, though perhaps not always in the way we hoped.

Our major crop was rye; in summer one saw endless expanses, moving like the sea, with clouds of pollen drifting like spray. Along the edges grew cornflowers and poppies. We also grew oats, barley, flax, potatoes, beet and various fodder crops, but only a few acres of wheat, which was a luxury because it depended on early snow providing a thick, protective covering before the hard frosts came. Summer wheat, sown in spring, had low, uneconomic yields.

Sheep, Pigs and their Keepers

Sheep helped with the pruning of seedlings in autumn, which was good enough for all cereals except wheat. The flock of sheep was a luxury in economic terms, but one that my father would not forego. Their wool provided clothing which was probably more expensive to produce than that sold in town shops, but sacred in the name of self-sufficiency and a romantic rural atmosphere of humming spinning-wheels and rattling shuttles of weaving looms. Their meat was not popular, but we did eat the odd Irish stew when a coup-de-grâce had to be administered to an old ewe. The workers' own sheep lived within our flock, but had different coloured ribbons round their necks for identification at shearing time.

Our shepherd tended the flock on the poorer pastures or on land that lay fallow for a season. We called the man Scheschel; his real name had too many consonants to be pronounced. He had wandered into Mikalbude from nowhere, carrying only a small bundle of clothes and a Bible. Nobody knew where he came from and no one pestered him for information: a man's past was his own affair. When he died, he was buried on the estate cemetery on the hill at the end of the birch avenue. His tombstone bore his unfamiliar real name, copied carefully from his papers.

Scheschel might have been seventy, eighty or even ninety years old when he came to us. His age was impossible to tell from his crinkled face, half hidden under a bushy beard and a moustache. His bright blue eyes always looked young and friendly. I loved sitting next to him on a grass verge, watching as he whittled willow or hazelnut branches to make baskets, or cutting ornaments and whistles from other wood. He rarely talked, but occasionally asked if I would like to hear a poem. He laughed when I joined in the recitation of those I had learnt from Omi, but when he recited poems in French or Polish, he looked at me seriously, as if to discover what I was thinking. He should have known that I was not thinking at all, just listening.

The only time I ever saw Scheschel's room was when Frau Schwarz told us that he appeared to be ill. He lived in the attic of the Schwarz family's cottage, and Mutti wanted to take him some hot soup. I was allowed to hold the bowl to his mouth, because he was too weak to hold it himself. His bed was a straw mattress on the floor; the Bible lay next to it. In one corner stood a small iron stove and a few utensils and clothes were hanging on pegs on the wall.

I would have liked to see him again next day, when he was dead, but Mutti told me that my first sight of a dead person must be that of someone I loved. I did love Scheschel, but apparently that was not the real love my mother meant.

Old Schwarz was a man whom I hated to love. He repelled me like my cousins' stink bombs and attracted me like a magnet. He was not as old as Scheschel and had no beard, only a long Bismarck-moustache with lots of yellowy-brownish smudges of snuff clinging to it. Once he tempted Claus and the Königsberg cousins to try the stuff, and they were sick. I was never tempted to try.

Schwarz looked after about sixty pigs, whom he loved and knew individually. My father insisted on essential breeding information being clearly entered on boards above every sow's stall, which was an arduous task for old Schwarz; and as soon as I had learnt to write, I offered to do the job for him. He knew all the details in his head and made a great fuss of anniversaries and other important occasions in a pig's life.

Birthdays were marked by a bunch of flowers suspended in a jar from a nail above the stall of the pig concerned. On the eve of the day which was the ultimate goal in a pig's life, a special stall was not only cleaned thoroughly – even freshly whitewashed at times – and lined with fresh straw, but profusely decorated with flowers. Schwarz chose the best pig for slaughter and comforted the ones that were not chosen by rubbing their backs and talking to them about the next occasion. Then he set about scrubbing the appointed sow himself. This he did with excessive vigour, and as the animal squealed, I screamed: "You would not like it if someone did that to you!" I knew of the trouble the Schwarz family had with the old man's objections to hygiene. He lived and slept in the same clothes as he wore for mucking out and had to be bribed before he allowed his daughter-in-law to wash them. I believe that he actually sometimes rinsed his hands in water, though he would try to wipe them on his trousers whenever he could get away with it. So I hoped that my words would sting – and I hoped in vain.

"When my time comes, the son's wife will do it to me," he replied quite calmly, and I suddenly felt sad at the thought of old Schwarz harnessed in a pure white shroud.

He had looked after the pigs of Mikalbude since he left school at the age of fourteen and at some date in the 1930s, when I was already at town school and Hitler was in charge of us all, old Schwarz was to be honoured for fifty years' service to German farming. For this he was to present himself at Hindenburg's mausoleum near Tannenberg. It was an order from above, and an order from his daughter-in-law forced the old man into a suit and leather shoes for the occasion. My father took him to the ceremony, which was held for a large number of similarly deserving people, all processing into the monument and all wearing shoes except for our man, who carried his in his hands and trudged wearily on socks. I could have hugged him for that.

The Coachman

Otto, the coachman, was the other man with whom I could spend time, because he was not on the move in the fields all day.

The carpenter did not count, because he did not like children in the vicinity of hammers, saws and axes. The blacksmith did not count either; for though he allowed me to work the bellows, there was such a din in the forge that it was no use trying to talk to the man. But Otto had plenty of time for me. He worked erratic hours: often my parents wanted to be driven to neighbours late at night; on other occasions, when neighbours visited us, Otto entertained their coachmen in the kitchen. They could have eaten in the room next to it, but rarely did. Coachmen had a wonderful way of sitting on the firewood box, legs wide apart and firmly on the floor, a mug of beer in one hand, and in the other holding – with enviable skill – a slice of bread the full width of a loaf, about as long as my forearm. Claus and I called such slices the "master bread", and it was one of our greatest ambitions in life to be able to eat like coachmen.

On most days Otto merely fed and groomed the carriage- and riding-horses, gave them fresh straw for bedding and polished my father's riding boots. He was happy when I sat on the big wooden box where the week's ration of oats was kept, watching and chatting.

Learning to be coachmen

Otto's daughter Anna, who was almost my age, never came to talk to him. She did not even bear her father's name, because when Otto's wife died in childbirth, her parents blamed the husband for making an ailing woman pregnant and insisted on bringing up the baby as their own. Otto saw her every day, yet for years the little girl did not know that he was her father. I knew; but Mutti told me to keep it a secret and to be specially kind to Otto.

Below

"Below" was the common name we used for the area that contained the cottages, their gardens and separate buildings for pigs, poultry and lavatories. There the grannies looked after babies when mothers worked in the fields. A warm, drowsy smell of drying wood filled the air where children played with dolls between cone-shaped stacks and chickens scratched holes for dust-baths in the sandy soil. The women sat on benches by their doors, knitting, darning, peeling potatoes. Early in the morning they had stuck a finger into the behind of each of their hens and released the egg-less ones and the cocks through the door. Inside the chicken house were nests with hinged flaps which fell shut when a bird entered and had to be re-opened at the appropriate time. Every now and then a cluck-cluck-cluck-shriek, cluck-cluck-cluck-shriek announced that this time had come; so a granny got up and went to the shed; moments later a hen would come fluttering out and silence would be restored. The eggs were left in the nests until all the birds had done their job of laying and were wandering round the cottages, in search of worms and other morsels.

Geese and ducks did not hang round houses or yards. Early every morning the big pond drew them like a magnet in straight lines from our yard and from the cottages, noisy ganders leading their broods, not-so-noisy drakes leading theirs. All day they stayed by the pond, swimming, ducking, eating grass on the verges, or just sitting under the shade of the big trees on the northern edge of the pond. Uninterested in roosting bars and unaware of the danger from night predators, they fiercely resisted attempts to herd them back.

Two of our maids had to goad them from the water every evening. They used a long string, coiled round short rods at either end, which they released while flapping the line on the water behind the geese, thus driving them to the other end. It was difficult to guide the string round trees which stood close by the water on the steep side of the pond; quite often the birds exploited those brief moments of a near-motionless string and retreated to where they had come from, so that the entire process had to start all over again. Even after they had been successfully manoeuvred on to dry land, it was a battle of skill and wits between women and children on the one hand and birds on the other, until the right ganders had been cornered and were chased home. The hissing and snapping of ganders could be disconcerting, but most country children are quite brave with regard to animals. The females always rushed to follow their ganders, and so did the goslings, stumbling as they ran; often they were caught and carried by children.

Not many goslings stayed with their own kind when they were very small, because geese rarely had the broody patience of good mothers. They often deserted their nests of eggs shortly before they were due to hatch, and this lack of instinct for imminent birth amazed me. It was usually easy to find a broody hen to accept surrogate motherhood. But on one occasion there simply was no such hen available, and so Frau Schalonka herself withdrew to bed with her deserted clutch. In the warmth provided by her body and by the goose-feather bedding the goslings were born; they were quickly trained to follow their biological mother.

I did not understand why other people on the farm thought this funny and joked about it.

27

"Wouldn't you have done the same?" I asked my mother.

"Certainly not," she laughed. And that, I thought, really *was* funny.

Frau Schalonka was the most expansively motherly of all farm matriarchs. In my view her greatness was most strikingly revealed in the way she cured anybody's hiccups immediately by inventing the kind of shock that would make us gasp. The second remarkable manifestation of motherly care and know-how was in her potato pancakes. They were so full of fat that the sugar stuck to them in thick layers, all of this being "good to clear you out", she said when Mutti found the very thought enough to make her sick. Mutti never actually ate them, of course; she just shuddered when Claus and I set off for the Schalonka cottage, because we could smell the cooking.

All cottages had a very small entrance hall, a pantry and two fairly large rooms, but no one could make such cosy use of their home as the Schalonkas. The pantry was the bedroom for Frau Schalonka's unmarried sister Auguste and her daughter Frieda, later our maid. The bedroom had a huge four-poster bed for the parents, a single bed for their son Fritz, a wardrobe, a chest-of-drawers, some chairs. The other room was totally dominated and almost entirely taken up by a huge weaving loom, dwarfing the kitchen range along one wall and the table next to it.

Around that table we sat, ate, played cards or, in winter, listened to Auguste telling us sad or frightening stories and singing many melodramatic songs. She had a thin, high-pitched voice which broadened into a trembling approximation of vibrato for the most melancholy passages: "On a Polish pond a corpse was floating, the most beautiful corpse in Poland; one hand carried a piece of paper, on which was written: 'I have kissed once and done penance'." Auguste's eyes filled with tears, but she took pains to assure us that the Cossack who had raped her would one day come back.

"What is rape?" I asked Mutti when I was about five years old. My poor mother blushed, stammered and said that Väti could explain.

But when my father said: "Like a stallion jumping a mare before she is ready" – which made good sense to me – Mutti was even more embarrassed. She never liked the way we were given access to all aspects of farming. "Children should remain children for as long as possible," was one of her favourite sayings. And Väti would reply that coming to terms with nature began at birth.

Farm life was our epitome of all nature. Dr Hassenstein, our vet, explained to me what he was doing when he gelded stallions, bulls or boars. It was always obvious to me that it was necessary for the survival of the species to keep the number of males within set limits. Once I had wondered why the same did not apply to humans, and my father explained that war kept a certain check on too great an increase in the male population. In any case, he added, human males kept a sense of proportion and did not dominate their females as in the animal world.

Cockerels were never castrated, and the idea of capons was offensive to the palates of farm people. To the end of her life my mother – and indeed most Germans – could not accept that a fowl of a year or more in age was good for anything but soup. So the cockerels were slaughtered while they were young and crisp. Old Schwarz chopped their heads off with an axe and assured me that they were completely dead immediately, even though some strange nervous system caused headless fowls to run frantically in circles before they dropped and were ready for bleeding, gutting and plucking.

All this happened by the wood-chopping block near our house; my parents were unable to hide such spectacles from me, much as they might have liked to. Nor could I avoid the newly-slaughtered pig hanging in the entrance room between kitchen stairs and bakehouse. It was suspended from a hook to facilitate the speedy drainage of its blood, which was later used for blood-sausage.

But I never witnessed an animal being shot, even though Väti liked to take me along for deer stalking. Evening after evening we went to meadows near the edge of the forest, sitting quietly downwind from the place where the beautiful creatures were expected, armed only with binoculars. Sometimes, when a gnat bit me and I said "Oh!" ever so softly, the deer would stand rigid and look in our direction; they might then leap back into the forest, or decide that they had made a mistake and start grazing again. It seemed to me that the hinds were more nervous than the bucks, and I often wished I could tell them that it was only one particular buck that my father had singled out for the kill. I also wished that my father would take me along on that final night and that I could say "Oh!" more loudly to warn the prey, but I was not given the chance and accepted venison as a natural part of our diet.

The same applied to roast hare and partridge, though these were shot without discrimination with regard to their sex, mainly to keep the numbers down, but also, I think, as an excuse for a big party with pea soup from a large copper pan, and with schnapps.

My parents held strong convictions that one should never introduce fear into children's lives and warned us in rational terms not to get into the peat bog. But life without fear was not much fun. Auguste told us the horrifying story of a rider who lost his way on a dark and stormy night and was sucked into the quagmire, horse and all, before he understood what was happening to him. "And there, deep down, he still stands today, well preserved in the peat. But don't tell your parents that you know it," Auguste ended her story. We loved it, but every time I watched men cutting peat, I had a strange flutter in my stomach region, half expecting them to come up with a chopped-off head on their long blades.

School

A few weeks before my sixth birthday I was allowed to go to school by special concession from the schoolmaster in the nearest village. Normally children could go to school only after their sixth birthday, and since the starting date was the beginning of the school year, at Easter, it frequently meant that children were nearly seven years old by the time they entered school. Mutti would have been quite content with that; in fact she would not have minded at all if formal education had only begun in our teens. If it had to be earlier, it could have been a governess, as in the houses of all our relations and neighbours at the time, except for those who lived in a town. But as always, Väti asked for advice, listened to it and then did precisely what he had decided to do anyhow. Herr Ziegler, the headmaster of the village school, felt flattered, and I was very pleased.

29

We all had an exciting shopping day in our district town of Darkehmen. Claus stared at me in admiration when I tried out the leather satchel for my back and the small leather sandwich box which hung from a long narrow strap round my neck, bouncing on my stomach. The most interesting items inside the satchel were purchased by us at the bookshop. There was the *Fibel,* the first reading book for any child, be it at school, or with a governess at home. I loved the colourful illustrations which matched each letter in alphabetical order, and I tried to learn most of the basic words when Mutti was not looking. Then there was the slate with a small hole in its wooden frame, through which Mutti put a string with a small sponge at one end, a home-sewn drying pad at the other. The wooden pencil-box had two layers, held in place by the lid that slid over the top compartment, thus joining the long grooves to a small space for the rubber – which in fact we did not require for another year. I had one ordinary pencil in the box; all the others were slate pencils. Crayons were bought in a metal container of their own.

Väti was carrying a parcel that was nearly as long as I was. I pretended not to know what it was and to be curious, while he pretended that I was not pretending. Of course, we were all familiar with the cone-shaped bag which every child carried on the first day of school – a cone made of cardboard covered with shiny paper and decorated with shiny pictures; it was lined with tissue paper, which was drawn together at the top by a cord. The content of the bags varied from home-made sweets and lollypops from the village inn to more expensive chocolates and 'Russian bread' – crisp, letter-shaped biscuits.

Our shopping spree ended with a meal in Hotel Reimers Hof, where we stabled our horses. Mutti, Claus and I had Frankfurters and rolls (neither existed in the countryside), and Väti had tripe with a pile of marjoram, a dish that could have been made at home but was never as tasty as in the hotel (at least, that was his comment). Otto chose beer and ham in the coachmen's room.

Our school had two classrooms at one end of the building. Next to them was a cloakroom, from which stairs led up to the assistant's flat; and the headmaster's rooms lay at the other end of the house. The latrines were situated across the yard, next to the headmaster's sheds and stables.

Our playgrounds were the deep sand of the road that led past the school and down to the village of Skirlack, or the large field behind the outbuildings. The latter had parallel bars, single high bars, swings, beams and other gymnastics apparatus on the flat top of the hill and plenty of grass slope all the way to the post office, or rather to the smallholding where someone's grandfather had taken on the postman's job. How the boys could play football on such a field was beyond my comprehension, as was the game itself, so it did not really matter. Instead of tossing for positions, the two team leaders said "az, paz, tri," and immediately produced their hand in a fist (meaning a stone), a flat palm (meaning paper) or outstretched middle and index fingers (meaning scissors); scissors cut paper, paper wrapped up the stone, the stone smashed scissors, but the process had to be repeated three times to make sure there was no cheating.

Every morning began with the entrance of the teacher, who said loudly: "Good morning, children," whereupon we all jumped up and shouted back in unison:

"Good morning, Mr Teacher." Then lessons began, up to playtime at 10 o'clock, then lessons again till midday, just under four full working hours. The school day ended with the same song every day: "When school is over, we merrily run home to Mother, who is overjoyed to see us and ladles out the soup."

Mutti was indeed always overjoyed at my return; and since she suffered from the delusion that I had been subjected to great strain, she always cooked my favourite meals.

After lunch I had to do homework every day, six days a week. For the first few weeks this was intensely boring, and it brought my mother close to tears to watch me struggle for hours with neat lines of one single letter per day on one side of the slate: capital A's fitted into the two top spaces of three-space formations; on the other side the figure 1 fitted into little squares, ever so many squares for ever so many neat 1's.

If I had not finished by '*Vesper*'-time (4 o'clock), Mutti offered to do the rest of the letters or numbers for me, so that I could run along with the other children. We all took sandwiches and a hot drink in ordinary bottles, kept warm by various layers of cloth wrapped round them. The labourers' children carried baskets for their own families; I carried mine for Claus, the *Elève* (a trainee farmer who was paid less than the Inspector and did not stay as long) and sometimes for a seasonal labourer. The afternoon break was always a special occasion in the fields, most particularly so during the corn harvest, when we could lean against corn stooks and chat, sing and watch how to make rings and bracelets from straw.

After our twenty-sixth piece of homework in Sütterlin script – the letter 'z' – we started on 'a' again in Latin script. Fortunately the German language is so phonetic that I could teach myself words simply by uttering the letters, and I learnt to read long before we reached the Latin 'z'.

Lessons at school more than compensated for the trauma of homework. I enjoyed every minute of every subject, most of all the gardening lessons, which horrified Mutti. It was just as she had expected: pupils provided cheap labour for the schoolmaster's smallholding. But I did not think that we were merely that. We did learn about plants and weeds. We had to draw them, identify their names, discover the functions of their different parts, stamens and pistils as well as the parts we knew already. I loved weeding among the sweet-scented lilies-of-the-valley, a very large patch of them, because they were Frau Ziegler's favourite flowers.

We also climbed the short, rickety ladder to the chicken coop and collected eggs. In the headmaster's kitchen we floated them in water to sort out the fertile from the infertile, the former for a broody hen, the latter for eating.

Boys learnt about pigs and cattle, including mucking-out skills, but not milking till some years later, when their hands had grown stronger.

Our mathematics progressed much faster than reading and writing. I could calculate averages, percentages, areas and volumes before I was ten years old, and this pleased my father.

Besides, we learnt a wealth of poetry, songs and stories. The assistant teacher's love of Greece infected me for life. We were lucky to have the von Fahrenheid estate of Beynuhnen so near, so that we could be taken there on rack wagons with benches for a day's excursion. We wandered round the park and were taken on a conducted tour of the house. The manor was built in the classical style, with a long hall supported by Dorian pillars along one side. In the park was a Dorian temple, amongst others, and everywhere we saw statues of marble or plaster, well spaced between pillars and shrubs. It was all so beautiful that it made me want to cry.

We learnt long passages from the Iliad in translation, and occasionally the teacher recited a few lines in Greek. How I wished I could learn that language! But the teacher said he did not know it well enough to instruct me and that I would have the chance to learn it all later, at another school.

The very thought of another school appalled me. No, not even for the sake of ancient Greek would anyone be allowed to dislodge me from rural life! I would stay, just as the other people stayed on our farm, going to school for eight years, then doing healthy outdoor work all the time. I would continue to have holidays with Omi and the odd week or two on the Baltic coast in Cranz, but go no further. So whence the sudden secret longing for Greece and Siberia, which I hated to acknowledge even to myself?

Communists

Much as my parents wanted me to acquire knowledge, they were worried about my love of reading. Children's brains were to them – or at least to Mutti – like delicate plants that had to be nurtured gently and slowly and should never be overtaxed. Most of all they feared for my eyes from the strain of excessive reading.

Of course, they never actually forbade reading, nor anything else for that matter. Only Oma, Opa and Uncle Egon laid down rules which were for us a challenge, to circumvent them or to be downright disobedient. My parents understood that very well. They expressed their wishes in terms of "It would be lovely if…" and their fears as "It would be really sad if…" or, more strongly in my father's words, "It would be absolutely senseless and stupid…" This made it hard to disappoint their expectations. I felt awfully guilty whenever I indulged in what Mutti called "the vulgarity of newspapers". Why then, I wondered, did they have the newspapers? Surely not just for the purpose of cutting them into quarter sheets for the latrine? I took those sheets from the hook and put them in order on the wide, wooden seat. Most of all I wanted to read the serialised novels, but I must have gathered some cryptic political information at the same time, unless it was my parents themselves who had told me about Communists. Or might I have overheard adult conversation? No matter where the ideas came from, they grew into our most exciting farm game ever. Someone had to shout: "The Communists are coming!" and to start running. Others followed, laughing at first because it was only a game; but gradually, as we began to run faster, our own footsteps began to sound like those of someone following, and we no longer dared to look back. We frightened ourselves into a frenzy, running round the back of the barn – "The Communists are coming, the Communists are coming!" – across the gate of a field, running behind the ox-shed, the heifer-shed, the sheep-sty, nearly incapable of braking when we came to the big pond, sharply turning into the farmyard, desperately looking for an adult who might save us; and still the Communists were coming… until at last there was a man or a woman into whose arms we could fly for comfort.

And then, when we had regained our breath, someone asked: "Shall we start again?" It was wonderful to have something to be really frightened of. The adults said we were silly, but when we asked them to explain what Communists really were, they could not find a way of putting it into simple terms, except for saying that they were Reds. It was a perfect explanation. Red as red devils, horns, hooves and all. What a marvellous game!

New Friendships

My friendships had shifted from adults to children. Otto rarely drove us to school after my first week or so, and we children had much time to talk on the long walk to Skirlack – in summer, when we picked wild strawberries on the way back, or in winter, when we towed our toboggans along for playtime. But we all enjoyed the treat when Otto did come along, sitting on a one-horse sledge and allowing us to sling our toboggans in a long chain behind.

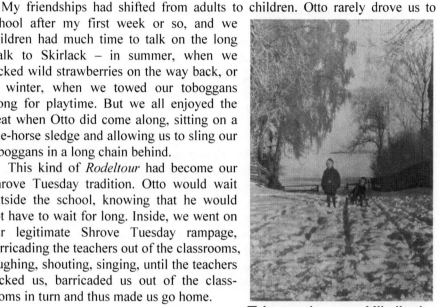

This kind of *Rodeltour* had become our Shrove Tuesday tradition. Otto would wait outside the school, knowing that he would not have to wait for long. Inside, we went on our legitimate Shrove Tuesday rampage, barricading the teachers out of the classrooms, laughing, shouting, singing, until the teachers tricked us, barricaded us out of the class-rooms in turn and thus made us go home.

Tobogganing near Mikalbude

This meant wild zigzag rides along the lanes, horse at a canter, us falling off, rolling in the snow, screaming "Wait, wait!" We would run after Otto, stumbling until we were out of breath and Otto really stopped, briefly, giving us a moment to set our toboggans upright again; and so on, and so on, until the horse was worn out and we were ready for the traditional Shrove Tuesday feasts of doughnuts and fritters in our house and in all the cottages. Most times Mutti had to bake these treats on her own, because the maids exploited their rights of Shrove Tuesday rebellion; but sometimes they actually wanted to help, both with the cooking and the eating.

School fêtes in summer were almost as good as our winter fun. I shall never forget the excitement of lining up in twos on the sandy road in front of our class-rooms, looking downhill towards the village proper, waiting, listening, until at last we heard the band of the local fire brigade. They were marching up towards us, the music growing louder and louder, until, just in front of us, they turned briskly and began to march down again without a break. We promptly took the cue and followed in equally orderly fashion, proudly nodding to parents and friends who lined the road from the bottom of the hill to the large garden of the village inn. There were stalls to buy fancy things, races to win more fancy things, folk dances to win applause.

My very best Skirlack school friend was not from Mikalbude. Hanne was the daughter of a small village farmer. She shared my mediocre ability in ball games and my infatuation with poetry. We did everything together at playtime, joining the games of others or simply sitting on the grass, whispering secrets. I was pleased when Hanne invited me to her birthday party and came home full of admiration for Hanne's mother's cooking.

"She made green jellies, really bright green!" I told Mutti, completely unaware of how this might frighten her.

"Bright green? What on earth could she have used? It must have been artificial. There is no woodruff about in November, and it isn't bright, anyhow."

Väti reassured her that there might be a perfectly natural explanation: she could have kept woodruff in an ice box, or something like that. But Mutti was by no means satisfied and scrutinized my face and body for days to find symptoms of illness.

I had actually felt just a little uncomfortable with Hanne's mother myself for reasons I could not quite define. She treated me with a certain deference which I had not encountered before. But this did not diminish my love for Hanne. I swore to myself that I would never have a different friend, whatever my parents hoped when they decided to send me to a town school.

I kept asking myself: Why me? Why only me and not all the other farm children? Frau Schalonka said that it was because *der gnädige Herr*, as she referred to my father, had more money than other men. I did not believe her. The only people I ever saw walking about with large sums of money in their wages' envelopes were our labourers on Saturday evenings. And yet, I could not believe that Frau Schalonka would lie.

YEARS OF SHOCK AND DOUBT: 1933–1939

"If I had been Eve, I would have taken the apple even before the snake tempted me", I told Claus angrily as we walked upstairs on the night of May Day 1933. It was a kind of new-life resolution that had come to me when I sensed that our parents' guests were waiting for us to leave in order that they might talk.

They had come for the traditional May Day punch of woodruff and champagne, just as they always did on the first of May. Carriages had driven up, one after another, with Frieda waiting on the veranda steps to take the guests' coats. The men kissed my mother's hand and gave her flowers. All of us shook hands, Claus with a deep bow, myself with curtsies bobbing along the line as if on a spring. Herr Lau pulled my plaits and joked about school – which was no joking matter for me at this particular stage – and Miss Mia chatted to Claus about horses. Väti poured the green punch into glasses while Frieda offered herring salad, cheese straws and various cold dishes. She was showing off the black dress and starched white apron which she wore on such occasions, and was much enjoying herself among the important people while the scullery maids giggled with the coachmen in the kitchen.

Yet in all this reassuring normality something was different this year. I strained my ears to catch remarks that might illuminate the events of the day: "I did not see your floats in Darkehmen…" – "I was busy, I had already made other plans…" – "Was that wise?" – "When all is said and done, this is the only alternative to Communism…" But though I played for time before doing my round of good-night curtsies, I gleaned no real information.

Hanne had told me of May Day processions years ago, but Väti then called them "rowdy socialist affairs at which decent people have no place". Now, suddenly, they seemed to have become respectable; May Day had been elevated to a public holiday this year, the Day of National Work, which in itself was a bit puzzling, since no one was supposed to work on that day.

"It is not *for* work, but *in honour of* work," Väti explained. I knew the word 'honour' from cheap newspaper novels in connection with gallant officers or shotgun weddings; so it required some adjustment to relate it to work and the lovely, gaudy floats which apparently represented it. They were beautifully decorated with fir branches, some early spring flowers like snow drops and hepatica, and others made of coloured tissue paper, such as we normally made only in November to decorate the moss between the double windows.

Väti had taken Claus and me to watch the procession. We stood not far from the town hall, at the corner where the pageant moved up the Gudwaller Straße, floats, bands, flags, ever so many flags. I knew the black-and-white Prussian flags and the black-white-red ones, which my father called 'imperial' or 'Hindenburg' flags, and which had always lined the Kowarren war cemetery for November ceremonies.

Then I saw a mass of red flags and seized my father's hand, urging him to run. "Communists!" I whispered.

Väti did not even laugh. "Look closer, Radish." He always called me a radish when my lack of observation irritated him. "They don't have hammers and sickles." As if I should have known that Communist flags had that particular design!

Those marching towards us had white circles with black hooked crosses in the centre, and the men carrying them had miniature flags of the same design around their arms. They were greeted with noisy shouts from the spectators, and I began to imagine that people were calling "*Heil Hitler!*" But I knew that could not be so, because my father showed no anger. It was less than a year since Claus had fought a boy called Arno for shouting these words at school. Väti had then been proud of his son, even though he had been the looser and Mutti had had to bathe his bruises and cuts.

And yet – for one brief moment I had the impression that Väti was about to greet those flags in the same way as other bystanders. He slowly raised his arm... and then put it round Claus and held him tight.

We did not follow the procession to the festivities in the sports ground, to which I had been looking forward, but were marched back across the square as soon as the last float had passed. Väti looked so cross that we did not dare to argue. He gave us no treats in Hotel Reimers Hof, but ordered Otto to harness up at once.

On the way back I dared to ask: "Were those Hitler people?"

"Yes, yes," Väti snapped, "but don't bother your little head about it. The main thing is that the Communists are finished."

There was so much more I would have liked to know...

Claus held my hand and looked up at me, waiting for more after my remark about Eve and the apple. Pity for my little brother and frustration with life in general nearly choked me.

"Would you prefer knowledge to paradise?" I cried. He hesitated before he replied in a tiny voice: "Not very much..." with the stress on 'very', which made his answer sound like half-agreement, the closest my good-natured brother ever came to disagreement.

"Then you just go on living in paradise; it's all phoney, anyhow. And I'm going to find things out."

"What things?" he wanted to know.

"If I knew that, I wouldn't have to find out, would I?"

We undressed in silence, the door adjoining our rooms open as always. We still felt a little frightened in our upstairs isolation, though we were proud of our independence and had lived in these new rooms for more than a year, ever since our baby sister had grown out of the basket cot. Little Marlene now slept in a proper bed, but next to our parents, since Oma and Opa had come to live at Mikalbude and needed downstairs rooms. The maids' room was also downstairs, near the kitchen. Cook, the Inspector and the *Elève* had their rooms upstairs, but at the other end of the house, beyond a number of store rooms, smoke room, incubator room, all around a dark, eerie place full of old furniture. A door at the end of our corridor separated us from that other part, which had a separate entrance by a stairway from a room near the kitchen. Occasionally we could hear the Inspector's gramophone, but we felt generally out of earshot from the rest of the house. So, just to be on the safe side, we had agreed that neither of us should ever fall asleep first.

We talked when we were in our beds, and when we were too tired to use our voices, we signalled our wakefulness by scratching on the eiderdown.

"Did you like today?" I called to my brother.

"Oh yes," he called back enthusiastically, "particularly the fire brigade."

I might have known that he would only remember the bands. He had conducted every one that marched past, waving his arms vigorously and stamping the rhythm with his feet.

"What game shall we play now if the Communists don't exist any longer?" I tried to resume the conversation.

"Wolves?" he yawned.

Hm, I thought, maybe. There had been no sightings of wolves since the year they shot the one hanging on the wall in Osznagorren – and that was in the year I was born; but one never knew... On the other hand, if the adults said that Hitler was the only alternative to Communists... Would we run if someone shouted "Hitler is coming"? I waited for Claus's answer, but he did not even scratch his eiderdown.

I decided to continue my thinking where it usually worked better than in bed, on my desk chair, by the window. I dragged my eiderdown along and wrapped it round me as I knelt on the chair, my elbows on the window-sill, my hands supporting my chin.

There was a smell of spring in the cool night air; the scent of freshly dug earth ascended from the rose bed, where the winter covering of straw and manure had only recently been removed. Pansies always showed their flowers as soon as the snow melted and were probably blooming all through the winter under a white blanket. I could see the yellow ones now in the light that fell from the drawing-room windows below on to the garden in the centre of the drive. The four arborvitae trees in the corners looked like hunched-up creatures keeping guard all through the seasons.

I could see the outlines of the farm buildings and hear the rattle of chains now and then. Beyond the bare branches of apple trees I noticed that the cottages were all dark. I too should sleep; there was nothing to worry about. All I needed to do was sit, breathe and enjoy paradise a little longer.

The coachmen were stamping across the yard, laughing. Then the sound of carriage wheels grinding round the drive, the flicker of coach lamps, a paraffin lamp appearing on the veranda below my window, the tinkling of coins on the plate for the maids. I heard good-byes and laughter, Herr Lau's high-pitched voice above the rest: "Come on, wifie!" As if she did not have a name, I thought angrily. But that mousy woman did not seem to mind.

Soon all was quiet and, one by one, the lights went off in the windows below. A stable lamp wound its way in and out of buildings round the yard; the Inspector was doing a last check on the animals before he too went to bed. I also decided to go to bed and to wait for the storks to wake me in the morning with their usual cheerful clatter of beaks.

They had come this year, as every year, punctually on the day which we called the storks' day, the 24th of March. On that day Mutti had sat on the yard veranda steps, darning stockings. Marlene had played in the sand near the stairs and I helped her to knock pies from metal moulds on to wooden boards. Claus had been amusing himself with pebbles in his catapult, but had this time actually decided to avoid the cellar windows which were his favourite targets. All of us squinted into the sky every now and then, all of us hoped to be the first person to see the birds arrive.

There they were at last: the unmistakable long lines of outstretched necks and long legs behind, bodies carried on wide wings, gliding in the sky, hardly ever flapping. Which of the two farm nests were they aiming for? We ran down to the old farm cottage and reached it just in time to see the birds alight on the old nest on top of an old wagon wheel that had been fixed on the roof for the storks years ago. There they stood proudly for a moment, stretching their necks high, then bending them across their backs to clatter their greetings — to each other? or to us? We clapped our hands in reply.

Playing near the veranda

When I was little, I used to stand on tiptoe to make sure the birds could see how big I had grown since the previous autumn; I was sure that they smiled at me.

The newly returned pair began at once to tidy the old nest. They both looked so alike that I could not tell their sex, but Väti told me that it was always the female who did the actual tidying, while the male carried new twigs, moss, grass, even paper and rags for the annual clean-up and possible extension of the nest. But on this first day after a long journey of about 10,000 km the male just stood still, watching and waiting for a good sleep.

38

While we had been absorbed in the joy of the first arrivals, we suddenly heard a clatter from the nest on the farm bell turret (opposite my bedroom window) and rushed up to the yard to apologize for our failure to receive the second pair in time. They went on clattering as if they were angry, but perhaps it had just been a prolonged greeting ceremony.

All that lovely springtime normality had been so real only one month ago and now? I suspected that the storks were guarding eggs, maybe even new babies? So I decided, this first of May, had been simply a figment of my imagination, a nightmare that had not really happened. And I fell asleep peacefully and happily and when I woke on a sunny May morning I laughed at the clattering storks from my bedroom window.

A Change of School

A week after May Day Omi gave me a diary for my tenth birthday; it was bound in red leather and had a lock. I confided my May Day worries to the clean white pages and turned the key. Then I opened the book again and added: "I am now alone. The door has closed on the Skirlack school."

Inviting Hanne for my birthday party had proved a disaster. I had sat on my 'throne', my chair which had been lovingly decorated with flowers tied around the back and sides. In front of me lay the cheerful red wooden ring with ten candles; inside the circle, on a lucky wooden toadstool of the fly agaric type, was the large 'life candle'. The table was full of cakes and biscuits. All that had been as on all other birthdays, and my friends from the farm chatted as usual. But Hanne, my guest of honour who should have remained my friend for life and who sat right next to me, did not know what to say and could only ask: "How's your school? Are you also learning to knit proper gloves with fingers?" I blushed and stuttered that we did not have needlework lessons at all at the moment. I did not dare tell her that at my new school in Darkehmen the subject was scorned like some inferior thing akin to housewifery, nor that we, boys and girls together, were making superfluous raffia serviette rings and might soon be painting china, for which we would have to buy expensive materials. Would she be able to share my excitement about learning French? I did not think so. Nor did I tell her the title of the essay I was struggling with, funny though it was: "A Drop of Water Falls from the Tap". I had already spent hours watching our one and only tap and had not yet discovered what I could possibly say; but as Hanne had never even seen a tap, she was unlikely to find it amusing.

So I said that the playground was surrounded by a solid wooden fence, that most of it was hard concrete for the boys to play rough games and that there was a small corner with gravel paths between shrubs where the girls walked. I did not tell Hanne that they walked in twos or threes while I walked alone; nor that they called me a tail, despite the fact that in such a small place I really had no option but to be behind someone.

These things I did not even tell my mother. I hated to see the questions in her eyes when I came back from school. I tried cheerful little stories to make her laugh and be proud: of Georg, Helmut and Joachim waiting by the school gate so that they could take my maths homework to the lavatory for copying. That did please my mother, particularly since Helmut was the son of the man in charge of the *An-und-Verkaufsgenossenschaft,* a kind of agricultural co-operative where Väti sold his surplus produce and bought his seeds.

I disliked the school music lessons, as they stressed formal, academic study of topics like the structure of a fugue, with letters A-B-A representing the various themes. I far preferred the times we sang rounds, especially a funny one which said: "C-A-F-F-E-E, Don't drink so much coffee! The Turks' drink is not for children: it weakens your nerves & makes you pale and ill. Don't be a Muslim who can't live without it". The first phrase cleverly uses the note names to spell the title, but it was only much later, as an adult, that I voluntarily went to a piano to pick out the tune.

C - A - F - F - E - E: trinkt nicht so viel__ Kaff - ee!

Nichts für Kin - der ist der Tür - ken - trank,

Schwächt die Ner - ven, macht dich blaß__ und__ krank.

Sei doch kein Mu - sel - man, der ihn nicht lass - en kann!

Carl Gottlieb Hering's "C-A-F-F-E-E"

Mutti cooked many of my favourite meals again, this time with justification: it was not that cherry soup with pancakes or semolina dumplings, or pea soup with ham and onions could really compensate for the social miseries of the town school, but it was pleasant to feel how much she cared. At the same time her worrying about me made my own worries worse. At least I never had to eat the three dishes I really hated: sorrel soup with a runny poached egg plonked into the middle, or sticky, milky pumpkin soup, or, worst of all, another milk soup called *'Klunkermus'*, in which lumps of sticky flour floated around like mucus.

I never mentioned a dark-eyed girl with a wild crop of brown curls who was always in the centre of the most vivacious group. Like a gipsy without the bangles, I thought, admiring her from a distance. She never called me a tail, because she did not even notice me. When I happened to walk behind her on my way to the bus, I noticed with amazement that she carried the school hat under her arm, which was against regulations. Those hats in their cheerful turquoise colour with silver braiding were the only kind of uniform we had and were a totally pointless, snobbish way of demonstrating our distinction as members of a fee-paying school. The boys wore peak caps, the girls a type of Basque beret with the right side pulled down over the ear, thus showing our silver braid class number, in our case VI for Sexta, the lowest class. I always put my hat on as soon as I climbed into our yellow postal bus at 7 a.m. and kept it on until I was inside the school grounds.

All townish rules were too bewildering for me even to consider rebellion, at least during those first few weeks.

Summer 1933

In May the birch leaves were still young green lights swinging on slender white and mottled branches. On the morning of Whit Sunday many of them were nailed to the banisters to form a festive arcade all the way down the veranda stairs. Our carpenter had a glass of schnapps with my father to reward him for his labours, and we all wished each other a happy Whitsun.

The wings of hundreds of cockchafers rattled noisily in the horse-chestnut trees. Sometimes we would climb up and shake the branches and laugh when the insects plopped to the ground like hailstones. They would quickly rise again and feed on the succulent buds. There was plenty of food for them and always enough left for conkers in the autumn, when we children traded them as horses, determining their value by the beauty of their dark saddle markings. The least pretty ones we would carve into little baskets.

But around Whitsun the chestnut trees were for the cockchafers, who were supposed to bring luck. Chocolate versions of these insects crawled along our dining table, some very large with split stomachs holding a variety of chocolates and with different-coloured ribbons holding the two parts together.

Sundays were family days. Occasionally my parents drove to church in the morning; certainly they did so on special festivals like Good Friday, Whit Sunday, Penance-and-Prayer Day. After the beds were made and vegetables prepared, the maids had a day of rest while Mutti cooked our lunch – which included a dessert on most Sundays, though not on the second Sunday of the winter months, which was the official *Eintopfsonntag* ('one-pot Sunday'), when we had to give an esti-mated saving, supposedly voluntary, to the *Winterhilfswerk* which catered for deprived people during the cold season. While Mutti cooked, Väti went to visit a few neighbours on horseback; he was always pleased when Claus and I accompa-nied him. Claus, though nearly three years younger, was a much better rider than I was and did not need Väti to tell him "Heels down, knees in, bottom in". I tried my best to obey these commands. My reward was that I was considered old enough to join Väti and a neighbour in drinking a stirrup cup. Claus did not envy me: the very smell of alcohol made him feel almost sick.

I frequently resented the superior expression of other farm children when they watched me horse riding. So I wanted to show them that I was every bit as good as Claus and, coming along the road between the big pond and the workers' cot-tages, I urged my pony to a gallop. It accepted my challenge only too well. I did not know how to slow it down and pulled hard on the rein... but the rein had come apart and only the right one was in my hand. And so I pulled the pony to the right, which guided it into the pond where it threw me into the water. My specta-tors roared with laughter. Served me right for showing off, I thought as I walked back to the house in my dripping clothes.

Herr Bagdahn patted the head of his Great Dane when he stood on the broad terrace of Lenkehlischken manor, talking agriculture and politics with Väti. Claus found him very boring and snobbish; I agreed with regard to the latter, but was fascinated nevertheless. His workmen and maids had to address Bagdahn as *Herr Rittmeister*, his military rank of captain-of-horse in the reserve, rather than *Gnädiger Herr*, ('Sir'), like my father. Even as he stood there in his casual British tweeds he looked every inch the old cavalry officer, far more so than Väti on his horse, though my father too had been a captain-of-horse during the War.

Väti on horseback

I heard the two men talk of Seldte and Duesterberg, the two leaders of the paramilitary *Stahlhelm*, also of "remaining Hohenzollern" and of the "Little Corporal" who was not doing too badly for the time being, as long as he was stoppable. On our way home I tried to find out what it all meant, but Väti only said that it was far too complicated to worry my young head about. After a while he added:

"However, you are old enough to understand that I do not share Bagdahn's bigoted views on humble origins, and a good little corporal could just be better than a bad big aristocrat – just as Opa has achieved more in fifty years than Bagdahn's ancestors did in centuries. We shall have to wait and see."

I was content to do just that.

After lunch I helped Mutti to take the dishes out. Väti sat in an armchair in the drawing room with Marlene on his lap. He never entered the kitchen, and Mutti would have considered it gross interference had he done so. Oma and Opa went to their separate rooms for an afternoon's rest. We sometimes went to neighbours for coffee and cake, staying on for supper (though Claus and I sometimes hid in straw-stacks, so that we would not have to go); but on most Sundays we only went for a long walk. Claus, Mutti and Väti, with Marlene riding high on his shoulders, inspected the fields and discussed their state, trying to make me take an interest in botanical details.

From June, when the animals lived outside, we counted their number and checked their fences. We listened to birds and grasshoppers. Harras, the retriever, chased partridges, but only for a little fun. He always came back immediately when Väti called him to heel.

Humpel, our St Bernard, never learned to obey and could only be let loose in our garden for short periods. He was such a beautiful, warm, cuddly creature with a kind growl and sonorous bark, lazy and to all appearances content to lie near his kennel, tied to a long chain, except for some irresistible urge to attack fluttering things. Stupid chickens which investigated Humpel's feeding bowl did so at their peril; many paid for their curiosity with their lives.

A little dachshund also walked with us, constantly yapping. She was Mutti's own pet, rather spoilt and not trained for digging badgers; the farm badger population was too small to cause the kind of damage that would justify badger shoots.

On warm summer evenings we sat on the sunny, open garden veranda for our supper: black bread, butter, various cold meats, Tilsiter cheese from the dairy and caraway cheese which Mutti had boiled herself. She also washed radishes and chopped fine chives which we piled on to our slices of bread and butter. We drank fresh milk or buttermilk at ordinary supper times.

As the shadows lengthened a mellow glow showed off the fields in what my father called "the mother-in-law illuminations". The garden scents deepened: lilac hedges on the upper terraces and a mass of pheasant-eye narcissi in the lowest garden, where vegetables and cut flowers grew. In June Mutti would load the carriage with buckets full of narcissi and take them to the housewives' co-operative in Darkehmen. It was her way of earning pocket money which she saved for special treats, such as citrus fruit or tins of sardines from Portugal.

The farm children's favourite game now was *Völkerball*, a ball game for two teams, in which small children could excel by dodging as much as their stronger, and occasionally skilled, elders could shine by throwing and catching; a game which we rarely played to the win-and-loose conclusion, because we all preferred undecided endings. We played in the large, flat space between our drive and the enclosure where yearlings were exercised or riding horses broken in. The rest of the yard had become less interesting since we had given up our Communist game.

I had never mentioned the Hitler alternative, which was evidently false. The man looked much too friendly to frighten anyone. We saw pictures of him, smiling as he bent to receive bunches of wild flowers from dirndl-clad little girls.

My parents no longer worried about children reading newspapers, and I could now do so openly and in comfort instead of withdrawing behind locked doors to the latrine, which had in any case become uncomfortable in the past year: the large wooden box-seat latrine had been replaced by a WC, and the position had changed from just under the reasonably bright window to the furthest corner, which extended into our hall and included my father's former darkroom. There were now eight sheets hanging from the wall, because the U-bend in the pipe could not cope with quarters; this made the assembly of pages extremely tedious. I saw myself forced to give up on cheap novels and current affairs; but when my parents wondered at my lack of enthusiasm for modernization, I only complained about the waste of manure.

I did, however, appreciate one part of the grand renovation – the bath. It was a real treat to have water running from a tap, particularly when it came out hot after

Frieda had lit the stove at the bottom of the long, cylindrical tank at one side of the bath.

On balance all was well. There was an air of optimism in that summer of 1933, and my father took pains to emphasize continuity and ordinariness.

Claus, who was home from the village school long before I came from town, gulped his lunch down quickly as soon as the hay harvest had begun in June. He rushed to the field where children were needed to take men's places on the saddle horses and to drive the wagons from rick to rick. Two men lifted the hay; two women arranged it into neat, box-shaped loads. A smoothly shaven tree-trunk trailed behind on a short rope until the wagon was full and the men saw fit to lift it between the two prongs of a fork to the horizontal centre of the load. The women on top helped to ease it along and then sat on it while ropes were thrown across at either end and simultaneously fastened to the railed sides of the rack wagon. "*Hau ruck!*" shouted the men when they pulled to make the rope taut. Then the women slid down, the boy came off the horse and they moved to the empty wagon behind, while the full one was taken back to the motorized elevator in the yard. It took as long to shift the hay up to the lofts above the stables and cowsheds as it had taken to fill the wagon in the field, and the total time of the journeys from and to the field was also approximately equal to the loading time. Hence three wagons circulated in an even rhythm, and another three built an open-air stack behind the barn in the same way.

To Claus all this was an absorbing adventure in spite of – or because of – the monotonous, repetitive rhythm. I was therefore surprised when he sacrificed the rush to the field one day in order to meet me at the bus stop. He was hopping from one foot to the other, and his words came out all jumbled in his excitement.

"Arno has invited us to his birthday party!"

This was indeed a surprise. Invitations from the innkeeper's son were the most coveted annual event at the village school. I had always loved those parties: the large hall echoed the thuds of children's feet, and we stamped about and jumped from the stage with deliberate vigour, because the noise on the floorboards was almost as good as that on the promenade along the Baltic. We enjoyed wearing imperial officers' boots which were too big for us and tripping on the hems of crinolines which were too long. We screamed to our hearts' delight when we bumped into each other because the powdered wigs had slipped across our eyes. Those wardrobes in the two stage rooms were full of clothes for amateur dramatics and meant for adults.

On Arno's birthday his guests played at being grown-ups all afternoon. We sat at scrubbed wooden tables thumping playing cards with the vigour of men at *Skat*, shouting "Trump!" every now and then without knowing the rules of the game. The innkeeper served us colourless lemonade in small schnapps-glasses, and orangeade which foamed with the help of carbonated tablets came in beer glasses. Arno's mother served cakes and sandwiches from trays. We could create noises from trumpets and hunting horns which were also among the stage props, or we could dance to proper music from a gramophone with a huge pink funnel.

I had often enthused about Arno's parties, but Claus had never been invited. At first he had been too young; then he had become Arno's enemy after the fist fight about Hitler. I was also out of favour by association. So why on earth were we invited now?

"Well, because we are all Nazis now, Arno said." Claus beamed at me happily.

"How dare he!" I shouted with rage while all the first-felt pleasure of the invitation drained away. "Whatever makes him say a thing like that?"

"He said that the *Stahlhelm* has joined Hitler's party," Claus stammered.

"You'd better tell him that there is Duesterberg as well as Seldte," I said without really knowing what the dual leadership of the *Stahlhelm* was all about.

Claus's lips puckered, but he was bravely holding back his tears when he whispered: "I thought you would be so happy."

I could have cried myself, feeling mean and disgusted at my stupid outburst. I wanted to hug Claus and say I was sorry, but I did not know how to bring back his initial enthusiasm. I really was sincerely happy to be invited, I said, and so glad that Claus too could at last have the experience. It was only that political remark which had annoyed me. Claus nodded assent, but I knew that I had destroyed his pleasure and that the party had gone sour before it started.

Nor did it come up to expectation. It was not so much that Arno greeted us in Hitler Youth uniform: many males like dressing up with ties, just as girls use ribbons, and I certainly had no political objections one way or the other; but somehow it became quite clear to me that I no longer belonged to a crowd I had left only a few months ago. There was no going back; nor, at that time, did there seem a way forward. The only constants remained my family, our farm people and country life.

Visitors from the Reich

My parents did not travel abroad to the Reich that summer, but all three of the foreigners we knew came to stay with us in turn.

Punktroller Putti von Paderborn was the first. She was a friend of Mutti's from her finishing school days. She lived in Paderborn, adored food – plenty of it – and, yes, she did bring along her *punktroller*. We were absolutely fascinated by the rolling-pin contraption, covered in rubber spikes which Putti drove along every line and into every nook and cranny of her vast body after every meal. When she had made sufficient impact on her layers of fat – not to speak of the impact she made on us, goggling at her performance – she was ready to come strawberry picking.

The best wild strawberries grew on the high banks of the ditches along the *chaussée*, and they were thickest where that road ran in the semi-shade of the forest. We picked them in small containers, which we tipped into a bucket when they were full. Strawberries with sugar and cream were frequently our main meal at supper-time in early summer. From the centrifugal separator in the kitchen flowed cream from one pipe and skimmed milk from another. The latter was partly for drinking as it was, but also used to stand in bowls at the back of the kitchen range until a curd formed, providing cheese for us and whey for the pigs.

Putti again ate with gusto, later punktrollering the surplus away with equal gusto.

Our next guest was Gretel from Berlin, also a finishing school friend of Mutti's. She and her two children came straight from their family holiday on the island of Rügen in Pomerania. The husband had by then returned to his work in Berlin.

Gretel was slim and of slightly townish, but pleasant appearance. Lori, the elder of the two children, was a lively tomboy with a naughty, dry sense of humour. Eberhard was a girlish little boy with long fair hair and a delicate, whimpering voice demanding constant attention, particularly from his sister, if I did not manage to abduct and hide her in time.

During the first few days of their stay the mother seemed nothing but a mother, devoted and fussy. Then she opened up to the rest of us and talked, talked, talked. Everything she said confirmed my belief in the awfulness of the metropolis. But she did not mean it that way. She loved her home and feared for it without apparently being able to define what she feared, at least not in a way that I could understand.

Sometimes she sounded as if frightened of the very things she hoped for, or even hopeful for frightening things. A strong hand – night patrols – keeping 'them' in check (whosoever 'they' might be) – calmer days – Communists, yes, she did mention Communists as if they still existed, lurking somewhere in dark corners... Maybe we could revive our old game after all, I thought.

"Make use of the lovely sunshine, children. Go out and play." I could not very well say that I would rather listen to adults when those two Berlin children had come specially for our country air. So I never made sense of the fragments of conversation and when our visitors left, I was quite happy to forget.

The third non-East Prussian we knew was a friend of my father's family. His name was Rudi and he came from Dresden. Long before my parents were married, he had come to Angerapp as part of a charitable arrangement to give underprivileged city children a farm holiday. In succeeding years he came as a private guest of my grandparents, who loved the friendly, well-mannered little boy.

He was the son of a war widow who lived in Dresden in a small, dark flat in a narrow, dark street and worked in a noisy, dark factory. Rudi had done well at school, gained a scholarship to study law and was now looking forward to a time when he could provide for his mother and sister. When he visited us in 1933 he was enjoying his last holiday before his final examination.

His round face sparkled with goodwill, gratitude and freckles. He was ever so gentle, with a handshake that made me think of soft skin on boiled milk gone tepid. His all-embracing kindness and consideration encompassed even me who made fun of him, or perhaps particularly me and that was why I made fun of him.

He came when the main corn harvest started, determined not to be a guest but a helper. But as he had neither the muscles nor the skill of a farm worker, it was difficult to find something to make him feel useful. Even I was better with the hand rake – and I was only just over ten years old!

I was on holiday then and beginning to harden the soles of my feet against the stubble. Rudi worked next to me; we were making piles of the long wads of corn which the horse-drawn rake deposited. When the last loads of the day were made fast, Rudi always insisted on giving me a leg-up, though I could climb the rope perfectly well on my own. He so pitied my scratches that I lived in real fear lest he should want to kiss them better. When the carts moved home, he walked behind, obviously enjoying the singing, but too shy to join in.

Marlene driving the horse rake

Frau Schalonka's sister Auguste did not work in the fields, but she never missed the musical drives. She came scampering along when she guessed that the working day was coming to an end – though we did not keep strict times – and scrambled up like a young girl. Then, sitting comfortably in the corn, she began to lead the singing. Her speciality was a medley of well-known sentimental songs of the *Home, Sweet Home* genre, and she joined each with a verse of her own invention which included a made-up word 'wupper' that sounded just right to describe the beating or fluttering of a heart in love: "Oh how wuppers, how wuppers, how wuppers my poor heart, so full of love and woe, so full of love and woe, and that not just in summer's glow, but in the deepest winter snow…" leading into the *Lorelei*, or Brahms's *Lullaby*, or songs about darkening fields and faithful or faithless lovers.

When we reached the yard, children rushed for the chance to take the work-horses for a swim. Men took off saddles and harnesses except for bridles and the long lines attached to the bits of the front horses. Being the master's daughter I always had the chance to take a foursome, even if others were there before me. It was unfair, but the men just lifted me on to a horse, shouted "Off you go" and smacked the saddle-less horse on the back. I did not have the inclination to insist on justice being done to other children.

It was glorious to have the water of the pond swirl up my legs, often soaking my dress up to my hips, and the difficulties of keeping the front horses of each of the six teams of four from getting entangled with the others added to the excitement.

In Alischken the current of the river added a dangerous touch to the challenge of giving horses a swim. At the edge of Omi's park, where the Droje tumbled across boulders underneath the stone road bridge, the waters had dug a wide pool that was deep even in the middle of summer. My heart was beating under my chin when I entered the almost sluggish side near the farmyard, for I could see the vigorous flow along the opposite shore. And once the thing I had dreaded happened: my front horses were caught up in the current. I let go of the reins and made a silent vow never to challenge the Droje again if by some miracle the horses were saved. I closed my eyes in horror, and when I opened them again I saw my pair galloping towards the yard, trailing their long reins. The men laughed:

"That will teach you; they always land just a few yards downstream."

It did teach me never to swear an oath again.

In Mikalbude leeches never seemed to attach themselves to our horses or to our bare legs, though the pond was supposed to be full of them and we were advised not to bathe in it. Only cook defied that advice; and only once did she have trouble tearing one of these creatures off her skin. It made her scream, but did nothing to deter her from swimming in the pond again, in her funny apron.

We preferred the lake in Kowarren, about 5 kilometres away on the other side of the forest. Sometimes we cycled there, but mostly we went in our small pony trap.

En route to a swim with the cows

When Rudi was in Mikalbude he accompanied us to Kowarren, striding behind the cart so as not to burden the small horse with his weight. We could see how Rudi shuddered with barely suppressed disgust when he followed us into the water, making our way across cows' muck and squeezing between the bodies of cows which stood absolutely motionless, up to their stomachs in the cooling water. In the middle of this small lake the water was very clean, deep and cold. There were no cattle at the opposite shore; nor could there have been, as a dense stretch of reeds blocked the access.

On some evenings when Väti felt the need for a swim after a hot day in the fields we went by carriage to Osznagorren. It was an attractive farm belonging to the Klaudat family. One could drive carriages all the way to the clearing in the forest surrounding the shores of the River Angerapp, but most times we stopped at the farm and walked the rest of the way.

On one of those occasions necessity taught me to climb a difficult, prickly tree. Whatever caused a herd of wild boar to stampede in our direction I do not know. Claus heard the thundering noise of their trotters, shouted to me, and before we had time even to reflect they were rushing past below our branches. Normally, however, that forest walk was quiet, cool and refreshing.

In the clearing the river had dug a calm bay on one side and the Klaudats had built a narrow stage close to where the current was fast. From there they dived and performed challenging feats of strength. Our family stuck to the calmer waters.

Väti had taught me to swim with perseverance rather than patience, first by making me do the breast stroke on the grass.

"For heavens' sake, have you never seen a frog?" he yelled at me more than once. Eventually, when I was about five, I learnt to swim as well as most three-year-olds. I never enjoyed swimming as a sport: I only wanted to move smoothly in a near-weightless state or float on my back with a sense of well-being that spread to the tree-tops and the sky above.

After bathing we had supper at the Klaudats. The old lady would have been very upset if we had not stayed. Hospitality was the raison d'être of Osznagorren. The house was crowded with relatives who had become impoverished or were just at a loose end for various reasons. Old man Klaudat offered asylum for all, cousins, nephews, nieces, stepchildren and of course his own children Mia and Anna, who belonged to the same musical circle as Väti's sister Frieda and her husband and held regular soirées in the farmhouse.

Their brother Gustav Klaudat fancied himself as a superior Icarus. He was convinced he could fly with no aids but his own legs and arms flapping his carefully constructed wings. His sisters had allowed him to build his own workshop on a slight rise in a field, and it was to that place that we had once been invited for his flight demonstration. He ran and pulled strings with his arms and legs and jumped upwards... and was very nearly airborne... but not quite! He ended down on his belly at the bottom of the hill. Most people thought he was crazy, but I admired his enterprising spirit.

The most interesting relative in the house was a man we called Uncle Max. He was only there during university vacations, because he was a student at Heidelberg, where he had studied for at least ten years without the slightest intention of taking any examinations, nor of joining a fencing 'fraternity' as most other male students did. The pride in scars which some eternal students had was totally alien to Uncle Max. He lived to discover and explore different aspects of life, and had no need to make a show of masculinity.

I loved his friendly, bearded face and happy eyes, his funny plus-fours and laced boots, his eagerness to listen, even to children; but most of all I loved the way he talked. It was like standing at a crossroads with all the signs pointing to nowhere beyond what one could see and having to choose arbitrarily which way to go.

Some years later Max was told that he could no longer remain a student unless he qualified in one of the many subjects he had studied. So he came home and worked on the farm.

Twice every year the entire farm population had an excursion, long before *Kraft durch Freude* was invented: one was a drive to the Trempen church in richly decorated rack wagons; the other, less decorative but more fun, was a day-trip to one of the nearest Mazurian lakes. Mutti prepared plenty of food for a picnic on the way; Väti fetched crates of beer from Skirlack. But the main meal of the day was in a restaurant, ordered in advance. I remember one such meal on the small island of Upalten, when we had left the horses stabled on the mainland and crossed in small motorboats. There we sat in a garden with peacocks wandering between tables, begging for crumbs. A band was playing and some people began to dance. All around us was water to make us relax in the feeling of detachment from the rest of the world which is peculiar to islands.

The new slogan of *'Blut und Boden'* ('blood and soil') had a romantic appeal for many farmers. It was beautiful to think of ourselves as trees with roots firmly implanted in our own land and nurtured by it while at the same time providing nourishment for others – the ideal life for mankind. And the ideal of expansion to the East, to the wide, rich plains of Russia, linked easily, albeit illogically, with that of being rooted in the earth. The *Volk ohne Raum* began to dream and to breed more Volk to require more room.

I too, totally oblivious of the political implications, began to create a dream world of those endless plains waiting for the plough. When Sholokhov's *And Quiet Flows the Don* came out, the romantic title made it compulsory reading; and while I read it, certain questions tentatively muddled the dreams. Communists were turning into people, which I found rather disconcerting.

It was natural for country people to be romantics and indulge in a sense of wonder at all natural phenomena. We all loved thunderstorms. The first one of the year told us that the frost had left the ground and that planting could begin. The later, sudden and violent storms on hot summer days split the nitrogen in the air and brought it down into the soil with the rain, which was a great blessing. Though we grew leguminous plants especially to plough them in for their nitrogen, and though we spread plenty of manure on the fields, Väti still sometimes had to buy artificial fertilizers to feed his land, and he felt uncomfortable about it.

The greater the cloudbursts, the more we rejoiced; we children ran about in the rain in our bathing suits. Only in the middle of the harvest did we not welcome storms, or at least Väti did not. For us they often provided special fun, because hurried work – either long into the evenings or on Sundays – to out-manoeuvre the approaching rain, was rewarded by celebrations.

My father could feel when particularly close, oppressive heat presaged a storm and the farm bell rang before we had sensed the danger. *"Arbeit, Arbeit"*, work time, work time, rang the bell: long-short, long-short was the rhythm. At dinner-time the rhythm changed to short-long-short, pause, short-long-short, pause, four times, then sharply short-long, short-long, short-long-short-short-long to fit the words "Come eat now, come eat now, you lazy old blighters; dish up, dish up, potatoes with soup." But this latter bell never rang when bad weather was threatening. Frantic work continued until the rain fell. Väti himself joined the loaders, his riding horse tied to the cart.

Meanwhile the blacksmith and the carpenter would put up trestle tables and benches in front of the house; Mutti and the maids prepared soup and potato salad and piled plates and glasses on the table in the yard veranda. I harnessed our little pony to the trap and made for the inn at Skirlack to collect crates of beer and schnapps.

Riding to Skirlack

After the downpour had washed the tables clean, the feast was spread and our Inspector brought his gramophone down for the dancing. We celebrated long into the night. Schalonka kept filling glasses of schnapps for me; Väti said I must not refuse, just discretely tip the stuff over my shoulder when we danced. The men were too drunk to notice that, but always sensitive to the insult of refusals.

Loud singing drowned the gramophone, and our normally taciturn men discovered that they could talk as well as their womenfolk. But when a woman decided that enough was enough, the husbands obeyed orders as always and swayed home on the arms of the matriarchs.

Rudi proved invaluable on such occasions. Observant, attentive, always on the spot where he could be most helpful, and glowing with happiness at his own usefulness.

"If only he were young enough to join the Hitler Youth, it would give him just the chance he needs to prove himself," I heard Väti tell Mutti.

"And it would take him away from Mummy's apron strings", Mutti added.

A few months later we had a happy letter from Dresden, saying that Rudi had been asked to become an instructor in the Hitler Youth. It was not clear what kind of instruction he would be giving. Surely he could not light a camp fire, and as for sports, the idea of Rudi even running seemed hilarious.

He was so completely different from Uncle Egon, who had joined the S.A. and now apparently divided all his spare time between musical evenings at home and dashing about to rallies on his motorbike. Or, as Aunt Anne put it, living between *Krach und Bach*, or brawl and Brahms.

I liked Anne's sarcasm and though I had never witnessed a brawl, I so much disliked Uncle Egon that I heartily agreed every time his sister-in-law attacked him. Such attacks became so frequent and vehement that they upset Mutti. Whenever possible, these two relatives were invited separately; but of course, that was not possible on my parents' or grandparents' birthdays.

Claus and I loved these verbal skirmishes and were half hoping that they would turn into fist fights. Rolf was a great admirer of Max Schmeling and hoped to become a boxer himself. Could he not teach his mother to be a little less lady-like?

Gisela

Baby storks had hatched, grown and learnt to fly by the time my holidays ended. They were ready for their journey south, and I was surprisingly ready for school. Lessons would be exciting, and I had adjusted to sad playtimes.

Suddenly, as I was walking behind her in the Gudwaller Straße, Gisela, the much-admired girl with the brown curly hair, turned round and asked why I was wearing that silly cap.

"Well, I don't really know," I stammered, totally taken by surprise.

"I know," Gisela said, "you think we have to live by rules. Do you know the Marseillaise?"

Without waiting for an answer, she went on: "Do you like freedom fighters?" I was quick to say that I did.

"Good," she said and then asked me if I knew of Bruno Walter. I imagined him to be some kind of freedom fighter, so I said: "No, I only know Kossuth." She pondered my answer for a moment, but before I could seize my chance to talk about Hungarian rebels, she said that I surely must know Gigli. I shook my head.

"Then what *do* you know?" she asked in desperation and quickly added, "apart from school things, of course."

"Storks… horses…", I said hesitatingly, but Gisela became excited. She adored horses; she was always dreaming of a day when she could learn to ride. Could she come to visit my home?

I could hardly believe my ears and invited her there and then, any time she wanted to come. How happy Mutti will be, I thought, and almost cried when I imagined her face.

"If you come with me now, I can play you my records of Bruno Walter and Gigli", Gisela suggested and then asked if I liked music.

"Yes", I replied. Unsure if I should tell her about songs from the Czardas Princess which Mutti loved to play on the piano, or about the Kowalewski/Klaudat kind of music, I just mentioned that we had a picture of the flute concert in Sanssouci hanging in our ballroom.

"Oh God!" Gisela sighed, and I thought I must have chosen the wrong topic; but she went on to ask if the thought of Frederick the Great made me want to cry with pity, too.

52

Gisela

"Very much so. I always hear him crying 'Katte, Katte' when his awful father made him watch his friend's execution."

"And all because he wanted to escape to a more civilized life," Gisela sighed.

From then on we became close friends. I went to Gisela's home whenever I had time between school and my return bus. She played her records and taught me the chorus of the Marseillaise. We decided to make it our signature tune for whenever we wanted to alert the other to come away from a crowd for some urgent discussion. The first one would whistle *"Aux armes, citoyens!"* – the other reply *"Formez les battalions!"* Then we would whistle the rest together and laugh when other children looked puzzled.

From that day Gisela often came home with me after school on Saturdays and stayed till Monday. At first I had felt apprehensive, thinking that she might find my mother too simple, without perm or lipstick, and fat by comparison with Gisela's own slim and elegant mother. I also worried that she might miss electricity now that the days were growing shorter. But Gisela was so enthusiastic that my own love for my mother and my home grew even stronger. She thought of Mutti as the kindest and warmest person in the world and adored the romantic glow of paraffin lamps. The painted china ones were her favourites, as they were mine, though Frieda spent hours every day polishing the brass ones until they shone like gold.

During the potato holidays Gisela came to join us for work. It was the time when children were paid wages, and paid at the same rate as adults one *Mark* per sack. We carried small baskets and the men tipped them into big baskets for us, chalking a mark by our name on the box wagon when they poured our potatoes into the carts, and often cheating in our favour.

The full loads were driven to the farm and emptied into sorting machines by the cellar windows. These machines rattled all day, shaking off surplus earth and directing the largest potatoes into the cellar, while small ones rolled from a lower

53

tray into sacks for seed and the tiny ones dropped through the grid for the pig swill.

Our labourers' potatoes were also harvested by communal effort, but taken to storage clamps instead of cellars. These had been dug to the depth of about 1 metre, thickly lined with straw, and eventually covered with more straw and a good layer of earth. Beets and turnips were stored in a similar fashion later in the autumn, each family having its own clamps in the space between the big pond and the cottages.

When our cellar was full, potatoes were directed into sacks and loaded on to wagons again for sale at the *An-und-Verkaufsgenossenschaft*.

Winter 1933-34

Winter began in November, when secondary windows were brought into the house and fixed inside the old frames.

The stubble had been ploughed long before, and autumn seeds of grain were beginning to show. Cattle were driven indoors during October, and threshing now began in earnest. Every year, much to Väti's delight, Frau Schalonka and Frau Heiland insisted on filling at least one token sack of corn with the aid of flails. They were determined to keep up their skills and strength, just in case the new-fangled machine broke down. The carpenter Brodien could easily repair damaged flails. Our threshing machine was still the only concession my father had made to the industrial age except for the hay loft elevators.

Horses could recover from the exertions of summer, and mares were taken to stallions at the Gudwallen stud. A few were required to take sacks of corn from the threshing machines to the granary, or to Wiechert's water-mill in Darkehmen. Others moved straw to stacks or back into the barn when the sheaves had been cleared. Now and then two would pull the long metal cylinder of liquid manure to a field, and occasionally a pair helped with the oxen's job of carting solid manure (both animal and human). Saddle girths were lengthened notch by notch when we took pregnant mares for gentle exercise rides.

The undercarriages with their wheels were hoisted to the ceiling of the coach house and sheds when those with runners came down, as did the smaller sleighs, which had no interchangeable parts.

Our woollies were hung on washing lines to disperse the smell of moth-balls. Children's liberty bodices called *Leibchen* came out. They were short, made of linen, with linen-covered buttons at the side, from which hung elastic button-hole strips to which we attached our stockings, boys' as well as girls'. The woollen stockings had the same type of buttons as the bodices. They were sewn to the upper edge; in our attempts to eliminate crinkles all along the legs we attached them high along the elastic strip, with the result that the lower edge curled and showed a bulge under the outer sides of Claus's shorts. Boys usually gave up *Leibchen* when they reached top class in Skirlack or went on to a town school. They were then considered old enough for knee-length socks under warm track-suits.

Fur coats also came out of moth-proof newspaper packaging, as did fur hats and ear-muffs. This started the ritual of my annual arguments with Mutti, who strongly believed in keeping heads warm. Väti never contradicted her in so many words, but he told me how I must rub ears and other parts of my face suffering from frost-bite with snow until the circulation came back, and that I must on no account enter a warm room before I had done so. I took that to mean that he understood I felt happier without hats or ear-muffs, which was reassuring, though I would not have worn them often anyway.

Clothing apart, winter was the most wonderful season of the year. White, blue, crunchy days and clear nights when millions of stars shone like polished lamps and sang a high-pitched metallic song which shivered in the frosty air. I listened to it from my open bedroom window with awe-struck abandon, the words of Omi's song in my mind: "God has counted them, every single one, making sure that none vanished out of sight; counted you, and counted me, too…"

I wondered how the shooting stars found their way back to God's sight. Claus suggested that they were turning round in Australia, where we could not see them. There were many of them in winter skies; they had the magic charm to fulfil wishes, if we wished quickly, before their trail vanished. I was careful never to wish the impossible, so as not to call the bluff of their beautiful myth.

Väti established some order in the heavens when he taught me the names of constellations. Mutti added that in ancient times eyesight was tested by looking for the little rider on the shaft of the Plough, Ursa Major.

Travelling back from neighbours at night, I lent back inside the warm sheep-skins of our sleigh and explored the patterns on the firmament. The prongs on the winter horse-shoes gripped the snow firmly, but softly, without the thud that hooves made on summer roads, and the runners slid silently behind. My father's voice became almost a whisper on such sleigh rides. Only the numerous little brass bells bounced on the leather backs of the sleigh harness and sang a gentle, continuous jingle.

Work sledges had big, single bells tied to their shafts. They produced heavier, more accentuated sounds, dinging and donging.

The way down to the cottages, along the chestnut avenue, was not very steep, but when the sledges had smoothed the snow and when an adult or a strong child gave us a good push, we could whiz down on our toboggans and, with luck, overshoot the road below, landing in the meadow beyond. Here we played when fresh snow had fallen and we could not skate on the ponds until the men had finished farm work and had time to clear the ice with shovels and brooms.

Skating was our favourite winter occupation and at its most exhilarating during times which were depressing from my father's point of view – when hard frosts came before snow had provided a protective covering on the fields, and when drainage pipes burst and flooded a wide area of fields, thus creating miles and miles of ice rinks. We would fly across at speeds which were only possible when braking problems did not exist. Väti loved to skate with us despite his better farmer self.

When we played catch on the ponds, we threw ourselves on to the snowy banks for home. But more often we only danced, side by side at first, crossing hands with our partners, until that proud day when we discovered how to skate backwards and turn as in a ballroom or, even better, glide in wide sweeps to the rhythm of Offenbach's *Barcarole*, Lehár's *Gold and Silver* or Strauss's *Blue Danube*. I learnt to play these myself when no adult obliged with the accordion and the Inspector had tired of winding his gramophone.

Skating with accordion and gramophone

One part of the big pond was fenced off, where the ice needed time to grow between twice-weekly harvests. Men sawed large blocks and sledged them to the shed in the orchard, where each layer was covered thickly with peat, ready for use in the ice boxes during hot summer months or for making ice cream in the soft fruit season.

Suppers were late in winter, because no parents could bring themselves to spoil our fun on the ice. Besides, they strongly believed in the power of frost to kill germs and rejoiced in the healthy glow on our cheeks when eventually they did call us indoors. On such days I loved every part of my tingling body and revelled in sensations of my own strength and freedom.

Skiing was a leisurely pastime, except for the start when we had to rub the wax in vigorously with the balls of our hands. It is a wonder we did not get splinters. When snow filled the hollows and grooves and turned our undulating fields into a vast, even plain, we slid in long, easy strides to visit our neighbours.

But when I was skiing alone, it was something other than a short cut to the next farm. Then I felt myself melting into an infinite light; a white peace with a million suns reflected in tiny crystals. My very existence dissolved in a light-headed dream. No longer conscious of moving, I could have lain down in the snow in elated oblivion.

Skis had been introduced to the East Prussian scene only recently, and knowledge of snow blindness and sunglasses had not come with them. It was entirely up to my guardian angel to confront me with a fence or a tree which would awake me to reality.

Whenever sunbeams burnt through the thin air with special intensity, icicles made a frieze along the tarred roof of the barn. On those very days they failed to form in men's moustaches. My father would forecast fog for the night and put his camera on the desk for the morning after. Before our bathroom extension, when Väti still had his darkroom, he had created some masterpieces of winter scenes. But now he was still experimenting with films instead of plates, to be developed by the Darkehmen chemist.

I never saw the fog at night, but I recognised its work in partnership with frost when I ran to my bus underneath a dome of hoarfrosted filigree birch branches. At school the art lesson timetable was re-arranged for all classes to have a chance to explore nature's overnight work. The teacher told us not to forget the tubes of silver paint when we took our water-colour boxes down to the river's edge.

I watched with admiration how weeping willows appeared on Gisela's paper, looking exactly like the real bushes in front of us with the sun highlighting the silver sparkle and intensifying the dark shadows on the snow. But try as I might, my own willows did not appear as I saw them, and all my white and silver smears would not create hoarfrost. Furiously I crumpled up my first paper and defiantly put little silver angels on the next bush I painted. They looked really silly, but as I was about to crush them, too, the teacher snatched my paper and held it up for all to see my "imaginative work". I could have cried with humiliation even before my classmates began to giggle. Gisela made it worse by telling me that her father had works of art which did not look at all like the real thing.

My only true comfort lay in the failure of my father's photographs.

In addition to Christmas, New Year and the season of masked balls and revels before Lent – rather tame in East Prussia by comparison with those in the Catholic regions of the Rhine and Bavaria – our social calendar in winter included ice-sailing regattas on Mazurian lakes, in particular on the Schwenzaitsee near Angerburg. Since these boats did not have to contend with the resistance of water, they moved at exhilarating speeds. My parents watched the bright and graceful spectacle for hours. Kiosks had been erected on the ice to provide hot food such as *Bratwurst* for the hungry and drinks for the thirsty. We enjoyed those treats, but soon became bored with the races and played our own games among the boats along the edge which were awaiting their turn.

Ice-sailing regatta

Christmas

The Christmas season began on the first Sunday in Advent, or rather on the evening before, when we volunteered to help Mutti with gingerbread biscuits. We cut out hearts and stars, moons, half-moons, angels, even Father Christmases, because he was beginning his rounds. He was checking on children's behaviour, and so we tried to be specially good in the weeks when adults were specially busy preparing for Christmas proper.

At coffee-time on Advent Sunday a fir wreath hung from a red stand on our table. Mutti had made it secretly while we were asleep, and though we always expected it, we made gasping noises of genuine surprise. Only one of the four candles was lit during the first week of Advent. Mutti played Advent carols on the piano and we sang.

Oma liked to sit on the bench by the tile stove, warming her back and asking for a baked apple from the stove hatch every now and then. Those apples had the cosy smell and flavour of winter evenings. Sometimes, after Oma had gone to bed, we played games at the small square table by the bench: Ludo, draughts, nine-men's-morris, Halma, or simple card games like Happy Families, rummy, *Doppelkopf*, even *Skat* without the serious conventions.

Later, just before we went to bed, we would each put a slipper on the window-sill, behind the rug of felt with a richly embroidered wool counterpane which hung on hooks several inches above the level of the sill as an extra precaution against winter draughts and added an air of secrecy to our hidden slippers. In the mornings we would find a biscuit, an apple or on occasions even a piece of chocolate – a treat normally reserved for when we lined up by Väti's cupboard to swallow a teaspoon-full of cod-liver oil. Sometimes, when one of us had been naughty during the previous day, Father Christmas put nothing but a twig into the slipper to indicate that we deserved a beating from our parents. Neither Väti or Mutti could have done such a cruel thing, so we were sure that it had been one of the maids playing Father Christmas that night. It did not greatly matter, because we had always known that the mysterious figure was only a metaphor for the idea of giving presents without expectation of thanks. Catholic children spoke of the Baby Jesus doing his rounds instead of Father Christmas, except on the night of the 6th of December, when Protestants and Catholics alike received presents from St Nicholas.

Our daily Advent celebrations became more exciting with each new candle that increased the anticipation of the most brilliant light on Christmas Eve. We were all preparing for it secretly in many different ways and hoping that others were almost dying with curiosity.

Our parents now made frequent shopping expeditions to town while we created our own presents for all our family and, most important of all, began to choose, learn, write and decorate our Christmas poems. The maids helped those of us who had not yet learnt to write. On the cover of a folded sheet of paper we put the words "To my dear parents from their grateful daughter (or son)…" and then our name and the year of that particular Christmas. We decorated the page with crayons, paint or ready-bought glossy, adhesive pictures of cherubs and flowers. On the second sheet we wrote our poem. Special Christmas books provided a wide choice ranging from two-liners for little children to lengthy epics; but when I grew older, I found all of them too impersonal and made up my own.

On the morning before Christmas Eve we hung around the dining room, walking up and down casually, never far from the ballroom door. A rustling noise behind that door made Claus run to the key hole. We heard male voices muttering and Mutti laughing.

"It's bigger than ever," Claus shouted excitedly.

"How can that be when it is always up to the ceiling?" I tried to be clever while enjoying the pounding of my heart.

"Wider, much wider," Claus insisted.

I took a turn at the keyhole, but saw only the dark blot of the key at the other side. Lacking that forceful conviction which enabled Claus to see what he wanted to see, I shrugged my shoulders: "There is nothing to see."

"There is a teeny-weeny slit at the side of the key," Claus persevered. But neither of us really wanted to spoil the secrecy of waiting for the sight of the tree in all its glory later that night.

Claus went outside to watch the carp fishing. Nothing on earth could have persuaded me to follow. It was not just the sight of wriggling fish that put me off, but fear of the hole in the ice. Long ago I had heard of a child in the Darkehmen district who had slipped into such a hole and disappeared so quickly under the thick ice that she could not be rescued alive. Ever since I had prayed to God to kill me any way he liked, but please, not by drowning.

For days we had helped to prepare the Christmas sweetmeats. On thin marzipan hearts, full moons, crescents and diamonds, we had stuck serrated strips with rose water around the edges; and after these had been baked, we had filled the cavities with lemon-flavoured icing and decorated them with one or two small diamonds of red currant jelly and strips of angelica; we had given the chocolate coating to peppermint creams; had put almonds and nuts on other confectionery. But on Christmas Eve, when Mutti carried them from the kitchen to the ballroom, she covered the trays secretively with a cloth as if we had never seen them before. When we pretended that we wanted to peep underneath the cloth, she wagged her finger as if to threaten us for being curious.

Shortly before supper Otto went to Beynuhnen station to fetch Omi, who had spent Christmas with us every year since Omut died. I wrapped up warmly to join Otto on the high green one-horse sleigh, which had runners that curved elegantly in front. It was a tight squeeze after Omi had bundled in with us; her luggage was tied to the superfluous footmen's seat. On our way home I recited fragments of French from school and Omi was delighted.

She left the heaviest case for Mutti to take to the Christmas room, and I carried the small one up to the visitors' room opposite mine. Claus walked ahead with a candle to show the way. We all changed into smart clothes for supper and walked downstairs together. Omi smelt pleasantly of 4711 eau-de-cologne.

We ate 'blue carp' with potatoes, vegetables and plenty of eye-watering horse-radish in whipped cream with lemon. The four candles of the Advent wreath were burning for the last time. Any moment now they would be replaced by dozens and dozens on a tree. When Mutti sneaked away to prepare the display, a funny feeling crept into my stomach. I became afraid that I might have forgotten the words of my poem and frantically tried to recite it to myself.

Then we heard the tiny tinkle of bells from the small silver steeple that always decorated the top of our tree. The doors to the ballroom opened; we moved forward, slowly, holding our breath. I felt a lump in my throat at the familiar sight of all those white candles shining on a dark green tree, the glitter of lametta and a few silver balls and the softly curling silken angels' hair. The light blurred when we sang 'Silent Night' and came into focus again when I wiped my eyes during the other carols. We sang many of them before someone gave me a nudge.

I stepped towards my parents and, with a curtsy, presented my Christmas sheet to them. (This was probably a precautionary tradition to ensure that adults could understand the words if a child mumbled incoherently.) I felt my legs shake as I turned to the tree and greeted it too with a curtsy, before I recited my poem. Väti and Mutti rewarded me with a big hug before Claus and Marlene had their turn. Then we all sang another carol before everyone moved to the places where their presents were displayed.

Children's gifts were under the tree. Claus, who had already given his toy horses an inspection from the distance, now rushed towards them. No presents were wrapped, and we did not require labels to recognize our places. Nor, of course, did we have to know who had inspired Father Christmas with particular ideas.

The adults had some difficulty in identifying their places on the long table with the white tablecloth in the centre of the room, but generally speaking the strictly hierarchical order was well known from previous years.

Ortlef, Helmut and Claus on Vollmacht, Silhouette and Loki

In 1933 it was I who was most confused, because I saw a beautiful new saddle close to things which were obviously for me. Could it have slipped over from Claus's side by mistake, I wondered? Väti was watching my hesitation with amusement and nodded, when I looked up. "You will have the horse to match the saddle later," he smiled, "if Sitalia's foal turns out the way I expect her to."

Claus looked up at me, his eyes beaming with happiness at my promotion. "She is called Silhouette; Väti said she had the makings of a lady's horse," he whispered with proud stress on the word 'lady'.

I ran to throw myself into my father's arms.

Everyone had their own *bunte Teller,* cardboard dishes with fluted or corrugated edges and a Christmas design, on which were distributed a variety of sweetmeats, nuts and special delicacies such as Karlsbad plums, figs and dates, which we nibbled all night. Fruit was piled on a large communal dish.

We all had new books and new games which we would play with others a little later. Over the past few years I had collected sets of Happy Family cards, starting with simple, pictorial versions and gradually becoming more educational. This year it was based on composers and their operas, but Mutti quickly warned me not to boast to Gisela that I now knew all the operas which Beethoven had written, because most of them had never gone beyond the overtures.

At that moment we heard a loud knock at the door from the garden veranda, and in came Father Christmas with a big sack and a long stick.

"Good evening," said a growly version of Otto's voice.

"Good evening, Father Christmas," we chorused and someone pushed me forward. I knew what I had to say, because I said it every year:

> *"Father Christmas, dear old man,*
> *Put your stick away! You can*
> *Look with kindness upon me,*
> *For a good girl I shall be –*
> *And so will Claus and Marlene."*

The last bit was not general tradition, but a family compromise to spare the adults the same old rhyme in triplicate.

"Very good, very good. Let's see what I have for you," came the voice from within a mass of beard, hair and fur. Father Christmas rummaged in his sack, extracted oranges, puzzles, pencils, crayons, small bottles of eau-de-cologne for Omi, Oma, Mutti, the maids and cook, and pocket diaries for Opa, Väti and the Inspector. Then he folded his empty sack, accepted a glass of schnapps, sang a carol with us and departed.

When the candles were burning low, Väti lit several sparklers which had hung unnoticed among the branches. Marlene jumped with joy and asked for more. There were plenty, and we had five or six sparklers simultaneously many times over. Then Mutti bent a fir branch close to a flame until it began to smoulder and shoot up small, crackling explosions while tiny dots of fire flickered along the twig like the tongue of a snake and died in a thread of smoke. It spiralled to the ceiling, filling the room with the scent of conifer forests. Its fragrance lingered for a long time, and when it weakened Mutti repeated the process once more before we blew out the last candles.

We played games and read new books by the paraffin lamp on the round table. Frieda and Hilde joined the games for a short time only, before they went downhill to their families to start Christmas Eve all over again. We were all ready for bed by midnight.

Christmas Day was not very different from a Sunday, except that we said "Happy Christmas" to each other instead of "Good morning", and the Bagdahns did not stay on their horses for a stirrup cup but came indoors for wine and nibbles and to look at our presents.

We had goose for lunch, because geese were bigger than ducks, though less palatable. Most geese were used for smoking their hams and breasts, the liver turned into pâté, lesser parts preserved in aspic, and the neck, wings, head, heart and blood cooked with dried apples, prunes and dumplings as a slightly sour-sweet soup called *Schwarzsauer*; Väti then usually split the head along the seam on the skull and dug out the brain from the two halves. The roast goose on Christmas Day was served with roast potatoes and hot red cabbage, followed by home-made *Fürst Pückler* ice cream, frozen over ice cut from our pond.

Later that afternoon I visited the Schalonkas to taste their baking and admire their tree, which was quite unlike any other I had seen, being absolutely smothered with coloured glass balls and glass birds.

"So vulgar," Mutti said to me once.

So fascinatingly gaudy, I thought; but I would not have wished to exchange it for our own dignified tree, on which new white candles glowed every night until we took it out to the garden and decorated it with bird food from the Three Kings on the 6th of January.

I am sure that Mutti prayed all year to be spared the evening of Boxing Day, but she prayed in vain. The *'Schimmelreiter'* could not be exorcised that easily.

He was a rider on a white hobby-horse, who invaded the house together with a man dressed as a stork, another as a goat, bearing the head of a real dead goat, and others simply dressed as ruffians. There was total pandemonium. Chairs were knocked over, tables collapsed, doors slammed; men made goaty and horsey noises and the stork kept clattering his enormous beak while trying to bite one of the maids. The maids ran and screeched and slammed doors, because superstition had it that whoever was bitten by that stork would have a baby during the following year.

Eventually, but not before all were out of breath and near collapse, the invaders consented to be bought off with alcohol and food. Kitchen, dining room and drawing room looked as if a hurricane had swept through the house. It all took place by the light of battery-operated torches, because one could not risk open flames on such occasions. Väti turned an armchair the right way up for Mutti to recover from the trauma while we set about tidying up. Order was restored within a few minutes, except for the odd broken piece of furniture which the carpenter would mend in the new year.

The sad news at the end of the old year was that our merry aunt Toni had been diagnosed as showing the first symptoms of multiple sclerosis. We just could not accept this. Jean Guerlin, the husband of Väti's cousin Trudchen, had had the illness ever since I had known him. Doctors guessed that it might have started as an after-effect of severe malaria which he contracted in Africa during the War. He was helpless at times; but at least he had a wife who was always at home to care for him. How would Aunt Toni cope, having a husband who was out at work all day? Would Omi manage to persuade her to move to Alischken?

Omi did not succeed. Her sister stayed with a husband who propped her up in a chair every morning and left food on a table within her reach. She sat there alone all day. It was heartbreaking to see her.

New Year

For New Year's Eve Mutti gave me a surprise which I thought lovely until I heard the sad explanation: she had invited Gisela to celebrate with me. Väti took me aside to explain the circumstances before my friend arrived:

"New Year's Eve is going to be terrible in their house; that's why Gisela's father asked me if we could have her. Uncle Heinz has been sent to prison for homosexual offences. I want you to know this just in case your friend wants to talk about it; but don't mention it unless she does."

"What is a homosexual offence?" I naturally wanted to know.

"It's when a man tries to marry another man instead of a woman."

"And why must such people be sent to prison?"

"Search me," Väti sighed. "It isn't the normal way for men to act, so someone made a law to forbid it."

"And whom did Uncle Heinz want to marry?" I had been told to call him uncle when I had been staying with Gisela.

"Herr Flaischer. He is in prison, too."

"But…" Now I was really puzzled. Herr Flaischer, an apothecary in Darkehmen, was married to a real woman and had two children.

"I know what you are thinking," Väti said, "and there is some sense in punishing him, though he has not done any real harm. It is terribly sad for his wife, and we must try to be as kind as we can to them all."

Gisela did not talk to me of her uncle, and we celebrated New Year's Eve in the usual way. Mutti had baked heaps of doughnuts, a few of them containing mustard instead of jam. In some years we held a big ball at our house; this year it was taking place on a neighbouring farm, and my parents prepared everything for our celebrations before they themselves went out, dressed as Domino and Pierrette.

Paper chains decorated the drawing room and dining room, but not the ballroom, as such things would not have been in harmony with our tree. Cartons of crackers and bags of confetti were put ready on Väti's desk. There was also a carton of lucky charms made of lead and the appropriate shallow spoon next to a candle. Apples were attached to strings for bob-apple games and others lay near a large bowl of water for duck-apple.

When my parents had left, Frieda served our supper and she and Hilde joined us at our table. After the meal Opa and Oma withdrew to their own celebrations. Marlene had been put to bed long before by Mutti herself. We others played games in the drawing room and danced in the dining room, having pushed the table to the wall. Throwing confetti and streamers began early, while we were dancing. Foxtrots, tangos, English waltzes in slow 3/4 time and fast Viennese waltzes. Ravel's *Bolero* and Bizet's *Habanera* were the Inspector's favourites. I liked a slouchy record "Bright is Every Day That You Can Give, Marie-Louise", because I had never known anyone with a double name like that and found it romantic. Gisela preferred tunes from films she had seen, films which I absolutely must see when they came to Darkehmen! She had seen them with her grandmother in Königsberg; I had never been to a cinema at all. We made plans for the new year, almost all revolving around the chance of seeing films and nights of talking about them in Gisela's room afterwards.

So I knew what to wish for when we floated tiny candles stuck inside halves of walnut shells. Two of these boats were afloat at anyone's turn, at opposite ends of the bowl; then we stirred the water slightly and watched them move. If they were close together when all movement of the water stopped, our wish would be fulfilled. Strictly speaking it should simply have been an oracle game for lovers, secretly naming one of the boats after whichever partner they would have liked to join by the end of the following year.

The hot punch we drank was spicy, but consisted mainly of fruit juices. The champagne was kept on ice for midnight. Then, as we lifted the glasses – they could hardly have been described as full – the farm bell began to ring and we went outside to join the crowd.

"Prost Neujahr! Prost Neujahr!" to you, and to you, and to you. Shaking hands, hugging, kissing, singing. Far away we could hear the church bells from Trempen when Brodien stopped ringing ours. Further still we heard the explosion of fireworks from Darkehmen, too far to see.

Our first deed in 1934 was to consult the lead charms about our fortunes. We had the choice of a four-leafed clover, a horse-shoe, a toadstool, a pig, a chimney sweep, the replica of a pfennig; there were two of each. One after the other, we melted the lead over the candle and then poured it quickly into the cold water. It was up to our imagination to interpret the resulting shapes; and so, happily assured of an exciting future, we went to bed.

On New Year's Day we made doubly sure of bright prospects by eating pig: the meat kind for lunch, the marzipan sort with a clover-leaf or toadstool in its snout at any time of the day. The real chimney-sweep obliged us by his arrival and let us touch the soot on his dark suit and top hat for an extra dose of luck after he had swept our chimneys.

Early in the year a law was passed, forbidding films which "did not relate to the national-social emotions of the German people", whatever that was supposed to mean. Gisela and I were warned by several friendly adults that we should hurry to see as many good films as possible while they were still on release. We had, of course, no idea what a 'good' film might be and where we could possibly see it. We liked melodramas and romances, and these were virtually all that the Darkehmen cinema provided, because there were few inhabitants who wanted to pay for challenging problem cinema.

Our favourite star was Heli Finkenzeller, particularly in a film called *'Königswalzer'*; but we loved many others, too. We bought artistic postcards of their faces and cut out pictures of scenes from our favourite films to stick them into thick exercise books made of good, smooth paper. Not content with the already strong sentimental appeal of such films, I enhanced the stories by adding yet more emotions when I re-told them in my scrap-book. Gisela then calligraphed artistic headlines and bound each book for me in cheerful scraps of coloured materials. We spent most of our spare time sitting at my desk or at Gisela's in Darkehmen, absorbed in film-related tasks.

Gretel wrote from Berlin that it had now become a pleasure to go out with the family again, because the cinema had been cleaned up. I did not know what she meant; and since I had no intention of visiting Berlin, it did not concern me.

Easter

Easter 1934, like all other Easters, started with the traditional Maundy Thursday bretzel: small B-shaped salt sticks to accompany drinks, mainly for adults; medium-sized sweet bretzel of puff pastry; and very large ones made of yeast dough, the size of harvest loaves, but sweet and often covered with almonds.

On Good Friday my parents never failed to go to church. Sometimes I accompanied them and had our dressmaker sew a special black garment for the occasion. It felt totally unlike myself to wear black and gave me a sense of drama. But I did not keep it up for more than about two or three years.

Easter Saturday was a big baking day – for bread, of course, but also for numerous cakes after the heat of the big oven had gone down. Hens' eggs were cracked carefully, so that the shells could be used for little vases to decorate the festive table on the following day. We painted them with our crayons or water colours and stuck them to sturdy small disks of card with Väti's sealing wax. Goose-eggs were pierced at the ends and blown into the cake mixes, then washed, dried, painted and filled with small sugar eggs through the slightly larger of the two openings before we patched it shut with coloured sticky paper. Dozens and dozens of eggs were hard-boiled, then dyed in special bright egg colours and rubbed with bacon rind until they shone.

In the afternoon we walked to the forest to pick hepatica. We also gathered snowdrops in our garden and, very carefully, cut branches of pussy-willow at the edges of the peat bog, some for big vases, others to keep under our beds for Easter Monday.

Our Königsberg relations stayed with us during the holidays, and we all gathered round the breakfast table, peeling coloured boiled eggs, putting them on to our slices of black bread and all waiting for the operative word from Mutti: "You won't guess what I just saw," she called out, looking at the window.

"Oh yes, we can! It was the Easter hare!"

Off we ran to the garden, because the hare never hid eggs in the yard, nor in the orchards. We looked for small nests made of straw, each with a variety of boiled eggs and sugar or chocolate eggs, hares and chickens. Our little baskets were filled with goodies: some we ate straight away, some we kept for later in the day, and a few we kept safe for the following morning, just in case we were caught in bed by an early invader come to *schmackoster* us.

For me the real and unforgettable treat of Easter was the first cucumber salad of the year. It tasted like no other cucumber, so fresh and full of the promise of spring after a long winter. We grew cucumber in forcing beds along the south-facing wall of the forge, in a special little garden surrounded by a high fence of closely overlapping wooden planks. The compost beds were surrounded by thick walls of straw and dung – in fact these forcing frames were literally called 'dung beds'. Two people had to roll up the straw matting every morning, far enough to the sides for the sun to shine on the glass all day. We had watered them on the previous evening and opened the frames just wide enough to release some of the condensation in the morning, or pulled them off completely if the weather was very good. A wonderfully warm, musty smell exuded from the young plants, and every day we watched how big cucumbers had grown in readiness for Easter; but we never used them before then, however large they might be. There were also some dill plants, not in the forcing beds, but close to the forge wall, so that they could flavour the sour-cream dressing. Roast young chicken was the main dish on the Easter table.

In the evening we began bidding for our Inspector's alarm clock, because no one else would lend us theirs. I did not mind if Claus won, as I would hear his alarm in my room, and in any case, I could trust him to wake me. Nor was it too bad if Rolf won the bidding, because there was a good chance that he would keep it safely under his pillow so that he could sneak out of the guest room without waking his brother. He would always come to me for company on our rounds, though he made it a condition that I should not wake Claus, at least not deliberately. I had to do it accidentally, because I could not allow my brother to be caught out in bed and have his legs smacked with willow branches. It was all very complicated; and if Frank won the bidding, I could hardly sleep at all.

We did our rounds of all the rooms of the house, lifting the bottoms of eiderdowns to reach the sleepers' bare legs with our sticks and reciting the verse asking for "eggs, lard and a chunk of cake", but quite happy to be bought off with Easter eggs and chocolate. I think we would have been unpleasantly surprised if someone had really presented us with lard!

Excursion to Rossitten

After Easter the new school year began. There was no great change in the content of lessons when I moved from Sexta to Quinta. Physics, geometry, and English were not introduced until we reached Quarta. The I part of the VI on my hat was carefully removed and left a slightly faded line. The really exciting difference was the quality of the annual school outing: whereas we had had only a day-trip to the Mazurian lakes in the previous year, we were now promised a fortnight in Rossitten.

Rossitten was a village on the 'Kurische Nehrung', the narrow strip of land that separated the inland sea of the 'Kurische Haff' from the Baltic. Its greatest claim to fame was a bird sanctuary founded by a man called Thienemann, and it was the first place in the world to introduce the ringing of birds for the study of their migration. My father was particularly thrilled at the prospect of my visit to the place, and – though I did not know it at the time and would have objected most strongly if I had – Uncle Egon mentioned my name to the warden of the sanctuary, who happened to be a friend of his. He apparently told him that I was seriously interested in ornithology.

It was not compulsory to take part in school outings, and Gisela was adamant that she would not come. "To be organised day and night like a herd of cows and worse, because everybody will be of the same age…": she shuddered at the very thought.

I was undeterred by her words. It was exciting to buy a rucksack and wonderful to have my plaits cut off, so that I could now manage my hair without Mutti's help. I felt proudly independent to be going away without parents or grandparents to look after my safety. In my excitement I almost forgot to kiss Mutti and Väti good-bye on the station platform.

During the seemingly endless train journey in a compartment full of giggling class-mates I began to envy Gisela her wisdom. My heart sank lower and lower until we reached Tapiau and boarded the steamer for the first boat trip of my life. The ship chugged along in warm June sunshine. Shallow-bottomed broad boats drifted alongside, loaded like floating hay-wains. Rows of small houses stood on both sides, right up to the water's edge like a colourful dam supporting the banks.

Then the water widened and the land disappeared. The *Kurische Haff* was smooth and very blue. Seagulls swooped and screeched and grew in numbers when white mountains of sand appeared on the horizon. Then we saw forests, some houses, a landing stage and boats, ever so many boats. Some were sailing on the *Haff*, others were moored in the little harbour, their red sails filling the hulls like crumpled feather beds. All of them had long wooden pennants on their masts – carved rows of houses, or rows of trees, or birds, all painted in gay colours and each representing the home villages of fishermen, Dr Gebhard told us.

But we could not see any villages other than the few houses of Rossitten, nor did I come across any houses when I walked for hours every day during our holidays. In small bays on the Baltic side we sometimes stumbled on a shed between dunes and long wooden bars fixed to posts. Rows upon rows of flounders hung there in pairs, tied by their tails. They were smoked over juniper fires and were the staple diet for locals, the most delicate treat for visitors and the main export of the village. They were taken to Königsberg in small boats and from there to the distant Reich in large ships.

Sometimes the smell of creosote mingled with the wood smoke in the bays. Fishermen worked bare-chested and barefoot, preparing their boats for the next trip while the women tended the fires or patched torn sails. It amazed us to see men's almost naked bodies gleam with sweat while their wives looked cool under layers of long black clothes, aprons, kerchiefs, even shawls. Why were those women always in black?

Dr Gebhard thought it was probably not worth their while to invest in other colours: bereavements were frequent even in this day and age, when the dunes had been almost stabilized. He read us a poem called 'The Women of Nidden', based on a true story about a village further along on the *Nehrung* towards the Lithuanian border. It happened at a time when the plague was ravaging the mainland. The people of the *Nehrung* trusted in the *Haff* to protect them. "God who gave us the constant threat from the wandering dune will save us from this other suffering…" the poem began. But the elks, swimming across as they often did, imported the plague. Seven women were the last to survive and pleaded with the dune to take on the jobs of the dead priest and the dead undertaker:

"... 'God forgot us, let us perish.
You, the dune, His house inherits
Cross and Bible be your toys!
Mother dune, come, bury us!
Wrap us in your thickest shroud.
You, our saviour, once our curse,
come and see us lie in peace.'
And the dune came and covered them."

Quite close to Rossitten, in an area called 'the humps', the sand had formed peaks around invisible obstacles of former houses, trees, a church. At another spot the dune had wandered along towards the *Haff* and gradually liberated the ruins, showing broken masonry, scorched tops of former trees and, we were told, human skeletons, too. Else and I walked there one night, not searching for physical remains, but dreaming of ghosts coming alive in the white moonlight on the white sands. It was beautifully frightening until the fear became real. We discovered that we had lost all sense of direction and could see nothing but sand and stumps; when we saw glints of water, we did not know if it was the Haff or the Baltic. We decided to take our chance with the equivalent of tossing a coin: "One, two, three, Schiller or Goethe?" As we both said "Goethe", we had to go left, which proved lucky. The entire village of Rossitten seemed like a ghost settlement except for one light shining from the youth hostel, where our kind class master and French teacher Dr Gebhard had waited up for us with a thermos of hot cocoa.

Gisela's warning about regimentation proved totally unfounded. Apart from hot drinks our breakfasts and suppers were cold meals, buffet style, and not restricted in time. The midday meals were cooked by teachers on camp fires by the sea. We were free to plan our own days or join special events which Dr Gebhard arranged for those who wanted to be educated.

I watched the activities of the gliding school on the highest dune. The planes were pulled by men in white suits, who dragged the gliders up to the top on a two-wheel contraption. When the pilot had settled in his seat, eight men, four on each of two ropes, ran downhill, pulling the glider with them until it was catapulted into the air and floated above the *Haff* like a great white, silent bird.

The *Haff* looked so blue that it made the Baltic seem green. I do not know why this was so. Nor do I know which was more fun for bathing. The breakers whipped our bodies and made us shout with joy when we were in the sea; the smooth, sometimes slightly curly water of the *Haff* was for relaxing, dreamy swims. Actually, on the return journey I changed my mind about relaxation when our steamer bounced on the short, vigorous waves and made us all sick.

Before then, we visited the bird research station and I had the most embarrassing experience of the holiday: the warden asked for me by name! My friends stared in astonishment and I wished for the earth to open up and swallow me. How could Uncle Egon have done this to me? It was ridiculous that I should be treated like a budding ornithologist when I could hardly tell a blackbird from a swallow and was not in the least interested in 400 Latin names for the various indigenous and migratory visiting species.

Among the various exhibits we also saw things that were not connected with birds, amongst them the eggs of the gadfly, which killed elks because they were laid in their nostrils and drove the big creatures berserk. I recalled my own great encounter with an elk one holiday in the sand dunes not far from Cranz. I walked alone on a very hot summer's day, my bare feet in the Baltic which was slowly beginning to change colour to a darker hue. I stared at the threatening water in admiration, and heard the first claps of thunder in the distance. Then I looked upwards to the dunes and saw there, on the peak, a magnificent big elk standing with his head held high and a wild noise calling from his throat. Torn between fear and awe I beat a swift retreat.

Elk near Cranz

Storks

At the end of our inspection I forgave Uncle Egon his indiscretion, because the warden asked me if I had ever noticed ringed storks in our fields. When I confirmed that I had seen such visitors, he wondered if I would work for the migration department on a voluntary basis on our farm by recording the numbers on those rings.

I had seen paintings of green-blue peacocks with perfectly designed fans and of elegant pink flamingos in the Camargue. The Darkehmen tailor had a parrot with bright plumage which could say "Hallo"; Uncle Karl had a canary of a startling yellow colour and with a rich vocabulary; Väti had pointed out an eagle in the sky, calling it "proud and strong"; we heard stories of wise owls, rarely visible in daytime, aloof and dignified; we knew that robins were friendly and cheeky and that nightingales sang beautiful songs. Yet these birds were as nothing compared with our beloved storks, which could neither talk nor sing, because they had no voices at all; whose plumage was plain white with a black border on their wings; whose long red legs and beaks looked grotesque rather than beautiful; which were neither cheeky nor friendly, neither aloof nor dignified.

69

Every morning I watched for the pair from the belfry nest to return after its early foraging trip, and the clatter was my signal to get dressed. The nest was so deep that I never saw the eggs, but I knew that they had been laid when the pair ceased to go out together. Male and female looked so alike that I never knew which was keeping the eggs warm at any particular time. When one returned from the feeding grounds, both would bend their necks until they touched their backs and clatter, clatter, clatter. Then they would sit together for a while in their wide home before the other bird went to look for food.

The babies did make chirping noises; so storks must have something like vocal chords, I thought. But even the warden at Rossitten would not confirm this. Perhaps they had certain embryonic chords which withered as their necks grew.

I thought it sweet when I saw parents put their beaks inside their babies' tiny ones for feeding, but when Mutti informed me that they were providing regurgitated food I felt quite sick. Fortunately that stage did not last very long. When parents brought whole frogs and tore them to pieces on the nest – probably still alive, certainly wriggling – I was not in the least disgusted. Long ago Auguste had told me that it was the frogs' goal in life to become food for baby storks in order to make them strong for their long journey south in the autumn. She had also told me that the will-o'-the-wisps on the bog on summer nights were the happily dancing souls of such frogs.

After the visit to Rossitten my stork observations acquired a more scientific, though no less romantic, dimension. The telescope sent to me looked like a machine gun. I cheerfully lugged it to the meadows at crack of dawn and again at dusk. Dozens of storks from the neighbourhood gathered daily in certain favourite places. They preferred open meadows and the edge of the bog, hardly, if ever, wandering among the bushes. They walked with a funny gait, bending their knees almost at right angles before they waded to another spot. Their partially webbed feet held them steadily at ground level while their beaks plunged into the morass. It was easy to see if they had any rings. I did not have to stand downwind, hide or even be specially quiet: storks allowed humans to within a few metres of their presence without showing any fear. But alas, amongst our regulars there was only one which had been to Rossitten. It was a female which had been born there, as I discovered later, when I had deciphered the number and sent it to the ringing station.

In August two more appeared, from Lithuania, already on their way to Africa. They stayed in Mikalbude for just over a week, an ever-increasing crowd, until one day they all departed and our nests were once again deserted.

I could now follow their journey with regular reports from Rossitten whenever my numbers had been sighted elsewhere. I thought of them foraging in the Danube Delta at the Black Sea – our very own storks among them, I was sure of that – then close to the River Jordan, later along the Nile and all the way to Lake Victoria… Geography, at school a boring succession of weather-and-vegetation charts, lists of the world's capital cities or stuffy ordeals of slides in windowless rooms, now became real and interesting.

The reports kept coming long after the telescope had gone back to Rossitten. In the spring I was informed how far our storks had travelled on their return journey. Then the practical fun began all over again.

Towards the Third Reich

Not long after I had come back from the school holiday in Rossitten, Gisela whistled our usual code and then spoke to me about Uncle Heinz's predicament for the first time.

"Did you hear the news on the radio last night?" she began.

I had not, but now I remembered that Väti had become agitated while listening with his earphones. Gisela was very angry and, I thought, really frightened.

"I hate that man Hitler. Promise that you will also hate that man Hitler, now and forever," she kept repeating. "He is a murderer, murdering people just because they are different. And he does not even marry a woman himself!"

Eventually she told me that Hitler had killed Röhm and his friends simply because they were homosexuals and that he was therefore likely to kill Uncle Heinz, too. I was aghast, frightened and full of hate.

Not so our newspapers, or the radio for that matter. They were full of praise for our high-minded leader, who had taken a stand for morality. It was all very strange. The adults added to my confusion when I overheard them whisper about there being more to it than meets the eye and about Himmler's SS having increased their power. (Not until more than ten years had passed did I learn the true facts of the 'Night of the Long Knives'.)

Uncle Heinz was not murdered. He was thin, pale and subdued when he had served his time, but he resumed his usual work at the Honskamp factory and the family could go away on holiday at last. They often went to the Free State of Danzig, because they were all opera fans and liked the open-air performances at Olivia. Gisela was hoping for 'Turandot', which was her favourite; but her mother feared that it would be 'Tristan und Isolde', which was most emphatically not Gisela's favourite.

Not knowing any operas at all, I had no preferences and not even a strong wish to go to performances. But since Gisela had told me that conversations were sung instead of spoken, I thought that Claus and I should try it at night, instead of talking in ordinary voices before we fell asleep; and so the thoughts and events of the preceding day floated melodiously through our adjoining door. I did not realize that singing voices were louder than normal talk and had no idea that Väti was listening to us, until he asked why we always shrieked cheerful things at a high pitch and made up soft, low tunes to tell of mishaps.

I was taken aback, but Claus answered promptly: "Because sunshine is high and bright and thunder growls."

It was Väti's turn to be taken aback. He had always thought of wise and friendly characters in bass voices and witches in high notes; but he agreed that Claus had a point. We discussed this seriously, in a way we had not talked to each other for a long time. My father had been irritable of late, even frightening at times. I had wondered why he had changed and now I felt guilty, because it might have been disappointment at our lack of musical aspirations that made him so bad-tempered.

In his youth Väti had badly wanted to learn a musical instrument, but had not been allowed to. Only his dreams persisted, and his own missed chances were turned into possibilities for us. We were expected to live the missing part of his childhood for him. We heard this often enough, not in so many words, but in hopeful dreams of *Hausmusik* with me playing the piano (I did not practise for my lessons) and Claus playing the oboe (the assistant master had introduced him to the recorder at Skirlack). Marlene had been allocated the role of a future string player while she was still in her cot. A home-grown trio to match our home-spun itchy clothes – and our nightly operas, which were meant to be a joke, had made Väti happy. I went to the lavatory for a long private cry.

On 2 August 1934 my father said "Hindenburg is dead" and unplugged his earphones so that we could hear the solemn music on the radio. I stared at the portrait above the chaise-longue as if the man had suddenly come alive, a legend turned to mere human flesh and blood. I must have heard before that Hindenburg was the German President who had shaken hands with Hitler at Potsdam a year earlier, but the connection with the hero of Tannenberg had never registered.

The picture had hung in the same place since before I was born: an old face, serious, somewhat distant, with a medal on a jacket which was sketched so lightly that it was not clear if it was a soldier's uniform or a country gentleman's tweed. Long before I was born he had been the saviour of East Prussia. Even before hearing the great story of the Trojan horse I had been told gruesomely fascinating ancient tales of how Hindenburg had driven the Russian army into the Mazurian lakes. In my mind was a vivid picture of thousands of Cossacks on their horses entering a big lake from all sides, riding deeper and deeper into the centre until the waters covered first the horses, then their riders; and on shore I saw that man Hindenburg, cracking a whip. Then, when all was quiet, he lowered his whip and bent his head in silent prayer.

'*Ora et labora*' was Hindenburg's motto, my father had told me in a reverent tone, adding: "a good motto for any life". I believed him, though there was no evidence of the *ora* bit in his behaviour. Protestants, and especially descendants of persecuted Salzburgers, heaped contempt on 'Catholic exhibitionists' who 'rattled off' grace at their dinner tables and openly fingered their rosaries in crisis situations. For me, too, prayer was an intensely private affair, a thanksgiving when I saw no obvious person to whom I could address my happiness. I felt such a prayer when I was certain that Hindenburg's portrait had been conclusively dispatched to the realms of legend.

Not so our captain-of-horse neighbour, who arrived in an ungentlemanly rage and did not even wait for us children to go to bed before he poured it out. He talked of the final seal on the death certificate, not of Hindenburg but of a thing called 'the German constitution' and urged my parents to vote 'no' when it came to a referendum.

"Why?" Väti asked, "I thought you did not have a high regard for it."

I decided I would ask Herr Pichotka, our mathematics teacher, about all this. The history teacher would be useless: he never deviated from our strictly chronological syllabus and we had only just reached Charlemagne. On second thoughts I wondered if there was a link. Our neighbour spoke of Hitler having now become absolute leader, president and supreme commander of the army, as well as chancellor... like Charlemagne?

Our teacher had mentioned that history books might soon be changed; he hoped that the 'great' attribute would be taken away from an emperor who massacred hundreds of Saxons at Verden just because they refused to become Christians. Maybe there was an opening for conversation with the history master, if Hitler now had that same power? My heart sank at the thought of Gisela's uncle Heinz.

But our captain-of-horse's real anger was about the order that army officers – noblemen, most of them – must swear an oath of allegiance to the Little Corporal's person: "Not even Napoleon made his men do that!" he shouted in fury.

"Does it matter", my father wondered, "if you swear to a person or to the constitution – or to the Fatherland or any other concept?"

In the course of this conversation it almost seemed to me that Väti was advocating the breaking of an oath when it was a question of conscience. Yet throughout the eleven years of my life he had made it absolutely clear that it was a supreme crime to break a promise. I should never use the words "I promise", not even in small matters; for, who knew, I might break my leg on the way to fetching a promised something, and then where would I be? Where indeed? I imagined the sky falling down on me or hell swallowing me up, and so I played safe and never made a promise.

It occurred to me that my father was talking nonsense solely to challenge our neighbour's obsession with Hitler's humble origins. I withdrew to bed with the not altogether unpleasant feeling that adults were behaving childishly.

On the rare occasions when I looked at newspapers I felt pangs of remorse at my unsympathetic grudge against my father's tempers. The forward-looking trends from natural living to mechanization frightened me, not so much because they were happening, but rather because there were no regrets. There were boastful statistics about increasing car ownership, radio ownership, electrification of houses, not to speak of financial jargon which I did not understand but found strangely cold and sinister. Väti was still resisting modernization; our lights were still soft except for the blue cold light of spirit lamps, which were used on some ceilings for large parties, when lively, well dressed people deflected from their harshness; and the Opel car still remained in a shed most of the time – for how much longer, I wondered?

Two zeppelins came cruising right across our farm – so light, so huge, so noiseless. Then I did marvel at modern inventions without sensing any fear.

Cousin Rolf was hopping with joy when his Max Schmeling beat Joe Louis. Gigli sang *Vergiss mein nicht*, looking tall and handsome through my tears, and I forgot how short and fat he was. Pola Negri was startlingly attractive in *Mazurka*. Heli Finkenzeller was fun again in *Boccaccio*, singing about romantic nights which are never spent alone. But I hated Shirley Temple, because she was meant to have consoled me after the humiliation of being turned away from the box office when I tried to pass for sixteen. I did not bring it off despite my adult-looking navy mackintosh and the wide-rimmed floppy white linen sunhat. Gisela was luckier and marched right into the cinema to see *Waldwinter*, which was not an exciting adult film at all, she later told me. The offensive bit was apparently the fact that the heroine was a married woman who fell in love with another man – but resisted her own feeling! I should have been grateful for seeing Shirley Temple instead, but I was sulking.

Newsreels preceded every film, and I found them fascinating. But Gisela had no political interests whatsoever. She only liked performances of medal-winning ice skaters like Sonia Hennie or the pair Ernst Baier and Maxi Herber, or certain riders who were occasionally shown as a current affairs feature.

At the end of 1936 Hitler Youth membership became compulsory. I felt almost suicidal with fear of weekly group activities in navy skirts and white blouses. Gisela managed to get a doctor's certificate stating her inability to take part in energetic pursuits on the grounds of tender health, and it suddenly occurred to me that the doctor might have been writing the truth. I began to watch anxiously how easily she tired when we were walking or riding, but my anxieties were dominated by my own good health. One day soon, somebody would come and ask why I was not with them; but perhaps the Darkehmen group left it to the Skirlack group, and since neither of them bothered, I remained free.

Threats of Expulsion

When I reached Quarta, we started geometry lessons, which I adored, physics, which I liked, and English, which I hated. Our English master (whom we nicknamed 'Pico' after a novella in the school library called 'Pico Sand's Mirror' – his real name was Dr Sand) had a strong lisp, which gave the English 'th' a special emphasis with a spray of spittle. I absolutely refused even to try a "th" and was generally becoming obnoxious. Pico, who was second master at the school, wrote to my parents to say that they saw themselves obliged to expel me. My parents were very upset and arranged that I should have a private talk with Pico. It was a very emotional interview.

"Why would you want to stay at this school?"

"Because my parents would be very hurt if I had to leave."

"So you love your parents?"

I was speechless.

Tears came to his eyes as he said: "This proves to me that deep down you are very good. Will you promise to behave well in future English lessons?"

"I can't," I stammered. "I don't know how strong I am. I would not want to break a promise." His emotional manner disgusted me, but I was close to tears myself. When he had composed himself a little, he said I could stay, because my honesty showed that I was a real Christian. He apologized for his own failure to convey the beauty of the English language and expressed the hope that one day I would hear an English actor speak, showing me all the rich varieties of English vowel sounds. He was well aware of his failings, ever so sorry… He really made me feel bad. Pico was unquestionably the kindest of all our teachers; he was also the weakest, the least respected.

Besides English he taught religion. He was so enthusiastic, so sincere, so full of life and a living God. I was a good, attentive pupil during those lessons. I remember the lessons on John IV, particularly verses 20-21.

"It is not Jerusalem, nor any temple, any sacred building. God's church is everywhere, all around us. In the meadows there" – he pointed across the school fence to where we could see grass from our upstairs classroom – "and down below that slope, in the running waters of the Angerapp…"

By contrast our religious instruction in the church hall was irrelevant. Those who wanted to be confirmed – i.e. all but Joachim the Mennonite and Irmgard the Jewess – had to be taught by the main pastor, the superintendent of Darkehmen Church. For the first year we had a two-hour lesson once a week; in the second we had two two-hour periods a week. In all that time we never discussed anything; indeed the pastor strongly objected to questions. He read to us from the Bible, gave a few set explanations of difficult expressions, and above all made sure that we learnt long passages from memory.

I enjoyed learning the psalms, some more than others; but when it came to "the most important things", the Confession of Faith, the Lord's Prayer (as if we did not know it) and the Ten Commandments, which included Luther's *'Was ist das?'* (What does this mean?) after every single commandment, I spent the lessons doodling, yawning loudly and chatting to my neighbour. Thus came the second threat of expulsion, at a time when our dressmaker at home was sewing my confirmation dress. She was already waiting for my next fitting, her mouth full of pins, so that she could not speak, when I told her that there was no point. She ignored my protestations and made me try on the nearly finished garment.

Väti laughed when the superintendent's letter came: "Just let him dare to exclude someone from confirmation!"

But Mutti took the threat seriously and was miserable, while at the same time assuring me that I would have my beautiful organdie dress anyhow, for future balls.

The following Monday both my parents were upset – furious rather than sad. The superintendent had included my name in the public prayer from the pulpit, loud and clear, just after Hitler's! What would people think of our family? Would they shun our company? My classmates, at any rate, thought the situation hilarious.

So I was not going to be confirmed, I thought, and since I might as well be hanged for a sheep as for a lamb, I determined to give that pastor a piece of my mind on a subject that had rankled since the summer of 1937. At that time the arrest and imprisonment of the Berlin-Dahlem pastor Niemöller had sent shockwaves across Germany. Niemöller was a highly respected man of integrity who had become popular through his biographical book on his change from submarine commander in the 1914-18 war to the pulpit. People were confused to discover that not only the Communists but also a man of undoubted patriotism had come into conflict with a government that had done so much good for his country. Our

Darkehmen pastor had kept totally silent in the matter, not even offering a prayer for Niemöller from the pulpit – just one for a girl who disrupted a confirmation class… That was going to be my line of attack.

But when I was called to the vicarage for a surprise interview and the superintendent told me that God had asked him to let me be confirmed, I kept quiet. When he further surprised me by asking that I choose my confirmation axiom there and then – it had to be one verse only, and that from the Old Testament, to which the pastor himself would find a response in the New Testament – I could only think of the Twenty-third Psalm: "He maketh me lie down in green pastures: he leadeth me beside still waters."

"Consider the lilies in the valley…", was his reply.

Did he know that we had ordered lilies-of-the-valley for my confirmation bouquet long before I was nearly excluded?

Confirmation

On 13 March 1938, a week before my confirmation, Germany became part of Austria. That, at least, was how I saw it. It would have been quite unbearable to think of grey Berlin as the capital of the land of the waltz kings. And there was my organdie dress, a frilly low neckline, huge puffed sleeves, a gathered, wide, full-length skirt, just waiting for a waltz under the chandeliers of the Vienna Hofburg… some day. What a lovely dream had begun!

Claus said that I rustled like an angel – that was the taffeta underskirt – and looked like one. I felt more like Lilian Harvey as I stepped into our open carriage. It was a warm, sunny day and I did not need a coat for the drive to Darkehmen. Claus kept turning round from his place near the coachman, just to admire me. "Your aquamarines sparkle brilliantly," he said.

The aquamarine was supposed to be my birth-stone, whatever that meant. Omi had given me one, hanging from a platinum chain, as a confirmation present. Mutti gave me a ring, part gold, part platinum, with the same stone, and Väti gave me a gold watch. Confirmation was the most important occasion in a person's life, and everybody gave the most precious gift they could afford.

I would have liked to wave to people along the roadside as princesses did in films, but there were no people lining the chaussée for me. When I saw the crowds near the vicarage, I suddenly did not feel in the least bit royal, but excited in an unexpected way.

The bells were ringing when we walked in procession from the vicarage to the church. I let my tears fall, because I had not brought a handkerchief and did not dare to use my new silk gloves. I clutched my bouquet and white, gold-embossed hymn book, trying desperately and unsuccessfully to think of something funny.

We sat in the front rows of the church. The girl next to me wet herself profusely. I saw the little stream running along the floor and noticed the big patch on the back of her dress when she went forward to the altar, but I was not aware of what had happened until long after we had quietly driven home and worldly thoughts reasserted themselves.

The first of those thoughts was a shock: the maids, cook, Frau Schalonka and Frau Schwarz ceremoniously lined up on the veranda steps to greet me, calling me "Miss" and addressing me by the formal "Sie".

Newly confirmed "adult"

Was this some kind of joke? Apparently not. A confirmed person was an adult, and the only way to return to familiar ways was to drink *Brüderschaft*.

"All right then, let's get on with it," I said, anxious to re-establish normality.

Väti brought champagne to the veranda. One after the other linked right arms with me – the arms which were holding the glass – drank the contents in this position, then introduced themselves informally: "Frieda". "Anneli", I replied. It was a ridiculous, but quite pleasant way of becoming tipsy.

Yet when Frau Schalonka said "Henriette," I nearly choked. "No", I said, unlinking my arm, "that is something I cannot say." How could I possibly, after my lifetime of looking up to the woman? I was nearly in tears, wishing I had never been confirmed, when Frau Schalonka insisted it was that or the new formality. Mutti suggested a compromise: the women of the farm should continue to call me by my Christian name, but change to the "Sie" form of address, while I was to continue as always. It still seemed silly, but was the best I could get.

That done, we feasted; speeches and humorous verses were read from the special confirmation magazine produced in a joint effort by Uncle Arnold and Uncle Karl. Then Gisela arrived and the dancing began.

Gisela could not have a party in her own house, because her grandmother had died a few days earlier. She came by car with Kurt Fuchslocher, an agricultural student from Chile who had spent the past three years experimenting with various methods of grass cultivation on the different soils of a number of farms in the district. He was a tall, handsome man and Gisela had a crush on him. But though he danced with her more often than with any other partner, and though she was now grown-up, she could not even tempt him to a kiss, nor to writing letters from Chile after he left East Prussia. So we later assumed that he had died in an earthquake which made headlines in our papers. We named clearings in our forest in his honour, Great-Chile and Little-Chile, according to the degree of earthquaky appearance of the felled trees that lay there.

But on our confirmation day we dreamt of Gisela's love while we danced until morning broke and we had to change for our first communion service at the Darkehmen church. I again had a special dress made for the occasion: navy blue silk with collar and cuffs in a chequered blue and pink weave of special ribbons. I felt really ladylike, though I never had any ambitions in that way. Then, when the pastor offered me the big silver chalice, I accepted it with both hands and drained the last drop of the red wine. My poor parents nearly sunk into the ground with embarrassment.

Thus we reached the official social – if not legal – status of adults at the age of barely fifteen. Teachers at school now addressed us in the formal manner, except for Herr Pichotka, who thought it crazy to change just for the few weeks we had left in Darkehmen. We were coming up to the *Einjährige* examinations which qualified pupils for most jobs and training courses, though not for university studies.

My Last School

The time for farewell parties had come. Angelic white underdresses gave way to pink or blue taffeta of the same pattern. Officers billeted in farmhouses during the annual manoeuvres joined the school leavers. I was jealous of Nucke, because the young man Nöh could not be distracted from adoring her. What was this thing called sex-appeal? Nucke was not at all beautiful, but men swarmed round her like flies – grown men, not our classmates. She had once written about my extreme "non-athleticism" in an end-of-year school magazine: "Sturmlauf ist das allerschönste! Schon die Nacht davor, da stöhnste… in der langen Ferienzeit, sammle Kraft zu neuem Streit!" ("The assault course is best of all! She already starts groaning the night before… Over the holidays, save up your strength for a new contest!")

Waves of joy superseded the depths of apprehension, only to plunge again to that sinking feeling of fear. A single-sex school was an alarming prospect, but Darkehmen did not continue beyond the *Einjährige*, and the Insterburg schools, the *Lyceum* for girls, the *Gymnasium* for boys, were our only chance to reach university entrance levels. For three whole years I would have to persevere. The only other Darkehmen girl would be in a different class.

Gisela was going to study graphic art in Königsberg. Her parents had already rented a studio flat for her, which sounded exciting, much though I should have hated to stay in a town all week. But Gisela was a town girl anyhow. She would see the opening nights of films which came to Darkehmen many months later; she would see many operas; and, best of all, she would write to me about it all. The prospect was exhilarating. The letters, when they came, were rather less so: she would draw cartoons, add a few words, then another cartoon on a totally unrelated subject. They were as Gisela talked, often changing topic in mid-sentence; but on paper it seemed more confusing.

I replied in lengthy, detailed accounts which probably bored Gisela: about the strain of giggly, all-female surroundings; about the history teacher, who was very

78

fat and sometimes stood against the classroom door (probably to catch a little draught to cool her down, we thought) and about her challenging, thought-provoking statements. Her nickname was 'Red Klara', because older people swore that they had seen her on the barricades in Berlin with the Spartacus group in the twenties. I also wrote about the maths teacher, who was so brilliant that she simply could not grasp the absence of brilliance in others. She would call out to me in desperation: "Anneli, can you explain it to them in simple words?" This worked all right in maths and in physics, where we Darkehmer were ahead of the lyceum pupils, but was a fiasco in chemistry, which we had never been taught at all.

Walking along birch avenue

I also wrote a magniloquent obituary on Thienemann, the founder of the Rossitten observatory, whose death spelt the end of my stork observations.

These letters of mine were written on bus journeys to and from town, which took well over an hour each way. I also did most of my homework on the bus, so that I was free to enjoy farm life after a late lunch.

A new machine had arrived which performed the astonishing feat of binding corn into sheaves even while cutting it. We marvelled at this technological miracle without undue worry. It required no more than one violent thunderstorm to make the self-binder redundant for the rest of the season. Out came the scythes to cut the flattened rye; the women walking behind, gathering large armfuls and twisting ropes of straw around the bundles in the old manner, their chatter following the friendly swooshing sound of the men, and the larks above sang loudly.

Lessons at Insterburg were far more stimulating than they had been in our old school. This was natural, given that we were preparing for university. We had heated arguments in class, and when I was not sure of my views, I deliberately contradicted other people's in order to discover my own.

Were Schiller's sympathies misplaced in his tragedy *Maria Stuart*? Should not the statesmanship of Elizabeth I be admired? All but one girl in the class came out in favour of the heroine Mary. We discussed freedom of thought, as requested by the Marquis Posa in Schiller's *Don Carlos*. We were encouraged to read *Wilhelm*

Tell, as it was still available in bookshops, although no longer permitted as part of the schools' literature syllabus.

That was the first official confirmation I had of the government making decisions about what people should read. Aunt Anne had always said this without giving definite examples. Soon I discovered a more sinister sign of such prohibitions.

Anneliese Bagdahn, our neighbour's daughter, had gone to a language school in Hamburg and was apparently moving in 'patrician' circles, a class peculiar to cities of the old Hanseatic League. Mutti thought that I would find it interesting to read about them and suggested that I try Thomas Mann's *The Buddenbrooks*. In a bookshop I was told politely that it was out of print; in the library the assistant shouted at me: "Is this your idea of a joke? Or is it more sinister?" Then, probably recognizing my innocence, she added: "Beware of the person who told you to ask for this. We certainly don't stock subversive literature; it would be a criminal offence."

"Stupid cow," Mutti said when I reported my experience, "covering up her own ignorance." She was quite adamant that no books could ever be forbidden in Germany; such things happened only in Communist states. But no, she would not come to the library with me: it was undignified to argue with stupid people. She added that I should resist Aunt Anne's influence because the latter had a bee in her bonnet about Hitler's lack of literary education.

I could have cried with frustration. Why would my mother never believe me when matters did not fit into her image of reality? Väti actually had the book on his shelves, but I found it hard to follow Mann's endlessly long sentences and gave up. There were more books I wanted to read than I had time for, and Hanseatic citizens did not rank high on my list.

In English we read *Hamlet* and *The Merchant of Venice*, which forced me to admit that Shakespeare was almost as good a writer as Goethe, despite the overdose of cruelty and deceit in his plays. We also read *Oliver Twist* and learnt Hood's '*Song of the Shirt*' by heart, both confirming my depressing vision of Britain. Shelley's *Ode to the West Wind* slightly improved my opinion of the distant island. My image of America was conjured up by *Uncle Tom's Cabin* and *Tom Sawyer*. It never occurred to me to admire these countries for the freedom of making unflattering stories available for all to read.

France came across as I wanted to see it, with Daudet's *Lettres de mon moulin*, Balzac's *La femme de trente* (trust the French to describe an old woman of thirty falling in love!), Lamartine, La Fontaine, Molière... I loved them all.

It made me angry that girls' schools were not considered fit for learning ancient Greek; the boys at the *Gymnasium* were equally angry at having to learn that language. But my real fury was directed against our headmaster, who made Latin a 'compulsory option' for the academic stream of the school. Officially it was regarded as a voluntary part of the syllabus. So why did he not leave it to us to decide?

"Because it provides valuable training in logic," he said when I confronted him.

"What kind of logic is there in compulsory choice?"

"None," he laughed, "but I had to find a way to give you foundations which you might one day be grateful for."

"Not I! Not unless I can also have lessons in Greek!" I explained. But there was no one at our school who could have volunteered to teach Greek.

I stubbornly refused to take part in learning Latin and read *Gone with the Wind* on my lap during the lessons. If some of the teacher's utterances entered my brain despite myself, I could not do much about it. One of the words I even liked: *urbs, urbis* suited the way we felt after a tray-full of Café Dünkel's cream cakes. We bought piles of these in our free periods and urb-urbised our way to a bench in the town park and back.

Signs of the Times

In biology we learnt to understand the value of Arian genes in the Indo-Germanic races. Good breeding on the Indian sub-continent and in Nordic areas of Europe had resulted in a pure concentration of mankind's most noble features, and certain genes for intelligence were most strongly attached to the blond and blue-eyed Europeans. Certain characteristics of size and bone structure excluded the Slavs from this category. As dark genes were dominant, my only chance of having gipsy-like children was to marry a man with black hair and black eyes and hope that he had not stored any of the recessive pale characteristics.

At least once a year gipsies came to visit our farm and others in the area. They were mostly treated with suspicion and fear of their possible thieving habits, but I really loved them: their dark hair, brown skin and sparkling dark eyes and their generally romantic behaviour. Remarks that they were probably not of strong moral nature did not worry me.

One man played either a violin or an accordion and another held a bear, standing on his hind haunches, by a collar which was round his neck; and with his head held high, the bear danced to the music in almost perfect rhythm. "How cruel!" some bystanders said. "How romantic!" I thought.

Our inspector had a gramophone record that sang "O come, you black gipsy, come play me a tune, so that I might forget what I have lost...", and although I had not lost anything, this song made me feel sad and happy at the same time. I was pleased to be given some coins to put into the man's begging bag, but even a good friend like Frau Schalonka shook her head disapprovingly. "Beggars," she muttered. Of course, she would say that, being such a hard-working woman herself.

Gisela's art college had potato holidays like ordinary schools, and so it happened that we were together in the Darkehmen cinema when the newsreel of the Sudetenland's 'homecoming' was shown. People were shouting and singing and crying with joy as Hitler drove through the streets of Eger, and we in the cinema cried with them. We were so moved, so thankful for Hitler, who had liberated the poor wretches without spilling a drop of blood.

I hated crying in front of other people, but it happened to me again, once more in a cinema, not long after the Sudetenland scenes. This time it was a feature film,

Ich klage an – I Accuse – which showed the suffering of terminally ill or severely handicapped people who were unable to die because the law prohibited euthanasia. Cinemas gave special morning performances for schools, to which we were taken as part of our education. The education worked: there was an outcry against that particular law and by public demand it was duly changed.

Tears again that autumn, privately howling this time, behind the locked doors of our lavatory. Furious, sad and rebellious tears. The name of my home was to be changed from Mikalbude to Mickelau; and, almost worse, Omi's dear Alischken was being turned into Walddorf. Many other places in East Prussia were thus 'Germanified'. At least, that was the official reason given; it had some validity in several cases, but none in the instance of our farm. Darkehmen, founded as a town by that name, registered in a Prussian royal charter of 1726, was now named after the River Angerapp, turning Opa's former estate into Klein-Angerapp.

All this was bad for sentimental reasons, but worse were the rumours that came with the re-naming: "It's to confuse the Russians..." "Hitler won't give them time to update their maps..." "War against the Bolsheviks must be imminent..."

War? How could that be? Hitler had achieved all his goals without bloodshed. Surely he could defeat Communism by our shining example, showing that even workers were better off without dictatorship? And besides, why did confusing maps matter unless he expected Russian troops to enter East Prussia? Questions, denials, rumours, even hopes. I for one was determined never to use the new place names.

10th November 1938

It was still dark when I took the 6 o'clock bus in the mornings, and as winter approached, it was dark when I arrived in Insterburg. But it had never been as dark as on that morning of 10 November 1938.

No lights shone from shops in the market square where the bus stopped as usual. There was an eerie silence, as if the plague had struck the town overnight and wiped out the entire population. The square, usually bustling at this hour, was totally empty. Whiffs of something smouldering drifted from somewhere. Automatically I set out for the school, hardly expecting it still to be there. Then I saw some girls up on the hill and felt normality coming back.

In front of our school was a small park. A woman sat on one of the benches, not dressed for November, I thought, perhaps wearing only a nightdress. Was she staring at me, asking something? I did not stop to look and listen. I just ran past her as fast as my shaking legs would carry me, towards the sanctuary of our school.

In my hurry I shut the big doors with a thunderous bang and waited for a teacher to come from the staff room to tell me off. No one came, and all the staff room doors were shut.

Half-way up the stairs I again stopped, panting for breath and watching with relief as the quadrangle of the inner courtyard came into focus through the hole I was blowing on the frosted window panes. The gym building on the left, the pre-*Secunda* classes opposite, the laboratory wing on my right, all still there and in perfect order.

Uschi, the poetess of our class, was hiding her head in her arms on the desk. I wondered if she was crying. Someone shouted: "I tell you, he has coped with anarchists before, he will put them in their place now." – "But what if he has lost control?" – "Then he will regain it. He is the Führer!"

"My father said he saw SA men there…" "Your father is a liar." "No, he isn't. But he might not have seen that clearly in the dark…"

What were they talking about? I listened from the door and was puzzled. Gerda was just coming in. I asked her what on earth had happened. She whispered in my ear that the synagogue had been burnt down last night, Jewish shops, too, furniture thrown into the street from Jewish houses, terrible happenings. No, she had not seen it herself, only the rubble now, on her way to school, but her parents had told her before.

"Who did this?" I whispered back.

"The shit-coloured people, but don't tell anyone I said so."

From inside the classroom a girl expressed her conviction that the anarchists had already been put in prison for the damage they caused the previous night.

Just then the school bell rang for the daily assembly in the *Aula*. As always, the teachers processed along the centre gangway, then turned towards us from the front, lifted their arms and shouted in unison "*Heil Hitler!*" We all replied in the same manner.

We sat down, holding our hymnbooks and waiting for the number to be announced. But there did not seem to be a hymn that morning. The headmaster began his announcements straight away: "There will be no school today," he began, but before we had time to shout "Hurray!", he continued: "We have received instructions to give you the chance to go and see what has been achieved last night. I know that none of our pupils will want to do so, but you have the day off, anyhow."

The music teacher started the national anthems on the piano, and the headmaster stopped half-way down the gangway to raise his arm. It seemed as if he had forgotten the normal endings of assemblies this morning. We all lifted our right arms and sang, first one verse of the *Deutschlandlied*, then the *Horst-Wessel* song, without a pause between the two to rest our arms. Everybody, regardless of the supposed stamina of Nordic genes, had to use their left arms to help support the right towards the end of the two anthems.

It was not until I found myself standing alone in our classroom that the impact of the headmaster's words hit me. And what was I to do now? It was not yet 9 o'clock and my bus did not leave until 2 p.m. All my classmates had disappeared.

I was just beginning to wonder if I might have been locked in when I heard a door creak downstairs. The headmaster was as startled as I was when, in my hurry, I fell from the last steps right into his arms.

"What are you still doing here?" he asked.

I tried to introduce myself. "I am from Class Secunda, my name…"

"I don't forget the name of the lady who tried to blackmail me into providing Greek lessons," he smiled.

I told him about my waiting time for the bus.

"I thought you had relatives in town," he said.

"Well, not very close ones," I stammered. The very last person I wanted to meet this morning was my Nazi uncle Egon, but I could not tell the headmaster that. Perhaps he knew. He nodded gravely and then asked if there were no trains before the bus. I knew that trains ran more frequently, but I had no money for a ticket. He offered me the money, but I turned back as he opened the door for me: "There is a woman on a bench..." I had only just remembered her and was frightened.

"A woman and a child," he replied, "but don't worry, they are all right now."

He did not explain, but he offered to walk to the station with me. He was a very nice man, I thought, and I would have liked to hold his hand for extra security, but I didn't.

When we had found out the time of my train the headmaster offered to phone my parents so that I could be met at Beynuhnen station.

"No thanks, it is only a 6-kilometre walk, which will be lovely, especially today."

He told me to take an extra day off; he would explain to my class mistress. I walked slowly from the station. The crisp November air was refreshing, and I tried to forget the morning. But the memories kept coming back, not like the exhilarating waves of the Baltic on days when we ignored the danger flag on the beach, but like Auguste's ghost stories.

My parents had heard on the radio what had happened: German people, outraged at the murder of a German diplomat by a Polish Jew in Paris, had taken the law into their own hands. But Hitler would know about it and would punish them.

"The headmaster said that he had instructions from above for us to celebrate", I told Mutti angrily, trying to hold back my tears.

"You must have misheard that," Mutti replied and made some cherry soup with semolina dumplings which did not taste as good as usual.

I went to bed early and lay there quietly, ignoring Claus.

From the distance I heard the Inspector's gramophone. "*Du schwarzer Zigeuner, komm, spiel mir was vor...*": Black gipsy, play for me so that I may forget what I lost... When had the gipsies last come to the farm, I wondered. I had not seen them for... was it years? I could not remember. I buried my head in the pillow and howled – for the dancing bear, for Mikalbude, for Alischken, for the woman on the park bench, for myself. I fell asleep.

But that same winter we started ballroom dancing lessons. Quadrilles, minuets, gavottes, as well as waltzes and tangos which I had enjoyed all my life. Short dresses in soft chiffons for ordinary lessons, a new orange slip under my organdie dress for the first coming-out ball, and then – oh what bliss! – a wide, tiered crinoline in light blue tulle for the big ball. Sometimes I spent the night at the Kowalewskis after a ball or after long evenings on the smooth ice of the specially flooded tennis courts, where we danced under spotlights to music from loudspeakers.

Dancing at the von Skepsgardhs in January 1939

In March the Memelland was re-joined to the German Reich. Then Czechoslovakia was "saved from internal conflict" by becoming a German "protectorate", and the Moravian minorities were given their long-desired freedom. The creation of the multi-national state of Czechoslovakia had flown in the face of all those principles that supposedly governed the Treaty of Versailles. Now, without shedding a drop of blood, Hitler was "restoring freedom" to the people.

Men in Uniform

Our school holiday in June 1939 was in Pillau. We were accompanied by our young sports teacher, Fräulein Paullun, and by our elderly Latin teacher, Dr Quasowski. The latter wanted to be matey on holiday and asked us either to call her by her nickname 'Quasi', or, worse still, to call her 'Mutti', as she was taking the place of our mothers for a fortnight. Moreover, we were to address her by the familiar 'Du' form. I found the request so unpleasantly undignified that I never addressed her at all. In other respects the holiday was good.

We made excursions to the *Frische Nehrung*, which separated the *Frische Haff* from the Baltic, similar to the *Kurische Nehrung* further north, but without the wandering sand dunes and the elks. There we explored the ruins of Balga, a fort built by the Teutonic Knights. In Pillau we wandered round the old citadel, taking photos of the statue of the Great Elector or of the harbour view from the lighthouse. We sat in fishing boats moored at the quay and painted watercolours, or just lay dreaming at the bottom of the rocking boats. Most of these things we did on our own or in small groups with special friends.

But the entire class joined an inspection of the battleship Scharnhorst, where we made individual dates with sailors who were coming on shore leave that night. We met them at an inn and some stayed there; others went to other inns; but my sailor did not like the stuffiness of such places and suggested a walk. He chatted incessantly, as if afraid to talk, and once he wove a random remark about the possibility of war into the chat. He did not really expect to die, but would I, please, accept his hatband to remember him by? I still have the navy band with the letters SCHARNHORST in golden thread, because on our refugee trek in 1945 a box of funny souvenirs accompanied me by accident.

On the farm a group of Hitler Youths from Danzig was helping with the harvest, "promoting understanding between town and country", and at the same time trying to inculcate a sense of the German-ness of their Free State. The older ones had been with us since the previous autumn, boys of fourteen or fifteen who had finished school and were too young for Labour Service in the RAD (*Reichsarbeitsdienst*). On Sundays they wore their uniforms and performed a flag drill which was not unlike that of the RAD; but on weekdays only Walter, their leader, wore Hitler Youth clothes, which in winter included a kind of trench coat and a cap. They all appeared to enjoy life on the farm, but the young schoolboys, who came from the same area just for the summer holidays and were doing light children's work, really had fun in the open air.

Scandinavian Visitors

Then Keijo arrived. Officialdom encouraged the mingling of Nordic races. Our family welcomed the chance of receiving a real-life foreigner in our midst, particularly one with the lustre of aurora borealis and midnight sun and the mysteries of wood nymphs and freedom fighters.

Keijo Heinonen came from Helsinki. His father was an engineer in charge of the construction of the stadium for the Helsinki Olympic Games, which were to take place the following year. He had gone to Berlin to see and discuss the 1936 stadium and Olympic village with German engineers while his son stayed with us for three weeks in order to learn our language.

Keijo was fifteen years old and the reality of his physical appearance was a far cry from our romantic expectations. I found it extremely difficult to ignore the chicken fluff where a beard or moustache was beginning to indicate his approaching manhood. Why on earth did he not shave? I politely refrained from asking that question for a time, but when I came to know him a little better, I asked it straight out.

"Why don't you wear a bra?" he laughed in reply and made me blush with embarrassment. How could he possibly have told? But I had to admit that there was a similarity, that I was as determined as he was not to cut short those few years of childhood for the long years of adulthood to come.

"And I have an even more specific reason," Keijo explained with that half-sad, half-mocking smile that I by now recognized as his special feature: "as soon as I see myself as a man, I will feel obliged to volunteer as a soldier for the coming war."

"But you are only fifteen!"

"It's not a question of years but of personality. Besides, I'm nearly sixteen like you."

As if I could imagine myself in a war! Or indeed imagine war at all. What was he talking about?

"It's coming, and it's coming soon. But we shall be on the same side," he added, as if to reassure me.

"Do you mean to say that Finland and Germany will fight a war against Communism soon?"

"Not exactly," he replied. "We have no common cause on the basis of that definition. But, ideology apart, Russia is our common enemy."

He tried to explain what he considered the values of 'real Communist societies' to be, adding that in fact he, or more precisely his father, very much desired such a society. Moreover, Finland owed her status as an independent state for the first time in her history precisely to the Russian Revolution. But Russia had remained a Czarist type of imperial and expansionist power despite the revolution. Finland would fight Czarism without a Czar.

I did not believe him. Keijo was prejudiced, and I would wait for what Claus might have to report after his visit to Keijo's homeland, close to the Russian border.

"I think it should be you instead of Claus. You'd get more out of it," Keijo suggested, and Claus enthusiastically chirped in: "Quite right!"

Much as my brother enjoyed having a foreigner as a guest, the reciprocal aspect of the scheme, involving his own journey to Helsinki, had never appealed to him. My heart missed a beat with excitement.

That same summer Gisela's family had children from Kristianstad in Sweden staying with them. They were two brothers, Torsten and Bengt, and their sister Harriet, whose parents had made friends with Gisela's father when he went to England the previous year.

We decided on a joint day excursion to show our guests the beauty of the Mazurian lakes. My father had bought a new car in spring, a 'Wanderer' with a folding roof. He no longer believed in the business-only potential of cars and had bought us all tight-fitting white linen caps with small ventilation studs in the earflaps. The car had been photographed, roof down and us inside, and people said that it looked very smart. I was still sulking – in sympathy with Mutti, who had always predicted that a car would mean the end of our coach trips – and said that a lake was a lake was a lake and that we had two perfectly good ones within reach by horse and carriage.

But I was proud to take Keijo and the Swedes to the further ones. We bathed in water so clear that one could have drunk it. We picnicked on sandy strips between dark forests and glittering lakes. While we stuffed ourselves with Mutti's yeast cakes and Frau Honskamp's cheese straws, the Swedish children told us of their journey through the Corridor, the strip of territory which, since the cession of West Prussia to Poland under the Treaty of Versailles, had constituted the sole link between East Prussia and the rest of the Reich. Travellers had to make this journey in sealed carriages.

"A girl called Britt-Inger pointed to a dirty pile of rubbish on the station platform, held her nose and laughed. She went on laughing when two policemen outside the carriage raised threatening fingers at her. We felt safe in our sealed carriage. Then, suddenly, the seal was undone and the policemen came in, shouting at the girl in Polish. We naturally did not understand what they were saying. Our teacher tried to intervene, but the girl was dragged out and taken to some station building with the teacher running after her. We all waited and waited. It seemed like hours before Britt-Inger and the teacher came back and the train moved on. Apparently it had all been some misunderstanding."

Gisela's father told us that the teacher who accompanied the transport of the Swedish exchange children was now trying to re-arrange their return journey by sea from Pillau or Danzig. Present conditions in the Corridor were frightening and untenable, the adults agreed. But was the idea of leaving from Danzig wise just now?

Keijo looked at me with an air of "I told you so"; yet he had talked of fighting Russia, not Poland, I thought.

"I'm going for another swim," Gisela said, and most of us joined her.

When the sun set into the lake a long red, rippled strip of light moved towards us and somewhere at the side there was a perfectly round reflection of light, as if from a second sun. The forests around the lake grew deep black. Fragments of music drifted across the lake. We walked along the shore to find it while our parents looked for a way round by car.

The bandstand was illuminated by strong electric lights which reflected on to the dance floor and attracted the mosquitoes away from the unlit guest tables of the lakeside garden. The violins were playing 'Bel ami', and Keijo asked me to dance with him. He was so serious, not in the least like Maupassant's hero. The thought made me giggle, or perhaps it was the wine.

"I didn't like your '*Carpe Diem*' motto when I first saw it above your desk," Keijo said, "but perhaps you're right. How long have you had it?"

"We have another motto, too, " Gisela interrupted: "*Aux armes, citoyens!*"

"Oh no, not now," I cried.

"You're right," she said, "not now."

The adults were still talking about the Corridor and Danzig, spoiling a beautiful summer night on the Mazurian lake.

A few days later, when we stood by the midsummer night fire on a field near the birch avenue, Keijo said: "Carpe Diem, will you jump with me?"

I was wearing my most colourful chequered skirt and my very bright scarlet blouse on purpose to be aglow in the light of the flames. The film *Black Roses* was in black and white, but I always imagined that Lilian Harvey was wearing red when she jumped across the fire with Willi Fritsch. I dreamt of imitating her, but when Keijo asked me, I did not have the courage to say yes.

Keijo's sadness was more than affectation and boastful projection of himself as a freedom fighter, though I tried to pretend it was only that. On his departure for Finland he said that he would shave and write to me from the trenches; I replied that I expected letters from Helsinki and his family log cabin in Karelia, and that I would come and see his school next year.

Fear and Hope

I was grimly determined to believe in peace and happiness, refusing to read the papers, listen to the radio, or snatch fragments of adult conversation lest they disturb my mind with doubts.

Mutti was on my side, cheerful and positive. Overcoming her natural aversion to arguments, she now frequently raised her optimistic voice to interrupt the gloom of conversation.

"Only a sharpened sword can deter aggression and keep peace": this slogan had long dictated the pace of German rearmament and proved successful in achieving many goals without bloodshed. Sharp words were part of that sword. There was no reason to fear that the problem of the Corridor would not be resolved in the same peaceful way as those of Austria, Sudetenland, Memelland... Except that the Poles were proud people who would die rather than succumb...? Except that Hitler had never retracted from the goal of Ukrainian cornfields and wide eastern living space...? And that the way to Russia was through Poland...?

Off the coast of Cranz we saw a minesweeper that summer. Holidaymakers congregated on shore to stare and guess at the apparition, mixing serious comments with sarcastic laughter.

"Blocking the way to Leningrad...?" I did not know the person who asked that question.

Cameras clicked, Väti's among them. When I stuck his photo into my album, I wrote Gretchen's last words to Faust as a caption, except that I used the letter H. instead of Heinrich: "*H., mir graut's vor Dir*" (H., I'm in dread of you).

Minesweeper in Baltic

Yet the sun was warm, the harvest good, and I had Silhouette, my own riding horse. There were so many reasons to be happy.

My father was realizing a years-old dream, the construction of his ideal room. He was extending and enclosing our garden veranda for that purpose. The room remained on stilts of brickwork. We did not mean to use the room in winter, so there was no need to extend the cellar from underneath the house for warmth. Windows all around and a glass door made it look like a conservatory, but we did not keep plants in the room, except for the usual vase of flowers on the table.

Our carpenter created sturdy window seats in oak all along the walls, and a table which was the right size for a game of ping-pong when not required for a meal. Curtains, tablecloths, and the covering of long cushions for the seats and backs of benches were all made of hand-woven materials in complementary rustic designs in red, brown, and cream tones. There were no other decorations. The picture we could see was the living, ever-changing expanse of lawns and fields, trees, flowers, shrubs. Here we sat long after we had finished supper, indulging intemperately in the beauty of sunsets.

No one wanted to give in to fear, yet no one could quite overcome despondency – not until the end of August 1939, when Ribbentrop concluded a non-aggression pact with the Soviet Union. The cloud lifted. Except as a stepping-stone into Russia, Poland could be of no interest even to Hitler. Even our most sceptical friends slept well again at night.

YEARS OF QUESTIONING: 1939–1944

Not many days passed before the radio told us we were at war. It was a surprise that was as unsurprising as the sudden conclusion of an argumentative chapter in a book. I felt nothing, except for a certain satisfaction which my little brother put into focus when he exclaimed triumphantly: "Serves him right." The boastful peacemaker who achieved all without bloodshed had exposed his weakness.

But our moment of triumph was cut short by Väti's angry and sarcastic outburst: Did we understand whose blood was going to be shed? Were we incapable of thinking? Did we perhaps imagine some medieval type of contest between two leaders to settle the dispute? No, we did not, we admitted, nor did we think that Hitler was going to shed his own blood. But we could not think any further, because we did not know a single soldier in person.

A war that was geographically so close to home remained distant for as long as the Polish campaign lasted, an almost abstract daily radio account of numbers in kilometres, tanks, prisoners, enemy dead, German heroes.

Central Europe in 1939

– – – – – – Boundary between Germany and U.S.S.R., 28 September 1939

The concrete effects of war had begun before we knew their meaning: rationing was introduced for certain goods, ostensibly to encourage thrift and fight waste in principle. Most of the measures we found thoroughly commendable, merely affirming the way we chose to live anyhow, but the withdrawal of our large passenger-carrying postal buses came as a great shock to Claus and me. Even if passenger trains had not been affected – and they were reduced by the new rules – it made no sense for us to spend more time travelling than actually at school. Our

91

parents were already looking for boarding establishments, for Claus in Darkehmen, for me in Insterburg.

Claus was placed together with two friends in the home of a family who eventually expelled them for making the family's Dachshund drunk on beer. He was later accepted as the only boarder in a *pension* where there was no dog.

Mutti tried to persuade me to go to the house where she had stayed as a schoolgirl and where my cousins Annelore and Ursel were happy now. Two jolly, elderly sisters were apparently looking after a jolly crowd of about a dozen girls and giving them a jolly time. That was an unbearable prospect for me. Fortunately my father found Fräulein Gramenz. She lived in a first-floor flat, and her only boarder apart from me was Felix Dirichlet.

I cannot pretend I was happy staying in town for five days a week, but I could bear it. Fräulein Gramenz was a lady in her late 40s. Very occasionally she was a little pathetic in her attempts to convince us that she had not been left on the shelf but was a spinster and a professional woman by choice – this fact was fairly obvious to us from her beauty and intelligence, anyhow. Generally, however, she was a sensible person and interesting to talk to whenever we chose to join her in the drawing room in the evening. She checked our homework if we had problems and left us alone when we did not ask for help. Thanks to her I began to understand a little chemistry, but I never caught up well enough to shine in that subject.

Fräulein Gramenz arrived home from work well before we came back for lunch; and we began to guess from the smells on the stairway what treats she had concocted. She did not expect us to do the washing up, but we had to polish our own shoes and make our beds, two jobs which I had not learnt before.

When our landlady had rushed back to her office, Felix and I did our homework, read books or played a board game. Sometimes I went to the cinema; in winter we both went to the ice rink and really forgot to be sorry for our town imprisonment. I should have done piano practice; my teacher tried her very best to encourage me, because for some absurd reason she was convinced of my musical potential. She would even go to such extremes as to come to the flat and give me a lesson when she – rightly – assumed that I would forget to go to her. But I was stubbornly committed to being unmusical.

My relationship to girls in my class was one of friendly indifference. I had not the slightest inclination to meet any of them in the afternoon, though once, from curiosity, Felix and I went to observe the crazy ritual which had been part of Insterburg school life since time immemorial and was called "walking the slipway". My mother had known the same pastime during her years in that town.

We could hardly believe what we saw. There were girls on the broad pavement on one side, boys on the other. They were walking up and down a particular stretch of the sloping main street, throwing glances at the opposite sex on the opposite side until, by some sign or intuition, a girl knew that a certain boy would follow her. Then she would detach herself from her giggling companions and carelessly amble away. A boy followed in that same careless manner and somehow, somewhere, they met, perhaps to walk in the park, sometimes even to kiss, I was told. Felix and I made fun of them all by walking together, changing from one side of the 'slipway' to the other, enjoying the consternation we caused for a while before it all became insufferably boring.

I was simply doing time in Insterburg, counting the months to the start of university life; and I was bearing it well. Only very occasionally did a certain sound, such as the clatter of a horse's hooves, the smell of earth from someone's window box or a special kind of light in the sky overpower me with homesickness. Then I would leave a note for Fräulein Gramenz and make for the station.

I still remember the intense happiness I felt on my night walks from Beynuhnen station, but I also recall my mother's worried face at my midnight arrivals. So I tried to wait until Saturday afternoons.

At least I was spared the Hitler Youth gatherings, which must have spoilt the weekends for most of my classmates. State Youth Day had been changed to Sundays, leaving Saturday mornings for ordinary school again. Not to have a single whole day in the week without being organized seemed to me quite outrageous; but there were people who actually enjoyed this, my cousin Lore among them.

Polish Prisoners

An awareness of war had come to our peaceful farm in the shape of prisoners. The Poles were the first. They were seven men in all, in uniforms which looked almost new and smart after a campaign which had been too short to wear out clothes. Our carpenter hastily put up bunk beds in one room of the old redundant farm cottage, and the Poles themselves filled large sacks with straw for mattresses.

Except for one man they could not speak German, and our German workers only remembered the Polish word for 'dirty dog', which they had learnt in the last war. When the prisoners learnt the German equivalent of the expression the two groups could converse. They socialized forever after, addressing each other by whichever name they found easier to pronounce, surname or Christian name. But the man whose surname was Zarod was always addressed as "Herr Zarod", because his gentlemanly manner forbade a more familiar form. Mutti in particular was so impressed by this Jewish lawyer that she would have offered him a single guestroom in our house if Väti had not forbidden such favours.

This gallant Mr Zarod delighted in arranging dry grasses and evergreens into bouquets, presenting them to the lady of the house with deep bows and a kiss of hand. He even discovered a berry-bearing spindle tree in a part of the forest which we had never explored. His job – the only one he was fit for – was to guard the sheep when they were out in the fields to nibble the tops of corn seedlings so that a blanket of snow could give them a protective covering before the frosts came.

Much as we enjoyed Zarod's conversations in his fluent German, our over-optimistic mother persuaded the authorities that such an educated man was ill-suited to farm work and should be sent home to Łódź to continue his own profession. He had two teenage children, whose crumpled photographs he carried in his breast pocket. Mutti cried when she saw them and offered to send a letter by civilian post. Zarod's family did not reply, but the authorities agreed to repatriate him.

Why was this Polish-Jewish lawyer not overjoyed at the news? We were puzzled in our naïvety, wondering if he had become really fond of us all. He almost cried when he said good-bye, and Mutti sent her best wishes to his daughter, expressing the hope that she might soon begin her studies at Warsaw University. Zarod thanked us and said he would write, but we never heard from him again.

War in Scandinavia

Meanwhile Keijo had changed his Helsinki address to a military number. I wondered how he might have felt fighting the Russians while writing to someone whose country had a friendship pact with the Soviet Union. He did not express his feelings other than personal affection for me, or if he did, I could not read them: large patches of black ink or paint blotted out most of his letters. I could tell that these were the work of German censors, as the envelopes were always re-stuck with officially printed *Wehrmacht* tapes.

A photo came through. It showed a man standing in front of a snow-covered bunker in a white camouflage suit. With the aid of a magnifying glass I discovered Keijo's features under the fur hat. He seemed to be clean-shaven, a soldier man of barely sixteen.

Later, in spring 1940, a letter came from the old Helsinki address. It had been opened by the censors like all the previous letters, but for the first time nothing was crossed out. Keijo wrote that he was back at school, happy to acquire more knowledge for the future. Yet there was a certain sarcasm in his letter, as if he considered his interlude of leisure a very short respite from the war. He was not enthusiastic about his young sister's return from her Danish exile and only changed his mind on that matter when German troops occupied Denmark.

We were told that the necessity of safeguarding trade with Sweden had made the occupation of Denmark and Norway unavoidable. The Danes seemed to accept this, but the Norwegians resisted strongly and created large numbers of German heroes. Marlene and Cousin Jutta stuck men with *Ritterkreuze* round their necks into scrapbooks in much the same way as Gisela and I were still sticking in film stars. The hero industry was in fierce competition with the film star industry; we two grown-up girls thought it sweet to watch the little ones' adoration of audacious supermen, but Marlene and Jutta found our condescension irritating and misplaced, since they considered our pursuit of romantic stars childish and frivolous.

My young sister was convinced that my brain did not contain a single serious idea, and in a sense she was right... at least as regarded *single* ideas. Ever since May Day 1933 a labyrinth of facts and fiction had played havoc in my mind, raising questions which received plausible and implausible answers, doubts and despair alternating with happy complacency, bouts of fervent desire for acts of positive defiance surpassed by love of luxurious enjoyment. How could I tell little girls about moral standards when I had none myself?

I hated Uncle Egon, Jutta's father, with all my guts, but only with all my guts; for when I tried to explain my reactions on a rational basis, I found none. I even had to admit that he was a greater idealist than his counterpart, Aunt Anne from Königsberg. Uncle Egon's commitment to the 'common good' was total: it left no room for any concessions to individuality unless these served the virtuous life-style of hard work, loyalty, responsibility. I disagreed vehemently on all counts: hard work, in my view, was no more than self-indulgence on the part of those endowed with energy, stamina and a certain restlessness, myself amongst them. I was far more impressed by people who knew how to enjoy leisure; I even had a certain liking for thieving gipsies who did no harm. (The gipsies had disappeared, and nobody could say where they had gone.) As for loyalty, I firmly believed the concept to be no more than an excuse for not using one's own head, and my father agreed with me. 'Responsibility' was a word some parents seemed to use when they bullied their children into living by their standards rather than discovering their own. Uncle Egon was one of them.

His most outrageous – and yet idealistic – statement was made when the adults talked about the war. "I hope that Hitler will conquer the world," he said, "because a single leader would bring peace and stability to the world, such as the Habsburg Empire provided for most of Europe."

I interrupted in fury: "Have you forgotten that you taught me to admire Kossuth when I was little?"

"Oh, I still admire freedom fighters; we need them even now in Germany."

I stared at him open-mouthed, not comprehending.

"… to feel sure that a tyrant could not gain power if Hitler died," he explained – and he meant it.

At a later date, because I could not stop thinking about Uncle Egon's remarks, I asked Aunt Anne what she thought of the possibility of Hitler conquering the world.

"Heaven forbid," she groaned. "Certainly not."

"Then how will it all end?"

"So much has ended already," Anne said, "but as for him, he will sink in Russia, like Napoleon."

"But Russia and Germany…"

"What a joke!" she laughed. "Even a man like Seldte attending a reception at which the red flags were flying! How he must have hated it! And for what? I am quite sure that if it had not been for Hitler's pact with Russia, Britain and France would never have entered the war and Poland would have gone the way Czechoslovakia went."

"You really believe that?"

"I do, and it serves him right. But he will attack Russia anyhow; he has never lost track of his real goals."

"So you have no hope?"

Aunt Anne only snorted in reply, and I hated her cynicism almost as much as Uncle Egon's absurd faith. Neither of them could help me to discover what was happening to us all. Perhaps Mutti's warm and simple humanity was the only illumination of a grim puzzle.

Prisoners from the West

By the time the Belgian prisoners arrived in June 1940 only two of the Poles were left; they were considered civilians, no longer in need of a guard.

In the intervening months the distant war in the West had seemed unreal, hardly more than a recitation of figures of meaningless tonnage sunk in remote seas. The sudden confrontation with the human aspect of the western front failed to suppress my pleasure at the sound of the French tongue on our farm, a pleasure that was not shared by my father. In fact, he was horrified: "Twenty versions of gentleman Zarod," he complained. "Whatever possessed you to choose such men?" he asked the foreman Heiland, who had brought the prisoners from Darkehmen.

"They look quite healthy," Heiland replied meekly.

"A chemistry student, a professor, an engineer, a shopkeeper, umpteen civil servants, even a Count..."

"You could have gone to choose your own workers," Mutti interjected, knowing quite well that nothing could have persuaded my father to muster men like cattle on the market square. Väti shrugged his shoulders and did not reply.

Belgian POWs

Window grills outside and straw mattresses inside had converted the end house of the old farm cottage into the Belgian prison. Later the men built some furniture for themselves. The German soldier who was their guard lived in the cowman's spare room. How much guarding he was supposed to do was not clear to anyone, least of all to the man himself. With lavatories at some distance from their house, he could not very well lock prisoners in at night. Besides, where could they escape to when their own country was occupied by the German army and probably controlled in a more rigorous way than our farm? And if anyone had the authority to make these gentlemen work, it was obviously my father, not the guard. By the rules of international law the soldiers could not be forced to work, but they could be sent back to the Stalag camp from which they had volunteered for farm jobs. It often took all my diplomatic cunning to deflect the threat of such deportation from the chemistry student, Monsieur Valère Pironnet, who was truly the most hopeless worker as well as the most handsome man, in a languid Mediterranean way. I did like his company – among others – and our poor guard was totally at sea with the interpretation of the non-fraternization rules when prisoners helped me to work for my final French exam. But I was furious to find that the humanitarian aspect of my relationship with the prisoners was totally ignored by the men themselves. Could these Westerners not understand any affection other than in terms of attraction between the sexes?

The question arose when the guard panicked before an official inspection and hastily collected all the Belgians' papers for my safe-keeping. There were my own summaries of romantic films, written in French, ostensibly for corrections, but really because I assumed that all people would enjoy reading the sentimental stuff I loved. There were also notebooks of the prisoners' own writings, essays and verses. I could not resist nosing out the men's private thoughts. I enjoyed many funny verses about various people, but suddenly my blood boiled in fury:

> *"Le Don Juan de Pironnet*
> *Tisse toujours ses filets,*
> *Et maintenant, sa dernière prise*
> *Est la belle Anneliese..."*

That was not how I liked to regard myself, and Claus heartily agreed: not a conquest but a conqueror, that was what he wanted his big sister to be. But Mutti only laughed when we told her. She suggested that one ought to have the kindness to leave some illusions to men whose pride had been badly hurt by the defeat of their country; as she saw it, humiliation can only be felt by people without self-respect. I had to try and treat provocation with a sense of humour.

It was not easy to grin when *le professeur* Louis Gustot went out of his way to pretend that a certain Suzanne was "no more than an old family friend", even though she made regular use of the civilian post that I had arranged for him, sending him at least one letter a week and many parcels at odd occasions.

Officially prisoners were only allowed to send a certain number of aero-gramme-type letters via the main camp, where they were censored for information that might betray a man's whereabouts. Their addresses were numbers. Such mail took a long time to reach its destination. Väti thought this a proper regulation and objected to the civilian letters received directly from Belgium. But Mutti insisted that we were not doing "anything seriously illegal", since M. Gustot was not only a personal friend of our family but also a friend of the Belgian fascist Léon Degrelle. To give Gustot his due, he had not called Degrelle his friend, but mentioned their time together at university quite frequently. I hoped that there was no close association; but when Gustot was prematurely repatriated, I began to wonder. It did not sound right to call him Flemish – which was the official reason given for his release – when his name, his language and the language used in all the letters he received were Walloon.

Yet I accepted that it was not for me to judge collaborators on such a flimsy basis. First and foremost *le professeur* was a good teacher, who navigated Claus through maths and Latin exams. The coaching took place in Claus's own room every afternoon and was a good excuse for Mutti and me to arrange homely coffee breaks, with cakes and biscuits from Mutti's store, real coffee from Suzanne. If Gustot interpreted our get-togethers as part of my designs on his masculinity, I reluctantly let things be. He was fun, anyhow. A slim man of medium height, of slightly eccentric manner, with a long, narrow scarf hanging almost down to the floor; the bobbles at the ends of the scarf bounced cheerfully when Gustot, together with M. Pironnet, showed us how to dance the hokey-kokey to the words of "*Prenez donc un parapluie, et vous êtes comme Chamberlain...*"

My mother and I addressed all Belgian prisoners as "Monsieur so-and-so", while my father called the intellectuals by their plain surnames and the 'good ones' by their Christian names, these latter including the Count, who turned out to be good with horses. All of them, irrespective of their education, treated our gastronomy with contempt. The East Prussian farm diet genuinely made them suffer, though their rations were not only the same as ours, but supplemented by Red Cross parcels. The cigarettes provided a valuable black-market currency, buying many extras, but rarely sufficient to bribe the cowmen to provide full-cream milk. Our own family was so used to skimmed milk that we actually preferred it. Poor Lucien Lebrun, the engineer, lived in dread of loosing his surplus bulk from actual starvation and from exertions on the farm. He was hardly justified in his complaints about the unusually hard work in the open air, particularly as he was often given easy tasks normally done by one of the maids, such as sprinkling bleaching sheets on a lawn with a watering can.

Lebrun

Lebrun loved meringues, which Mutti provided as occasional treats. Whether or not he really liked raw apples, I cannot tell: he certainly liked my gesture of holding one out for him when he waited for me at the top of the cellar stairs.

"*La pomme d'Adam?*" he asked and kissed me passionately.

I enjoyed both, the funny remark and the kissing. It was refreshing, so much less hypocritical than the usual approach to fraternization.

Last Weeks at School

Carpets of hepatica covered the forest floor again, but I hardly noticed the blue brightness in the gloom of Spring 1941. I was afraid of life. The prospect of six months' Labour Service between school and university loomed large, coming closer every day.

Moreover, those of us who had stayed at school to the age of 18 were presumed intellectually corrupt and had to attend a compulsory course "*für intellektuell Verbildete*" before we took our final examinations. It was a three-day nightmare, much of it spent in a dark room with slide projectors. All those endless lectures seemed to be saying one thing: that we were the new emancipated women. Times of etiquette and passive female consent had passed. We had to actively propagate a new, healthy generation, and for this goal it was up to us to take the initiative instead of waiting for a male to propose. But we had to be selective in the context of genetic probabilities. These were shown on the screen in large diagrams.

"Most SS men are safe, because they have undergone rigorous tests! Go forth and breed Nordic specimens for your country!" That was the message, and it made me feel quite sick. Yet Mutti did not believe me. Nobody could possibly have meant such immoral things: my imagination was running riot as usual, she said when I would have liked to share my worries with her; and Väti firmly stated that it was up to me and my conscience to create my own future. That was no help either. How could I create a future when I no longer had a sense of what I wanted it to be? The way ahead looked bleak. I would have liked to crawl into a rabbit-hole and hide.

But preparations for the final examination, the *Abitur*, had begun in earnest. Much of it consisted of written tests and teachers' assessments, and I had nothing to fear from these. Even in Latin I had done so well by cribbing from miniature Caesar translations combined with lucky guesswork that our teacher chose me as one of two pupils to be presented to external examiners! I pleaded with her, admitted all my past sins of cheating, warning her that my dismal performance would reflect badly on her teaching. It was to no avail. She became so angry at my admissions that she stubbornly chose her own humiliation in order to punish me. Unfortunately I had discovered too late that I needed the basic 'Kleines Latinum' level for the study of history at university and had come to regret my rebellion against compulsory Latin.

I was pleased, though, when the headmaster chose me as his showpiece for an oral external examination in history. Alas, the final result of the orals depended heavily on the way the minutes were written during the proceedings, and the person chosen to keep the minutes of my history examination was our Latin teacher! I panicked. My parents and Omi stuffed me with glucose. The whole world began to smell of glucose. I jabbered quotes from Hitler's *Mein Kampf* and Rosenberg's *Myth of the 20th Century* to myself; the headmaster had told us the good ones to remember, because no one could possibly be expected to read the complete works. Then, faced with the minute-keeper, I jumbled the lot and had no idea what my voice was talking about.

Miraculously I passed in all subjects, including the voluntary 'Latinum' – my mark for the latter was only 5, but the failure mark was 6. I could wear the *Serevis*, a pill-box hat in red velvet with golden oak-leaves and acorns embroidered round the rim and my initials on the flat centre; and, because we were East Prussians, images of St Albert, the patron saint of Königsberg University, decked the front of our dresses and coats. These *Albertinen* were produced in gold, silver, brass or tin, as pendants, brooches and badges, large and small. They were presented to us by way of congratulations from relatives and friends. *Abitur*-balls and smaller parties continued for almost a month without a break. On isolated farms the celebrations were two-day events. Yet much as we danced, joked and drank champagne, that sinking feeling would not go away. It grew and grew when the parties stopped.

With Serevis & St Albert after the Abitur

Labour Service

I began to convince myself that I could not possibly survive six months of Labour Service. This premonition of early death drew me melodramatically close to Kleist and away from Goethe and all things positive. I began to envy Gisela for the comforts of her tuberculosis, which exempted her from the RAD (*Reichsarbeitsdienst*). She sat all day in a beautiful garden room which her father had built for her on a rotating floor so that the wide open doors and windows could always be turned to the shady side. Gisela was not permitted to feel the warmth of the sun. She could not go for walks and was often too weak even to sit and paint or read. I envied her, and the shame of my envy added to my misery.

Mutti was becoming seriously worried about me, but Väti was full of contempt for a daughter who made such an open exhibition of gloom. The Belgian prisoners expressed surprise that I should be so "anti-government". They really did not understand. I was much in favour of the RAD as an institution to make factory girls from the West mix with the sheltered daughters of rich East Prussian land-owners and to have them all work together in the open air, provided that the arrangement excluded me. I could not bear being in a crowd day and night, nor having the hours of my day organized. It was only fair to expect respect for my unique character! But others did not see it that way.

Both my parents came along to see me settled into camp at Wuttrienen, a tiny village in the south-western part of East Prussia. A large lake glittered in the sunlight, larch trees were sprouting fresh green tips, hepatica covered the ground as at home.

"Isn't it beautiful?" Mutti exclaimed.

"Nature has no feelings, says Goethe," I replied. It ought to have rained in sympathy.

"And Goethe goes on to say that only man can do the impossible, can discriminate, can choose," my father commented.

"Some choice!" I grumbled. "Run away from the RAD and forfeit all chance of going to university. Well, I might just make that choice."

"You could also choose to accept life with dignity…"

At that moment the camp came into view: a rectangle of wooden buildings around a lawn with the RAD flag fluttering from a pole in the centre. All around the camp was the forest.

A plump woman with a bun at the back of her head and a khaki suit came to meet us. "*Heil Hitler*", she shouted with a raised arm. My parents tried to copy her; this was easy for Väti, whereas Mutti looked pathetically clumsy, feeling so obviously foolish that I could have hugged her. But I saluted smartly instead.

"I am the camp leader", the woman introduced herself and then shook our hands so heartily that I was sure my fingers would be broken. I inwardly apologized to Rudi Haenig for abhorring his lukewarm handshakes.

We were taken to the office for me to sign on. Väti's eyes were roaming round the room with approval. The furniture was made of pine, a large desk, a small low table, several chairs, bookshelves and a cupboard. The curtains were of a rust-coloured weave that either was or pretended to be hand-woven. Arrangements of catkins and larch stood on the windowsills, a small vase of hepatica on the desk and another on the table. In the far corner stood a bed and on the bedside table was a book with a marker between the pages and an electric lamp. The title page of the book was turned down, so I could not tell what our leader was reading, but I was impressed to find electricity in this isolated place. Bookcases lined two walls; a rag-rug covered most of the floor. Everything was very clean and tidy.

There was a knock at the door, and a tall, slim woman in the same kind of khaki suit as the first one saluted as she entered. I noticed that both women wore brooches with the *R.A.D.* emblem on their white blouses. The second woman was the sub-leader. I was told to go with her while my parents waited in the office.

In the camp's clothes-store I was measured and then handed one uniform of the same type as the leaders wore, an extra khaki skirt in a rougher material, one felt hat, two white blouses, two bright blue cotton dresses, two red headscarves, several white aprons with red embroidery strips along the hemlines, a long weather-proof jacket with several deep pockets, two peculiar nightshirts, a track-suit, gym shorts and vests, several socks and tough stockings, sturdy lace-up boots, gum boots, gym shoes, towels, sheets, pillow cases, an *R.A.D.* brooch… It seemed an immense pile of items, the smaller of which I could stuff into a large new shoulder bag while the sub-leader helped me to carry the rest into my future dormitory, called a *Kameradschaft*.

Arbeitsdienst 1941; I am in the centre of the middle row

Five bunk beds along either side of two walls indicated that we would be twenty girls in the room. Chairs stood at the foot-ends, high narrow cupboards at the head-ends. A few girls were already assembled in the room, jumping up to salute the sub-leader and continuing with their change of clothes. Most had come without parents and were putting their civilian clothes into boxes for posting home. But I still had a chance to choose my bed and decided that the top ones would be marginally more private, albeit with a disadvantage for making the neat boxes we were supposed to create from our bedding. The pillows were much smaller than any I had ever seen; the blankets were grey and coarse.

In my cupboard were hangers for dresses and various shelves, one of which I was allowed to use for certain personal items, such as writing materials and a few photographs. My own toothbrush, flannels, hairbrush and comb I could later leave at my place in the large washroom, I was told. Girls who possessed such extraordinary things as lipstick were supposed to send them home with their clothes. We were allowed to keep a very small amount of money for postage stamps in case we exceeded the number of free letters we could send home.

I made my bed and changed into uniform. "You need not wear hats", the sub-leader told us; "they are only for special parades" (my heart sank) "and for travelling home on leave" (my heart lifted a little).

When I gave my parents my clothes I was brave and did not cry. I hugged Väti and Mutti, deliberately not using the Third Reich salute for our farewell despite the RAD leader's disapproving looks.

Soon we had a first small roll-call in our *Kameradschaft* by way of introduction; then the whistle blew for the big roll-call by the flagpole.

"Here, here, here…" came the replies as our names were read out in alphabetic order. The leader made a speech about the goals of the next six months, after which we raised our arms and sang the two national anthems while the sub-leader lowered the flag. The girls who would do that job on the following day had already been chosen.

Our supper was in the dining hall of the hut opposite our dormitories, next to the kitchen and store room. On this first night we were served by our leaders.

Next morning camp routine began in earnest. We were woken by a sharp whistle and jumped out of bed, pulling up blankets and sheets for airing and changing into track-suits. We assembled on the grass for morning gymnastics, after which another whistle dismissed us to the pumps in the washroom hut. We put on our cotton dresses and white aprons, tied the headscarves, made our beds and ran to the flagpole at the next whistle, which came rather too soon for me to finish making my bed according to regulations; I learnt to be faster on future mornings.

By the flag the motto for the day was read out; then arms were raised for the anthems while the flag ascended. We held hands and skipped round the pole ring-a-roses fashion, singing a folksong. It was not even funny.

Ilse, a school friend from Insterburg, kept her sense of humour and tried to persuade us that things could have been much worse. We should be grateful that we had not broken a leg or two while skipping on the bumpy grass and appreciate the simple food which would preserve us from dying of obesity. "Seriously," she said, "I know a fat person who did!"

A girl called Eva had a platonic incestuous relationship with her step-brother and felt guilty whenever she wrote him a letter. Ilse comforted her: "It would be far worse if he were a first-grade brother." Some of the girls from the Rhineland talked of sex at night. I tried to plug my ears against the sickening, unfamiliar talk.

Our first week of camp life and lectures was every bit as ghastly as I had expected, not to speak of all those roll-calls around the flag. We did have some free time to familiarize ourselves with the beautiful countryside around, even occasional short chances of escaping from the company of others, but it was a week of misery.

Then life changed dramatically for the better: we were allocated jobs for the next fortnight, and fortunately I was not among those chosen for camp duty, which comprised tasks like preparing and cooking food, washing up, cleaning other girls' boots and rooms, washing clothes. Only the task of making beds was part of the drill which every girl had to accept for herself. I remember an occasion when, during one of many random inspections our leader looked at my bunk and said in an almost admiring voice: "Very good indeed!" Before I had time to breathe a sigh of relief she tore down all my blankets and told me: "Now show how fast you can do it!" Did she not believe I had done it myself in the first place? I swallowed my pride and anger for the sake of a peaceful farming day ahead.

Our camp was central to a large number of small farmsteads, such as I had not known before. The population in this southern part of East Prussia had been Prussian before Germany existed and had become German, but traces of a different ethnic origin survived in religion and language. The farmers conversed in Polish among themselves, and I was happy to enjoy my privacy behind the language barrier while being part of a community which looked upon me with friendly smiles and the occasional encouraging word in German.

We received no wages, though I believe that the farmers paid certain rates for our work directly to the camp; but I worked hard just for the joy of being in the open. Some of the work I had done at home during school holidays; other tasks I had watched when we took *Vesper* to the fields. I was the only girl in the entire camp who came from a rural background; so it was not surprising that the farmers began to ask for me by name, for ordinary work hours and for overtime in the evenings or on Sundays. I was happy to avoid camp duties and many evening flag parades, but I did not tell this to our leader, who thought I was noble to accept such extra work.

The sweet smell of hay; later the delicious prick of stubble when I kicked off my boots for the corn harvest; the satisfying stickiness of sweat running along my deeply tanned arms and legs and soaking my blue dress; the taste of home-cured bacon on large slices of dark black bread; the refreshing sips of *Ersatz* coffee when the bottle was passed round!

My parents delighted in my health and happiness when I went home for a long weekend's leave and was eager to return again to "my farmers". I had taken leave on purpose at the time between the hay and corn harvests, when my absence would least inconvenience them. Other girls had gone home at other times; some had not yet taken their home leave and were in doubt about doing so because of the frequent air raids in their towns, which lay in the western part of the Reich.

It was hard to imagine the war still going on in the distant West when East Prussia was so peaceful. We had no black-out regulations and found it difficult to accept that we were not allowed to light St John's fires to celebrate Midsummer. But on midsummer night we began to wonder. It seemed like the eerie drone of aeroplanes crossing in waves, though we could not see any despite the clear sky.

"Jupiter is close to Mars, and Mars is very red," a girl from the Rhineland commented; "this means a bloodbath is imminent."

I had no sympathy for people who showed off about reading astrology. But I felt a heaviness of fear paralysing my body and could not shake it off.

War on Two Fronts

When we gathered round the flag the following morning our leader told us that Hitler had pre-empted a Russian strike against Germany and that our troops were now advancing inside the Soviet Union. So Aunt Anne had been right! I felt stunned. War had come to us, and the names of Hindenburg, Napoleon, Tolstoy, Sholokhov were running riot in my mind. It did not make sense.

As it was Sunday I was walking in the forest with Rita Eggers, a girl from Hamburg. We had taken our swimming suits and were walking to the edge of the lake, but we did not swim. The lake glittered peacefully in the sun.

As so often before, Rita had taken along her accordion, on which she played jazz tunes she had learnt from forbidden radio. She was infatuated with Americans and even the British despite their bombings, and being a great pianist, played classics alongside anglophone pop pieces such as the Boogie-Woogie or "Alexander's Ragtime Band". Later I was to write about her "Ich liebe Beethoven und Bach, und ein englischer Schlager macht mich ganz schwach!" ('I love Beethoven and Bach, but an English hit-song makes me feel weak at the knees'). But on this 22 June 1941 she did not play. We were staring at the water in silence. Once Rita fingered the beginning of the Volga Boat Song and grinned a little helplessly.

A subdued mood clouded camp life from that day on, which was almost a pleasant change. Less ring-a-roses cheer, fewer jollified social events; and farm work was as satisfying as ever. Only occasionally, when the farmers talked with serious faces, did I wish I could understand Polish.

Then came August. We began to boil with fury which we could hardly control in front of our leaders: we had been told that we should not be able to go home after our *RAD* service, but would be sent for voluntary war service (*Kriegshilfsdienst*, KHD for short) in certain towns. Voluntary? As with my Latin lessons at school…

"What if we refuse?" I asked.

"Where would you go then?"

"Well, if they don't let me go to university I could stay at home on the farm. Maybe I'd even enjoy that better," I replied.

"You wouldn't, you know; you'd be packed off to a concentration camp," someone clever explained.

"That could hardly be worse than working in an office," I insisted.

"The Lord preserve the innocent and ignorant," groaned a girl from Hamburg; "Have you no idea what concentration camps are?"

"Not much," I admitted.

"Day in, day out they'd teach you how to be patriotic."

"How could they indoctrinate me if I simply didn't listen?"

"By starving your body and feeding your mind with nasty lectures," the girl explained, and the terrible memory of the course for '*intellektuell Verbildete*' came back to me. It was probably not worth resisting *KHD*. I shrugged my shoulders.

Another girl from Hamburg, Karla, later approached me. She had noticed my ignorance and wanted to illuminate me. I had long been impressed by the knowledge that these Hamburg girls had acquired from foreign radio, and much of what Karla said made sense. But when she said we were ruled by an imbecile "who could not even write his own speeches if he tried", I could not take it. An entire nation hoodwinked into subjugation by a lunatic? What did that make us? More lunatics? No, I insisted. We could be tricked only by a clever villain, not by one who could not write his own speeches! For the sake of my own self-respect and that of my parents I needed to feel assured of Hitler's intelligence.

Karla laughed; but when I said I would go to the leader for an opinion on the matter, the laughing stopped and Karla pleaded with me not to do it if I did not want to get both of us into trouble. I was so furious and so careless of the threat of trouble that I stormed out and went straight to the leader's office, where I was re-assured that Hitler had written more than just his own speeches. So all was well in that respect: at least we were not ruled by a lunatic. I was satisfied that this was the end of the subject.

Or so I thought until, a few weeks later, Karla and I were told to travel up to some high office in Königsberg. We were puzzled and a little apprehensive, but not seriously worried.

On arrival we were interviewed separately, myself first. Did I know that Hitler had written important books and articles as well as speeches? Then I knew what our appointment was all about. Quotes from *Mein Kampf* which I had muddled so badly during my *Abitur* suddenly came out fluently and in perfect order. But then I was not sure if our interview had anything to do with our ruler's mental state. I was asked about my father, his job, whether he belonged to the party, whether he had belonged to another party before, who his friends were, who my mother's family were, even quite crazy questions as to what pictures were hanging on the walls of our house. I was getting confused.

Karla's interview apparently ran on similar lines, as she told me later when we sat in the train on our journey back to camp. Suddenly we hugged each other, clung to each other, crying without understanding why. We were still in close, sobbing embrace when we heard the name of our station called out.

Work for the State and my Father

A few days later we received our civilian clothes and moved to the war-service town of our prescribed destinations. Only three girls from our RAD camp came to Mohrungen with me; one of them, fortunately, was Rita. We lived in a youth hostel, a former water tower, and were independent except for being locked in – or out – at 11 p.m. Our 'hostel mother' cooked our breakfasts and suppers and cleaned our rooms.

I worked in the food office, where I lost my RAD tan and regained the weight I had successfully shed in field work. For most of my working hours I was bored. We were given free lunches in the office canteen and some pocket money on top of this, so that we could go to cinemas and riding stables at the weekends.

About twice a week I was a little less bored, because my boss chose my company for going round the district in his car to check on farming produce, livestock, slaughter and such things. Farms in the Mohrungen district were different from those around the RAD camp and more like those I was used to at home. The large estates belonged to the aristocracy and it was probably on account of my personal acquaintance with some of those families that I was taken on the inspection trips.

The castle of the eccentric Countess von Dohna-Lauck was the most interesting by far. It was a strange sight to find her dressed in coarse trousers and gum boots while stories of her extraordinary wealth circulated far and wide. She was reputed to have invited the entire company of the Berlin State Opera to provide entertainment at her parties; she drove to town with an African footman on her carriage, perhaps the only black man living in the German Reich. But the most remarkable feature of the Countess was her integrity: she would not bribe officials from the Ministry of Food! Whereas we returned from other estates loaded with hams, butter, eggs, poultry and game, we went away from the Countess of Dohna-Lauck empty-handed. And when my boss had to sign a certificate for emergency slaughter the carcass looked genuinely sick.

"Delve deep into the fullness of human life, and where you grasp it, it's interesting", Goethe had written. Unless I wanted to be miserable, I had to do just that, and on balance I enjoyed the Mohrungen experience. When the six months ended, I had no wish to go on to university immediately. I needed time to unwind, to reflect, time to submerge and to regain my roots.

Väti did not altogether approve of my intention of staying at home until the winter semester began. The long interval between school and proper academic studies seemed wasteful to him; I agreed, though I could not see what difference an extra six months would make when I had already wasted a year. I assured Väti that I had no intention of opting out altogether.

He was really quite glad to have my help, since he had not managed to find a secretary after my grandfather's death and book-keeping was becoming a nightmare that grew with every new official decree. Artificial fertilizers had to be used and accounted for by ever-increasing production results, painstakingly recorded. Moreover, the calculation of wages was complicated by different rates and different types of money: Poles were paid in German currency, but at a much lower rate than even German children; Belgians were paid a German adult wage, but in vouchers which had to be ordered from the Stalag organization and for which the prisoners could then order goods from the same place; *RAD* and Hitler Youth groups were paid a little pocket money while their earnings went to the state.

Then there were the ration cards to be sorted out, not only for the different categories of people but for butter, cheese and skimmed milk of our own produce, not to speak of slaughter allowances per person and estimated egg yields from our poultry; seeds and fertilizers also had to be entered. Calculations and regulations were a full-time job, but one that I could do at hours of my own choosing. Time stood still for this long summer.

Helmut

"Make three curtsies and you can have a wish," Helmut said when we saw the first small sickle of the waxing moon.

I thought for a while, but could not find a wish. It was a perfect night in a perfect summer. Through the open doors of ballroom and veranda I could hear the sound of Bizet's *Habanera* and the shuffle of dancing feet. Helmut and I had left the dancers for a short walk in the cool air, and only a moment ago our noses had touched inside the dewy fragrance of a purple lilac umbel. I had no wishes.

"I would like to be up there," Helmut said.

"Among the stars or in heaven?"

"In the dark spaces between twinkling memories of extinct places," he replied.

Then I wished that Helmut should not want such things, but I had missed my chance to curtsy. I so much wanted our earth to be important, our garden, our own fields, our forests and ponds each to be larger than any star.

The summer of 1942 had begun in May, when Rose invited me to a party in Insterburg. An army doctor in charge of the officers' convalescent home wanted to provide respite and distraction for his charges, and Rose's father arranged dances at his house. I was invited as soon as I was discharged from the *KHD*; I realised it was not for my person (I had hardly known Rose when we were at school together) but for the contact with a farm. So I obliged with weekend invitations to Mikalbude. Helmut had sat opposite me during that first dinner and had sung Czech words to *Roll Down the Barrel* when we danced.

Dance party at the Nieters; I am second from left

By the rules of etiquette it was not done to dance more often with one partner than another, nor did it make sense to have large gatherings unless we wanted to alternate partners and subjects of conversation. But after several big parties Rose decided that she, Ortlef, Helmut and I should form the 'consortium of four' and occasionally have a more intimate weekend just for ourselves. Apart from the couch in my room and the chaise-longue in the drawing room we now had only five spare beds for visitors. But my guests never tired of dancing all through the night, and the sheets stayed clean for future visitors. We went for long walks at dawn or watched the sunrise from horseback.

Helmut had studied law in Vienna and Prague and, as a self-appointed gramophone-winder, often chose records that suited his own nostalgia. He made me guess before he put the needle down. I always got it right and happily convinced myself of strong telepathic ties with the young lieutenant of my perfect summer.

He made me dream of Vienna much in the way my great-grandmother had made me dream of aristocratic Prussian balls. When I closed my eyes, the scratchy gramophone turned into Johann Strauss's own string orchestra and sparkling chandeliers grew out of our humble gas lights. Our plain ceiling metamorphosed into elaborate baroque splendour and Helmut's field grey uniform was transformed to gleaming white with gold braids. I could hear the swish of my crinoline on marble and forgot that Frieda and Hilde had been on their knees, polishing plain wooden boards not so many hours ago. I learnt to say "*Servus*", that friendly, melancholy-happy greeting and farewell of the Viennese.

Sometimes, when my heart would burst with happiness or take wing and float lightly with contentment, I felt sudden pangs of guilt that it should be so when somewhere, in distant lands, a war was raging; indeed, that very war had sent us the wounded to convalesce, to dance, to gain strength for… No, I did not want to think that far.

"Should we be more serious?" I once asked. Helmut replied that light and music were the most serious things on earth. He kept urging me to study in Vienna, where people knew the art of living.

Then he told me about the day he was wounded: "The first reaction was sadness, not so much for loosing my life, but for having it taken away by the very people I loved most, the people of Tolstoy, Pushkin, Tchaikovsky… Then I called out that I wanted to see the sun. A soldier who was crouching nearby got up and turned my body. As the sunlight fell on to my eyes, I felt light and happy and died… or so I thought. It was disappointing to wake up in a hospital bed."

"They don't make songs about soldiers who stop fighting so as to let a dying man see the sun," I said, "only about so-called Good Comrades who have no time even to hold a dying man's hand because they are too busy re-loading the rifle." I had long felt bitter about that particular song.

Helmut thought I was unfair to our poets and songwriters, who had given much praise to beautiful humanity. "It is only in times like these that the adulation of duty has become so popular," he said.

But if that was true, "times like these" had existed for as long as I could remember. The song about the Good Comrade had been written by Ludwig Uhland in the early nineteenth century and was played at all military funerals. It had a moving, solemn tune which made my mother cry even at the first bar while I usually managed to control my tears till the third or fourth bar. It happened to me still, even though I had long since analysed the words and begun to hate them; but it had affected me most strongly as a small child, every year on the 9th of November, when we commemorated the 1918 'Stab in the Back' which had ended the First World War. The *Stahlhelm* organization always held a ceremony to honour the fallen soldiers in the Kowarren war cemetery, or *Heroes' Cemetery*, as it was referred to in German.

High on a hill overlooking the countryside and the forest that separated our farm from Kowarren stood an old, sturdy oak, whose crown had camouflaged a Russian machine gun in 1914. Next to the tree and exceeding it in height stood a cross of the Western kind, while below, neatly arranged all the way downhill, stood small crosses of both the Western and the double-barred Eastern species. They marked single graves with names, some even in Cyrillic script, and mass graves with numbers. I shuddered at the thought of the mutilations that had rendered so many hundreds into nameless heaps.

But the speeches held by men with little silver helmets on their lapels – the badges of *Stahlhelm* members – did not mention the horrors. They proclaimed rhapsodic visions of fearless youths, perhaps singing their national anthems as they fell. "Hail, thou with the victor's laurel-wreath, saviour of the Fatherland, hail, thou, the Emperor…" Hail Kaiser, or perhaps in retrospect, hail Czar, since the Russian Emperor, too, had fallen victim to the stab in the back brought by the Revolution.

Remembrance of the dead also meant dedication to the fight against Communism, which had caused the humiliation of a lost war. When the black-white-red imperial flags and the black-and-white Prussian flags were dipped, I used to feel waves of reverence flow down my spine and gooseflesh cover my arms. I felt that still, every time I entered the cemetery, although now at the age of nineteen I scorned heroes and heard no music to whip up my emotions.

On a fine summer morning, when we were walking to the Kowarren Lake after a night's dancing, someone decided to deviate and follow the path leading up to the old oak tree. There was no sound but for the song of larks and the shuffle of our feet on the gravel. We stood in silence among the crosses. Then Lieutenant von Burkersrode asked: "Will they mark our places with simple crosses or double bars, or do their carpenters shape hammers and sickles?"

He looked so young and vulnerable as he spoke, I longed to hug and comfort him. But Helmut firmly held on to my hand and Ortlef laughed aloud: "They use stonemasons now, and they will fashion an impressive bust of Stalin to sit on our mass graves."

None of us thought the remark funny, but it dispersed in the mist of sentimentality.

Soon after, we were floating in the calm, clean centre of the lake, Helmut and I drifting indolently on our backs, side by side.

"These waters don't move," Helmut said, "yet I feel as if a tide were pushing us from living water to dry land. We are too lazy to resist."

"I only know tides from Theodor Storm's novellas," I replied.

Helmut chuckled. He had never even seen the Baltic, let alone a sea that had tides. "It's only a metaphor with the physical strength to pull me, to drag me away from singing mermaids."

He held out his hand and sang Don Giovanni's "Give Me Your Hand, My Sweetheart." I recognized the tune, though Helmut's words were Czech. The sun was warm on my face, our legs were kicking rhythmic ripples across our bodies. I was happy.

With Helmut at Mikalbude

I asked the question that had long been on my mind: "Why do you always sing in Czech?"

Helmut hesitated before he replied: "Perhaps it's my penance; I don't really know. One day, when we are alone, I might try to explain."

He often came alone mid-week, in an armoured car, accompanied by a driver who was more concerned with our maids than with me. Then we would saddle two horses and gallop across the stubble, or amble along woodland paths. I had shown Helmut Great-Chile and Little-Chile, and once we had visited Gisela together.

One day, when the leaves were beginning to turn yellow, Helmut suggested that we dismount and sit in Little-Chile on the warm logs for a while.

"I spent my childhood in the Sudetenland," he began. "My parents often conversed in German, but we children spoke mostly Czech. All our friends were Czech… or at least I thought of them as Czech, as indeed I thought of myself."

"How can that be? Your parents must have been German, or else why did they give you a German Christian name? Were you not persecuted and ill-treated?" I vividly remembered newsreels of exalted scenes of jubilation among liberated Sudeten Germans when Hitler drove through the streets of Eger.

"There were acts of true horror, but not all of them were as straightforward as you were perhaps led to believe. One of my own uncles was a Nazi *agent provocateur*."

Helmut described some events preceding the liberation of the Sudetenland, or the invasion, as I began to call it after I had heard his story. My skin bristled with anger and frustration, not so much at what had happened in Czechoslovakia as at the way Gisela and I had been taken in. I swore to myself that no one, not even Helmut, should persuade me that the way to truth was through music. There had to be another way to penetrate the nets of propaganda, and I was determined to find it. If only the real adults around me would stop thinking of me as a child and trust me with their schemes! Herr Bagdahn, for one – and Aunt Anne and her relatives… the sudden silences in their conversations when I entered a room… They must be plotting, I thought, perhaps to overthrow Hitler's regime? Surely there were tasks for someone like myself somewhere? Surely they could trust me?

I vented my fury on Helmut: "How can you be here in that uniform when you felt you were Czech?"

"Well may you ask," he replied sadly. "Yes, we did have the choice of opting for our nationality. Ethnically we are Germans, and my parents realistically opted to confirm that fact. It made our lives easier than those of Czech people."

"So you chose the easy way that landed you in the German army," I mocked him.

"Do you think that is worse than fighting for the Czech resistance?"

"That depends on what you believe in. What do you believe in? Did you not have a personal option? Did you have to go along with your parents?"

"In theory I did have a personal option, but such a positive stand against German nationality from a son could have harmed my parents more than you are able to imagine."

"So you sacrificed your Czech friends instead?"

"Friends... yes... and the love of a girl who meant very much to me," he said simply. After a while he added: "But that is over now. I sing in Czech because I am not at all sure if I really opted for my parents' well-being or my own easy life. Well, all that brought me here, to such peace, such beauty. I have no regrets."

I apologized for my unfair bad temper, and when Helmut held me close for a long time I wished that the world would end before it turned humdrum.

On that same evening Helmut did not say "*Servus*" when we shook hands on the veranda steps, but "*Auf Wiedersehen*". See you again? What a sad way of telling me that he would not come again, as I felt suddenly quite sure he would not. I understood his message, but could not reply because my voice stuck in my throat. Helmut climbed into the armoured car and waved.

Ortlef came on another day to tell me that Helmut had been sent to Stalingrad.

Russian Prisoners

All through my summer of 1942 I had taken little notice of the prisoners. Despite their exotic culinary fads the Belgians, like the Poles before them, had been assimilated into everyday farm life. Even their uniforms became a rare sight since Stalag had run out of booty and we gradually replaced worn-out clothes with old civilian substitutes on which the men had to sew a small identity label.

The arrival of twenty Russian prisoners momentarily jolted my mind into a frightening comprehension of bias and injustice on a hitherto unimaginable scale. The 'basic wage' for a Russian was fixed at 1/4 of that of Western prisoners. The explanation was that Russians were used to a considerably lower standard of living. From this sum we had to deduct 50% in the form of *Reichsmittel*, a payment sent to a government department presumably in recognition of services rendered in capturing our additional workforce; no such payment was made for Western prisoners. From the remaining 50% we were obliged to deduct 1 *pfennig* per working hour for board and lodging, as compared with 1 *pfennig* per working day for Western prisoners, despite the fact that both food and living quarters provided for Soviet prisoners were of a far lower standard than any other. The remainder of such wages was paid in *Lagergeld* as for the Belgians, but those few *pfennigs* could not have bought a bar of soap per month, let alone such luxuries as cigarettes. And of course, since the Soviet Union was not a member of the International Red Cross, there were no parcels to subsidize the Russian prisoners' rations. Food rations for the Russians excluded meat, butter and cheese other than that made of skimmed milk; their bread ration was also considerably lower than that of the Belgians.

"How do you expect a good day's work out of half-starved men?" my father enquired, only to be told that the workforce from the Soviet Union was infinitely renewable. Farmers were thus forced into cheating with emergency killings and false counting of poultry, as well as concealing the number of game after shoots. My father did this reluctantly and on a much smaller scale than I had experienced on the estates around Mohrungen.

Living accommodation for Russian prisoners was arranged in two adjoining cottages of the building where the Belgians lived. Their compound was heavily fortified, not only by barred windows but also by a fence of chain-link and barbed wire surrounding the compound, including the path to the outdoor lavatories. This enclosure provided a small recreation area, a place to stand in the open air, even to dance on summer evenings until the armed guard decided it was time for 'bed'. Then the prisoners had to give him all their outdoor clothing and were locked into their two rooms, which had straw mattresses all over the floor and nothing else.

Officially all Red Army prisoners had to work in a single group under the supervision of a guard. Any man detaching himself from that group could be shot without warning for attempted escape. The arrangement offended my father's desire for efficiency, particularly when it became obvious that many of the Russians were used to farm work and could easily handle horses, which was more than most Belgians were likely to learn in a million years – at least, that was what he felt. He persuaded the guard to make a few concessions to common sense. My father's manner of persuasion was probably more intimidating than the prospect of Stalag inspectors coming to check on compliance with the rules.

Eventually Mutti also made use of such concessions for her own gardening arrangements. Her schemes had nothing to do with efficiency and were made many months after the Russians arrived, because it took a long time to get to know them as individuals. At first it seemed that none of them knew any German at all, and official rules forbade that they be taught anything other than the understanding of very basic and necessary commands.

In the autumn of 1942 I decided on a first semester at Vienna University and managed to persuade Anni, a girl I had met in the KHD, to take over my work. She was a trained secretary, pretty, quite bright, willing to work hard and generally lively and pleasant. I introduced her to all the complicated paper work and the weighing of grain, both as part of the German workers' wage and as a weekly ration for farm animals. Then I packed for university.

Berlin

I had lived in Insterburg, had visited Königsberg, but was not prepared for Berlin. Even as our overnight train stopped and propelled us on to the platform in a stream of hustling, bustling, pushing passengers who were immediately swallowed up in the anonymity of greater crowds, I could have shouted for joy. Considering my contempt for townies, this was a remarkable reaction, and for safety's sake I grabbed my mother's arm. I was only just beginning to wonder how we should ever discover our friends when we heard our names shouted out.

"Berlin, Berlin, you wonderful city, placed by the Lord at the hub of the world", said a song. Our two days en route to Vienna were like living on a film set. Gretel Schneider took good care that it should be so. We travelled by underground and S-Bahn, deliberately stopping at the station Gleisdreieck, made famous by a Heli Finkenzeller film of the same name; we joined the hardy customers at outdoor tables on the Kurfürstendamm, drank *Berliner Weisse* in the cool October sun and at night watched the flashing lights of the Alexanderplatz, "just a token sparkle compared with peace-time", Gretel said. We went to the Metropol Theatre to see '*Hochzeitsnacht im Paradies*' with Johannes Heesters, a film star in real life and blood! I marvelled at it all, and the sense of occasion was enhanced by wearing lipstick, borrowed from Lori.

We also went to Potsdam and saw Sanssouci, which lay inside depressing air-raid camouflage, thus belying its name. I wondered if it had ever been without worry, if Frederick the Great – or Bach, or Voltaire – had ever really relaxed. There were air-raid shelters in all the Berlin houses, our friends told us, but we had no wish to inspect one. I would not have wanted to live in Berlin, but was happy to be swept along on its wave of exhilaration and fascination.

The Schneiders introduced us to a friend of theirs, who was Göring's adjutant. I think his name was von Kusenow; I know his little daughter was called Edda, one of those Nordic names which had become fashionable in Nazi families. It was intriguing to hear this man say openly that he was seriously considering escape to Sweden in order to ensure some future for his little girl. And that in front of strangers like us!

Having just returned from one of the frequent arguments between Göring and Himmler, he was depressed, because he felt that the latter was gaining the upper hand. To me the very name of Himmler had become synonymous with that of the Devil, though I would have been hard pushed to explain why. It was rather like the frightening childhood fantasies of Communists: I imagined Himmler to have the stature of Max Schmeling, Joe Louis or Dracula. But while "Communists!" had been shouted loudly, "Himmler!" or "SS!" were expressions of terror in whispers. Kaltenbrunner, the Head of Security, later acquired that same aura.

Introduction to Vienna

"I find it rather repugnant to hear an adjutant of Göring contemplate desertion of Germany", Mutti said when we were in our train for Vienna. I did not argue, because I had all but forgotten Berlin and my heart was pounding in anticipation of Vienna – "forever the city of my dreams". I was still dreaming, but more than a little apprehensive lest reality should shatter my dreams.

"I'm happy to think that Gerda and you will become friends", Mutti said, suddenly adding to my anxieties. I hardly knew Gerda, though we had been in the same class in Insterburg for three years. She had not taken a term off between war service and university and had already spent one semester at Vienna University. Her parents had told mine that I could have her lodgings when she moved on to another university, and when Gerda decided to extend her stay in Vienna I was offered the chance to share her flatlet. My trunk had already been sent there.

My fears evaporated when Gerda greeted us with a friendly "*Servus*" on the quiet platform of the Vienna *Westbahnhof*. She suggested that we take a tram along the fairly uninteresting Mariahilfer Straße and then walk along the Ringstraße.

"There is the Opera House; there the Art Museum and the Natural History Museum; and there, beyond the gate, you can just see the Hofburg – renaissance, neo-classical, neo-Gothic." Art styles, dates – I let Gerda ramble on as we strolled between two rows of trees lining the pavement, and Vienna flowed into me. The bare twigs blended with wrought iron gates, and beyond the filigree patterns the buildings were white and grey and palatial. We paused for a while by the steps of the university building, watching students in fur coats sunbathing on benches in the little park. Then, at the Votivkirche (neo-Gothic, Gerda explained), we

114

seemed to be turning right and then left again, and Gerda pointed at Liechtensteinstraße No. 30: "That's where we live. But first I'll take you to your hotel."

The hotel was situated in a small side-street nearby. In the dark entrance hall, which was hardly large enough to be called a foyer, a round, friendly woman sat behind a desk. We had to fill in our registration papers, and the woman examined our identity cards. I was proud of my brand new document, complete with finger-prints. Now and then, among the hectic crowds of Berlin, I had fumbled in my shoulder-bag for it, just to reassure myself that it was still there; a verification of my identity gave me a sense of security. Here in Vienna it suddenly seemed a superfluous, even ridiculous piece of paper.

Walls papered with dark roses on gold and hung with portraits of Habsburg imperial bourgeoisie, red plush curtains, red plush chairs, a sofa, a table-cloth to match, some cream-coloured crocheted lace squares on our bedside tables and in various other places, large covers on our twin beds, an electric lamp with a shade of beads: that was our room.

The Andexlingers' apartment at Liechtensteinstraße 30 was a large-scale version of our hotel. One of our rooms there was as big as the drawing room at Mikalbude. A grand piano stood by the two windows; there was a big desk, several bookshelves and cupboards, plush-covered chairs (including two comfortable armchairs), a long table and a convertible couch, which Gerda used as her bed.

My bed was in the small adjoining room and had a large, solid desk instead of a bedside table. Gerda had put the university prospectus there for me, and I would have liked to delve into it straight away, but Mutti would not let me. While she was with us I would have to forget academic things and enjoy an extravagant way of exploring which I would not be able to afford later. Mutti was only staying for a few days.

"*Kaiserlich-königlich*", she said with mock admiration when she stroked the genuine silk velvet of the Hotel Sacher furniture; "and so is the table service, and the china, and the glasses... but the soup is not up to Omi's standard." In fact, Mutti did not like *Leberknödelsuppe* at all.

In the Opera House we had a box: only a small one, but a box nonetheless. Gerda pointed to the galleries where students normally sat, and I could not help thinking that the metamorphosis of the heroine into a tree might have looked more real from that height, where it was not obvious how curtain after curtain with patterns of leaves were drawn in front of the singer like shimmering veils.

On Mutti's last day we had to see mountains, and the Semmering was the nearest. I was so excited and afraid we might miss the train that I could hardly eat our breakfast *Kipferl*, the crescent-shaped rolls which commemorate Vienna's salvation from the Turks. Mountains at last! Gisela had been on holiday in Garmisch and sent me a card of the Partnachklamm; I would write her a card from the Semmering and urge her to come for a visit. She had almost recovered from tuberculosis and was going to resume her art studies in Königsberg, but how she would love Vienna and the Semmering! It was snowing hard, and Mutti was disappointed not to see the mountains; but I did not mind at all, as I could feel them in my legs and visualize their splendour and tremendous height. In the wind I heard non-existent waterfalls; it was wonderful!

We made our way along the serpentine road from the station up to Hotel Panhans, walking, climbing, slipping, staggering, heads at right-angles to our hips. At Mutti's insistence we drank a glass of hot lemon-juice even before we had our soup. Since we had not come all the way just for a meal in a hotel, Mutti agreed that Gerda and I should do some mountain walking until coffee time.

We enjoyed some hours in the snow, but when we saw the lit-up sign for Hotel Panhans we were suddenly really hungry for cake and coffee; so we ran the last stretch, only to discover that Mutti was not there. It was hard to ask other people if they had seen her, because whatever description we gave seemed to fit several women. We waited, one of us in the lobby, the other in the restaurant, just in case Mutti was having a lengthy session on the lavatory. But she could not have been there *that* long, we decided. We felt miserably helpless, until someone asked if we had agreed to meet in the *Grosse* or the *Kleine* Panhans.

We looked a bit blank and began to examine the foyer, trying to recall the one where we had left Mutti. Neither Gerda nor I was an observant person, but we agreed that it was possible that my mother was in the other hotel, apparently on the same side of the mountain but accessible only by going all the way down to the village. We ran, stumbled, panted, and when at last I threw myself into Mutti's arms, she only grumbled that she had begun to feel quite sick with the amount of coffee she had drunk. Although waiters would constantly renew a glass of water at no extra charge, nothing could have persuaded my mother to drink it. She could not accept the idea of making use of a restaurant's comforts without continually ordering some item or other.

Alas, there was no time to consume the cakes we had looked forward to. We took Mutti downhill, hooked into our arms on either side, running for the last train to Vienna. Glowing, invigorated, happy, we were ready for a big meal from the huge menu at the Rathauskeller.

Mutti handed me her remaining coupons and some banknotes, which I accepted with thanks but without counting, because I still could not persuade myself that it was proper to look at money. I would now, for the first time in my life, have to cater and calculate for myself.

The allowance which my father sent every month was the same as Gerda's – far more than we needed, though no more than we could spend. I did enjoy Viennese cakes for as long as my extra coupons lasted; I enjoyed theatres and operas; but probably more than anything else I enjoyed buying books. When I discovered that other students borrowed books from libraries, I had a shock and began to watch their spending with a feeling of guilt. Apparently they ate one-course meals in the students' canteen or possibly in the Rathauskeller, where one could survive till evening on a single *Kaiserschmarrn*, a kind of torn-up omelette with jam and/or raisins. When I discovered how many students were actually doing menial work to support themselves, I decided to hide my riches in a post office account, so that I could pretend to be poor without hurting my well-meaning father. (Three years later, when East Prussian bank accounts were frozen, our family managed to live on my post office savings[*].)

My rent was sent to the Andexlinger family directly and included breakfast, which our friendly, chatty, Czech-born landlady brought to our beds in the morning, after her own two daughters and her husband had already gone to work.

Student Life

In Vienna I lived simultaneously in two different centuries. This caused me no problems, since May Day 1933 had inserted twentieth-century worries into my romantic, nineteenth-century mind. Now I ambled along 'K & K' ('*Kaiserlich und königlich*') Habsburg streets and parks, made them my own, lingered and flirted in coffee-houses, abandoned myself in music and dance, and all the while pursued my quest for truth beyond the slogans of our time. This pursuit was more noteworthy for the determination that characterised it than for any success.

Students generally inscribed and paid for one major subject and two minor courses of study. There had never been any doubt in my mind that history should be my first priority, and the most eminent historian at Vienna University was Professor Ritter Heinrich von Srbik. He was lecturing on absolutism that semester, so I searched the university prospectus for other lectures to complement Srbik's topic and widen my understanding of the seventeenth and eighteenth centuries.

"Fantastic, absolutely fantastic", Gerda exclaimed when she learnt which period I was hoping to explore; "you couldn't have chosen a better time for the history of art in Austria! We'll look at it all together, here and in places outside Vienna. In Salzburg – oh! – Fischer von Erlach!" Gerda almost swooned with enthusiasm, and her exaltation was infectious. So I decided to study Austrian Baroque. Little did I know how art historians tended to divide beautiful things into vertical, horizontal and diagonal lines, making it impossible for me to see entities.

"You will", Gerda kept encouraging me; "once you grasp the details of composition, you'll see the completeness as you've never seen it before." That was certainly true for her, but by the end of my first semester I knew that art history was not a subject for me.

Nor did I fare much better in German literature, where I could not even blame Gerda for making the choice. I had the notion that no education is complete without the study of literature. Presumably I found lectures to blend into Srbik's centuries, but I cannot even remember which writers I studied.

Srbik was fascinating, and what he had to say was interesting – when I could hear the words! One had to arrive at least half an hour early for his lectures, as the Auditorium Maximum was always filled to capacity. The space for standing at the back of the big hall was almost out of earshot, for which the arrogant, famous man made no allowances. He sat at his table on the stage and articulated his wisdom in a quietly monotonous voice, seemingly oblivious of his audience. Or perhaps he was deliberately whispering, to enforce dead silence and strained ears. Yet he attracted not only students of history but large numbers from other faculties. Medical students made up at least a third of his audience.

---

[*] Post office accounts were valid nationwide, whereas most bank accounts were local

I was waiting for history to explain the present. Absolutism seemed right, explained as the centralization of power for a nation's self-defence and progress. Louis XIV removed the power of feudal lords by turning them into courtiers... like Hitler? Not quite. Was the difference only one of style, the frivolous Versailles compared with the austere, pompous grandeur of Third Reich architecture? The emphasis on harmony with nature of the Obersalzberg setting could perhaps be ignored as an optional extra. But had the time-scale simply been speeded up from Louis XIV to Louis XV, Louis XVI and then the Revolution? What revolution was possible in Germany? Who could overthrow the dictator and take him to the guillotine?

We argued long through the nights; but it was just a game, I thought, just a competition between optimists and cynics. We collapsed with exhaustion, some going to sleep on the floor, some wandering home through the silent streets of Vienna at dawn, others taking the first tram to Heiligenstadt to run up to the Cobenzl or the Kahlenberg for a glimpse of the sun rising above the Danube. The waters looked blue through my eyes, but others said they were grey; they teased me and liked me for my naïve good nature, which was the very last thing I wanted to be liked for.

There was Alois, who wanted to be called Loisl, writing poetry for me and about me, the simple nymph from the East Prussian backwoods – the kind of girl people wanted to marry, never just to flirt with. How I sometimes envied the sophisticated girls with their subtle caprices! Yet sophistication did not fit my nature, and the briefest encounters turned serious.

Some soldiers asked the flower girl at a café to present Gerda and me with a bunch of violets and a note asking permission to join us at our table. They started as flirts, just fun to talk to, to walk along the Ring with, a little diversion for their two-day leave. But whereas Gerda's young man kept kissing her even while we walked, my partner discussed the future in all seriousness and asked permission to write me letters. Only when we arrived at our door did he kiss my cheek... not without having first asked my consent. My irritation was appeased later, when a regular supply of large boxes of chocolates arrived from his father's factory, and I felt sincerely sorry and shaken when one of my thank-you letters came back with the words "Fallen for the Fatherland" stamped across it.

There were many others tying messages to violets, primroses, cowslips, tulips: soldiers given a two-day break in Vienna, wanting to forget the war. They were clean, courteous, gentle. Most came from war scenes which they did not understand at all, a mountain war without battle appointments. Rocks or trees suddenly moved from the shadows like mysterious killer phantoms, guided by an invisible force referred to as 'Tito'. The Yugoslav partisans rarely featured in official news bulletins, and our soldiers did not want to talk about their experiences. The aura of anonymity made ambushes in the mountains more frightening even than images of the Battle of Stalingrad.

Against my better judgment and all my sensible resolutions I still secretly hoped that Helmut might not yet be dead and that Paulus would surrender before the entire Sixth Army were slaughtered. I dreamt of Helmut, a prisoner in Moscow, speaking the language he loved, though deep down I knew this not to be so.

When the Stalingrad massacre ended in February 1943, I cried despite myself and for some reason crossed myself, as I had seen Roman Catholics do in films. Gerda turned the radio off and said: "Let's go to the Türkenschanzenpark; I think we have much in common."

Giver of violets

I had not told Gerda about my summer of 1942, and she had not previously told me about the convalescents' home near that park, where she had been in love and had walked every day that same summer. It was for those memories that she had stayed in Vienna another semester, though she had also agreed not to write letters, to have a clean-cut "*Servus*". We were happy to walk and exchange memories.

Far from objecting when we missed lectures, our teachers positively encouraged us to explore life with a capital 'L' – the sunshine, parks, mountains, theatres, concerts. Mutti need not have worried that I would overdo academic work, though I had to admit that I often found it difficult to choose between fresh air and the lovely, musty smell of the university library.

There was only one compulsory lecture, the 'pro-seminar' which was the prerequisite for attending seminars. Professor Lorenz was to equip us with the tools for our studies – bibliography and a general outline of historic events. He had published a book entitled '*Staat wider Willen*', which outlined Austria's reluctance to separate from an all-German state; and although he conscientiously – and boringly – fulfilled the task of his lectures, he often deviated to advocate his own philosophy of Prussian virtues as a standard measure of historic events. It was extremely difficult to follow his unfair and uninspired discourse, and after one such lecture a fellow student approached me:

"Excuse me, colleague; I saw you writing long notes and wondered if I might borrow them, because I simply could not make sense of what the man said."

I laughed and showed her my 'notes', which began: "Dear Mutti and Väti, I am making use of a boring lecture to write to you..."

Thus started my long friendship with the history student Edith. It did not worry me that she was attracted to meat coupons and, above all, to my social status. I had long given up explaining to people that life on the feudal estates of East Prussia was not as grand as its public image, and I was simply enjoying an ordinary student's life without inhibitions.

Edith and I worked together and tested each other before the pro-seminar examinations. I did not take hard work too far, but gambled instead on my Prussian-ness, learning dates and names of the Great Elector's predecessors for some name-dropping. The gamble came off, and my reward was an apparently unprecedented mark: 1 + with the words 'Very Good', the 'Very' underlined three times on the certificate. It was unfair, but I did not care any more than I cared about having the 'Kleines Latinum' certificate from school whilst poor Edith had to do things the hard way, taking private lessons while at university. After she passed the Latin exam her registration as a proper history student was back-dated and she could enjoy the same full course as I had had from the start.

Newspaper Science

One of the subjects we had in common, a kind of sub-subsidiary, was newspaper science. It was our insurance against being drafted into the teaching profession after our state examination. We treated the subject with contempt, although in our honest moments we had to admit that these lessons taught us more about the realities than all the academic lectures. We learnt the procedure and strategy of propaganda, devices, tricks, gimmicky ways of manipulating readers, thereby grasping Goebbels's tactics and becoming wary of his words.

Each of us had to produce some piece of original research for the examination, and I chose the title 'Propaganda through Newspaper Novels' from a list of suggested headings. Old memories of sitting on the lavatory, piecing together such novels and wallowing in melodrama, came back to me. I flushed with anger when I became conscious of stereotypes presented in an almost casual dramatic way. Propaganda addressing sentimentality; rich, ruthless, elegant Jewish moneylenders; even more ruthless, very calm and gentlemanly British businessmen; most elegant French connoisseurs of food, wine, women, art, frivolous in all things except their extreme nationalism; Hungarian and Polish freedom fighters, misguided at times, but proud; lazy Russian drunkards, never more happy than when they could be miserably exploited by Czars, churches, officialdom; Scandinavian nobles; Italian cowards (who disappeared in later novels); and then, of course, the blond, tall, blue-eyed German heroes who rescued those in distress and poverty and yet treated evil characters with dignified courtesy.

All this, our professor said, illustrated our duty as journalists to form and lead public opinion. Not to mirror it? No, certainly not, nor to pursue a quest for truth, for truth was irrelevant in comparison to ideals.

Some agreed, some disagreed; and so we argued, as students must argue if they are to change the world. We argued in houses and flats, in lecture rooms and the press club, on the grass slopes of the Kahlenberg, in a snowstorm inside the cable car which took us to the Raxalpe, in the wine taverns of Grinzing. We grew heated, furious and were happy.

There were arguments about the logic of *Lebensraum* and requests for us to breed more little Germans. This argument became very topical after students in Munich had rioted in response to an order for every female student to produce one child a year for the Führer. No such things were asked of Vienna students, who would have ignored the order without rioting. The Viennese had charming ways of ignoring interference.

Only a few members of our newspaper science group had always lived in Vienna. Among these were Kurt and his plump, pretty girlfriend Hedi. I sometimes wondered why Kurt did not wear a uniform, as he looked perfectly able-bodied; but it would have been tactless to ask. Herbert was equally puzzling: he did wear a soldier's outfit, but the sleeve of a missing arm was pinned inside a pocket. His girlfriend Mierle was plump like Hedi, and pretty, too. Both she and Herbert wanted to make films without political content, which struck us as very ambitious, at least for as long as Hitler lasted.

Nazi lecture at Newspaper Science Institute

Karl-Maria, a theology student from southern Austria, had obviously learnt to give Caesar his due (he wore military uniform) and his wife a child a year; she was a nondescript blonde who never argued.

Edith liked Gerd best, perhaps because he was from the Rhineland like herself, but more probably because he was tall and smart with polished shoes and polished buttons on his uniform. He was extremely hard-working, almost like those Japanese students who rushed about like bees, all wearing spectacles and all ignoring us – much to our relief. But Gerd was the only one who wore a Nazi Party badge, which I considered ridiculous. Edith told me I was petty.

Then there was Hubert from Silesia, also in uniform, on a year's study leave from the army. His landlady ran the ghost train in the Prater funfair, which I hated but made full use of, because we had rides for free. We all screamed as if we enjoyed ourselves.

Edith's flat-mate Hannelore, a medical student from Berlin, often joined our parties with Gerda. Edith was fascinated when Hannelore took us along to one of her anatomy lessons, but I felt sick. The sight of students peeling skin off human corpses was bad enough, but the sweet, chemical smell of the hall was really nauseating.

I might have felt sick in the stuffy room of Gerda's arty Turkish friends, had it not been for the distractions which took my mind off the heavy oriental perfumes: there was the problem of trying to sit in some kind of respectable position on a low couch when I was the only person in a short dress, and the room itself was covered in thick carpets and wall hangings, so that it was impossible to tell if there was any window. A small lamp with a red shade shed hardly any light, yet the colours all around us seemed to glow. Sweet black coffee was poured from brass jugs with straight handles into tiny mugs, which caught a ray of red light every now and then on their shiny polish. We were offered nuts and Turkish Delight, and I felt that I had landed inside a story from the Arabian Nights. Incomprehensible discussions of art were to me like exotic background music.

Gerda certainly did have interesting friends, and I was glad that we had agreed to spend the next years together at some university. We thought of Prague first, then perhaps Freiburg or Tübingen, finishing with two years of serious work for final examinations in Heidelberg.

"Soon all these roses will be in bloom", Gerda sighed as we walked through the Volksgarten.

"We don't really have to leave, do we?" I asked.

It did not seem very adventurous to spend yet another term at the same university; but when I went home for the Easter vacation, I left most of my belongings in Vienna. Who cared about enterprise when we were happy and longed to smell the scent of roses?

East Prussian Interlude

During the Easter vacation I began to suspect that the Russian prisoners Nicolay, Carp, one of the two Grigorys and perhaps some others understood and probably spoke fluent German. What was not clear was whether they were too proud to talk to us or too afraid. Officially it was forbidden for them to converse with us, as indeed it was for the Belgians, but the latter had always ignored this rule. In addition it was forbidden for any one Russian to talk to more than one other at the same time, presumably on the assumption that a group could be incited to create trouble. How anyone could prevent this at night was never clear.

The Belgians had no wish to establish contact with 'barbarian Slavs', but most East Prussians felt a certain affinity with Eastern people, not least because of a common taste in food. Lucien Lebrun thought I was joking when I expressed this view. How could I, a civilized person...? But although I was determined to make the acquaintance of at least the engineering student Nicolay, I did not succeed for some time. Little children like Marlene and our cousin Jutta had less difficulty and were already beginning to joke, even to flirt with Russian prisoners.

My own social breakthrough came with the arrival of Katya and Galya. In official jargon they were simply 'foreign workers', but in fact they were as much prisoners of the war as those in military uniform. German farmers were given vouchers entitling them to a certain number of additional labourers, either to replace Germans who had been called up or as a reward for increased production and an incentive to produce even more. When an assignment from the Soviet Union was due, farmers or their representatives would take their pick from the crowd on the market place in Darkehmen, mustering them like specimens on a slave market. Väti hated the very thought of such affairs and sent our Inspector, who hated them just as much but had no option, except that he refused to join the scramble for the strongest-looking men. So he took what was left: two girls aged fifteen and sixteen.

Many of us gathered and stared in disbelief when they descended from the pony trap. The pretty, dark-haired girl gaped back at us: "*Bah!*" she growled, copying the expression on our faces. "*Patchemu bah? Nix circus acrobat!*" Her black eyes flashed in fury. Everything about her sparkled with vitality: her cheeks glowed, her lips pouted, little curls burst out of her plaits. She was the younger of the two, and her name was Katya.

Galya looked dull and awkward by comparison. Her head was too small for her bulky figure, which was almost square except for her big bosom; and her nose was too large for her small face. Her fair hair was straight and neatly arranged in thin plaits. I did not notice her soft, sad, dark eyes that first day, but Mutti did and fell in love with Galya, while my heart went out to Katya.

Because I had since my earliest childhood enjoyed building houses and arranging rooms, Mutti gave me the task of preparing accommodation for the two new labourers. Since our blacksmith had married, the room next to the forge seemed just the right place. Although we had expected men, I had taken great care to make the place pretty and was looking forward to cries of delight when I took the girls there.

To my amazement Katya stopped dead on the doorstep and snorted contemptuously: "*Nyemyetski nix kultura!*" I knew that Nyemyetskis were Germans and could guess the culture bit, but was at a loss for why. Galya tried to make up for Katya's harsh words by uttering soft, incomprehensible phrases and stroking my beautiful, clean, starched tablecloth with admiration. I tried to think: What might have been lacking? The spring sun shone straight through the two south-facing windows; the entire room looked ever so bright and cheerful. The red-and-white chequered curtains, the blue-and-white tablecloth, white linen on the down-filled bed-cover and pillows – what was it that was not cultural? I had expected male workers, of course, so that it had to be some feminine aspect that was missing.

Nighties? Yes, it had to be nighties. I beckoned to the girls to wait while I rushed up to the farm and pulled two of my nightgowns out of the chest. I held them up to the girls expectantly: "Take them!" I hoped they understood my gestures. The girls held the gowns against their bodies and giggled: "*Rabota?*"

The language problem was depressing. Then Katya pointed to the table and said proudly: "*Kultura!*" While I was fetching the nighties she had picked dandelions and daisies and used one of the tooth-glasses as a vase. I nodded approval: yes, flowers were culture. But no, nightgowns were not meant for work and no, they were not yet meant to go to bed. Oh hell, how could we communicate? I had to restrain them physically from undressing. I gesticulated, mimed and said "*Niet rabota*" and "*Nye panimayo*" in turns; eventually I took them by the hand and marched them off in search of an interpreter.

My real hope was Nicolay, the reticent, proud prisoner who had not yet admitted to any knowledge of German. Carp, Vassily and Grigory had, but they were always joking and playing tricks on children, so I did not quite trust them. At a pinch I would rather ask the reliable Ivan, who at least knew a few words.

It was easy to find Nicolay, because the guard insisted on always keeping that particular prisoner within a group, in sight and within rifle range. He was convinced that the man had set his mind on escaping.

Nicolay listened to the girls and talked to them while I held my breath. Would he or would he not speak German to me? At last, either from compassion with the two girls or because he wanted to make us aware of German sins, he translated the girls' story. They came from a small town in the Ukraine. The inhabitants had been ordered to register their names in order to receive food rations, and extra food was promised for those able-bodied inhabitants who registered at the Labour Exchange. Katya and Galya were among the latter and were immediately hustled on to lorries. It was not what they expected, but while they thought they were going to a factory nearby, they were not worried. Only when they were taken to the railway station did they become suspicious. When they were directed to a cattle truck they became frightened and Galya began to cry, while Katya shouted at the German soldier that she was not an animal and would not go into the wagon. A soldier hit her with the rifle butt and pushed her in. "Katya wants me to tell you that *the soldier* was an animal and that *he* should have travelled in the truck", Nicolay inserted before continuing. The journey lasted several days. Occasionally they were let out at a station to relieve themselves and to be given some food and drink, but during the first two days they were not told where they were going. Eventually they heard that the destination was Germany, for one month's work, and that they would be able to write letters to their families. Nicolay looked at us: he knew, as we knew, that there was no postal service to the Soviet Union and no Red Cross there.

"But I thought we were told that they would work here till the end of the War, weren't we?" I asked my father. His reply was a grunt, and Nicolay said pointedly: "Precisely."

"They were also told that they would be given writing materials and working clothes", he continued. I thought of the nighties and burst out laughing despite the awfulness of the story. Nicolay explained our misunderstanding to the girls, and we took them to the house to find the promised working clothes. Galya chose the two plainest and most practical dresses from Mutti's wardrobe. Katya chose four pretty, flimsy dresses from my wardrobe and one practical one, a blue dirndl with a white, puff-sleeved blouse, which looked perfect on her. She was hopping about and dancing with joy during the dress-fitting, while Galya smiled kindly and sighed.

Neither girl believed Nicolay's warning about the mail service, and we could not refuse them paper and envelopes. Their faith was infectious, so I posted their letters with stamps of the same value as those I had used for Gustot's letters. The

Ukrainian ones came back, returned to sender; yet the girls continued to write, printing the addresses more clearly, making Nicolay write them in German script.

"What can I do?" I asked him. He shrugged his shoulders; so I kept the returned letters in my desk. None of them had been opened by censors. They were probably returned from Darkehmen sorting office.

Gradually, receiving no replies from their families, the girls did give up writing. In any case, their expected one-month stay was coming to an end. Katya was counting the days, setting her count-down songs to music on the guitar we had managed to procure for her: "Seven more days, only seven more days", then "Six more days…" I did not know if to be glad or worried about my return to Vienna before her zero-day.

"What is going to happen? How will Katya accept reality?" I asked Nicolay, and again he shrugged his shoulders. But it was not an unfriendly shrug: we were no longer enemies.

Mutti had persuaded the guard that Nicolay was a real gardener and that she would take full responsibility – in writing – if Nicolay escaped while working apart from the guarded group. Then she sent Galya to work in the garden, too. I was amazed that anyone, least of all Nicolay, should fall in love with Galya when an attractive girl like Katya was about; but my mother said she understood such things and would give the two lovers a chance.

Her scheme worked well in all respects. Those two, hidden from the rest of the world, laboured to justify Mutti's trust in their gardening skills and had plenty of time to sit on the bank that divided the lawns from the vegetable garden, or inside the tomato house. Mutti wrote to me at university, asking for Russian books on Nicolay's behalf; I managed to obtain a second-hand Lermontov and a volume of Pushkin which had a lovely picture of a troika on the cover.

Galya and Nicolay

Excursions from Vienna

The roses in the Volksgarten were profuse in exuberant colours and scent. Gerda and I did not regret our decision to stay in Vienna while Edith had moved on to Prague. Sometimes she came to visit us; we went to the Gänsehäufel island to swim in the pool and picnic, or to the Vienna Woods; and when Väti visited me together with Rudi, we made a two-day excursion into the Wachau and the Ötscher Gorge.

"I am studying Goethe", I gasped when I saw my first-ever waterfall, which was such an overpowering sight that my own feelings failed me. Gerda laughed, but I was quite serious:

> *"Falling from the steep wall of rock,*
> *Scatters delightfully,*
> *Touching lightly the smooth boulder*
> *Like wafts of cloud,*
> *Bubbling, murmuring softly,*
> *Sinking into the depths..."*

And Gerda continued:

> *"But when crags bar the path,*
> *The waters foam angrily..."*

I added:

> *"Soul of man, how like the water,*
> *Fate of man, how like the wind!"*

But Gerda did not want to hear this last part. Her mind was full of Mariazell, where we had spent a night before beginning our 25-kilometre walk through the gorge. The basilica, the twelve columns by Fischer von Erlach and, most important, the Romanesque statue of the Virgin just had to be the experience of a lifetime for all of us, Gerda thought.

It was a glorious, sunny day. In heavy mountain boots and with a rucksack full of food Herr Andexlinger jumped from boulder to boulder as nimbly as a mountain goat, never out of breath, much more agile than any of us, who were carrying no luggage at all. We also explored the Wachau, talked of Richard Lionheart and the faithful Blondel at Dürnstein, of Robin Hood's form of justice, of the Nibelungs further upstream. So many taverns with attractive wrought-iron signs tempted us, but we waited for our mountaineer landlord to suggest the one with the best *Heuriger*. Väti produced meat coupons, so that we could load our plates with large chunks of different kinds of pork in addition to a variety of salads, including, of course, the traditional cream cheese with paprika.

When we returned to Vienna I wanted to walk alone for a while, to unwind. Something drew me to the over-ornate Jesuits' church, and on an impulse I lit a candle. I sat for a long time, watching without seeing the flicker of the light. My excitement and Goethe drained away, and my overwhelming sense of gratitude dissolved into peaceful nothingness. I had no idea why I was doing this, and when I came out of the church I felt embarrassed, because on a normal day I was not a religious person. Gerda mentioned in a casual voice that she had dropped in at the Greek Orthodox church for a while; I replied "Oh?" and said no more.

Every day one of us said to the other: "We must make concrete plans for the winter semester before we get stuck in a rut", and then we discussed what we still wanted to see in Austria, leaving the future in the air. Gerda had no wish to see

Graz, but for some reason, possibly on account of the climate, Lori from Berlin wanted to go there with me. It turned out a very unmemorable occasion.

As we did not want to pay for first-class seats, we spent the long overnight journey standing in the corridor of the crowded train. By the time we reached Graz in the chilly hours, we could only think of the bell-tower as a sight we had read about. We plodded up the Schlossberg like two somnambulists and collapsed there in the grass, where we slept until it was time for the train back to Vienna.

Henceforth I left the planning of excursions to Gerda. It had to be Salzburg, she said. The Kollegienkirche was Fischer von Erlach's masterpiece, all white-on-white chiselled marble, bulging clouds, the cherubs' light and happy playground under the ceiling of the church.

"So be it", I agreed, "as long as I can also visit the Tomaselli Café." I remembered the film *Königswalzer*, in which Heli Finkenzeller had served royalty at tables under the beautiful trees, and I hoped to persuade Gisela to join our excursion for that reason. But Gisela was advised against the long journey by her parents.

My little sister Marlene, now aged eleven, came instead, together with Cousin Rolf, whose birthday was on the same day as hers. It was by then the beginning of the summer vacation, and our big trunks had already been sent home. We first let the children enjoy the sights of Vienna, then left for Salzburg and Berchtesgaden as our grand mountain finale. This time I had learnt my lesson: we booked seats on the train.

The old town of Salzburg was everything Gerda had promised, and more. The fountains gurgled and splashed water over our outstretched arms as if it had been peacetime, Imperial Habsburg peacetime. Gerda arranged our culture tour and restricted the offerings to suit our digestion, stopping while we were hungry for more. She wanted us to retain a longing to return to Salzburg one day in the future. Now it was time to take the bus to Berchtesgaden and thence the little narrow-gauge train to the Königsee.

We just caught the last boat for a circular trip on the lake. Somewhere in the middle, opposite high mountains whose flat faces dropped vertically into the water, the boat stopped and a man's trumpet-calls were answered by clear, eerie echoes which made me want to cry. This was the highlight of my student days, or so I thought. But later, when we were walking along the side of the lake and suddenly saw the Alpine glow turning the summit of the Watzmann bright red, I changed my mind. I gasped, and gooseflesh crept along my arms.

The gooseflesh refused to go away even after the spectacle had faded. It suddenly became terribly cold. We covered ourselves with the jackets which we had a short time earlier found so cumbersome; but we still shivered on a single bench, huddled together yet unable to sleep. Gerda's big overcoat wrapped round the four of us was of no use. We decided to move from the lake, hoping that the covered porch of the little station would provide more shelter. It was cold even there. We counted our money, wondering if we could afford a night in a hotel; but we had spent too much on ice creams and drinks during the heat of the day.

When we saw a lantern approach, we quickly hid under the benches. We knew it was against the law to sleep outside a station and feared it might be a night-watchman coming to check for vagabonds. We were right, but the old man kindly offered us accommodation in a stable, next to two horses whose breath provided warmth. A single round beam, suspended from the ceiling to about a metre above the ground, was all that separated us from the animals. Every now and then we heard the thud of a horse's hoof hitting this beam; but otherwise we slept undisturbed and warm in fresh straw. In the morning we were woken by the night-watchman bringing us mugs of hot *Ersatz* coffee. The horses were already munching the oats which he had brought while we slept.

Berchtesgaden

Rolf sat much closer to Gerda than was necessary in the warmth of the stable, and I felt sorry for her. But she only giggled when he told her that he wanted to marry her because she organized such friendly holidays.

A month later Wiener Neustadt was bombed and nearly 400 people died. Frau Andexlinger wrote that she had bought blackout curtains. Poor, beautiful Vienna!

Our Prisoners

When I arrived home for the summer vacation, my father warned me with a chuckle that my mother had been converted to Communism.

"Rubbish", Mutti protested; "I'm only impressed that an intelligent and interesting man like Nicolay should be a Communist. He has told me wonderful things about his education."

"Free holidays on the Black Sea coast", Väti laughed, "just like our *Kraft durch Freude* schemes; and you know how much such 'Strength through Joy' was appreciated!"

"Just because Sperling was seasick and too old to enjoy Madeira, it doesn't mean the idea was bad", Mutti retorted; "and Nicolay experienced far more, and much more exciting holidays together with his student friends."

"You see what I mean", my father grinned at me.

When I had more chance to talk to Nicolay, I became as impressed as my mother was. His general knowledge amazed me. When an engineer was as familiar with Goethe as I was – and more familiar with Shakespeare, Dante and Molière than I could ever hope to be – it said something for his education. I was

128

all the more puzzled by his love for Galya, who was so ignorant and simple. She was kind and gentle; her voice was soft and her heart so warm that even the terrible war could not freeze it. She longed for her mother and cried for her, but without a trace of hatred for those who had taken her away from home, without the slightest bitterness. And the sophisticated, cynical Nicolay loved this girl?

"No, he doesn't", Galya said, smiling with just a little sadness; "I'm for here and now. Later he'll look for a girl with a good head."

I wondered. Katya said she was crazy, but then, off and on, everybody was crazy (*dourna*) in Katya's view: "*Ti dourna*" was her way out of perplexities. She was a wild thing, looking for her mother. Once Katya came to me in the middle of the night, wearing only her vest and knickers and shivering. She cuddled up to me under the warm, down-filled bed-cover, crying and hugging me, saying: "*Slotka, moya slotka.*" I never found out exactly what those words meant, except that they were terms of endearment. And then, quite suddenly, I was no longer the mother-substitute, but a representative of those who had made her a prisoner, a *banditka*. She was passionately bewildered and helplessly repetitive in expressing her frustrations. Whether her general vocabulary was limited I could not tell: it was only the ever-recurring words that enabled me to understand a little Russian. In the same way she learnt German swearwords and words for certain items of food; and we both learnt "thank you" and "please" in each other's languages.

Once Katya folded the ends of her plaits under her nose, so that they hung around her mouth like a drooping moustache. She grinned mischievously and said in a deep, growly voice: "Me Papa Stalin. Will make all Nyemyetski *kaput* for what they have done to my children Katya and Galya."

"He has begun to do that already, at Stalingrad", I replied.

"*Kharasho*", Katya said with glee; but Galya looked miserable and sighed.

Ivan, Hilde, Galya

When Katya cursed me as a bandit, a madwoman, or in similar strong terms, I knew that she would suddenly change to affection again; but when she addressed me as plain *Nyemyetska* I knew we were in for a prolonged period of animosity. Yet all the time it was Katya I loved in preference to the forbearing, perhaps se-

129

rene Galya. Katya was like a storm tearing away cobwebs and like a child, making us see by asking questions about the obvious which we had not even noticed. There is a kind of freedom in slavery, an awareness of having nothing to loose, which made Katya bold or, as Mutti called it, impertinent.

When the girls were asked to take visitors' coats and hang them on the pegs in our hall, Galya obliged with a friendly smile while Katya planted herself grimly in front of a gentleman, pointed to the pegs and said: "You no dwarf, you no cripple, you see peg, you hang coat." My mother looked as if she would explode with anger, but good manners forbade reproach in front of strangers. My father chuckled; I looked over my shoulder while curtsying to another guest and held my breath; and the man did as Katya bade him.

On another occasion Katya approached a young gentleman who was dangling an ornate walking stick while crossing our yard: "You bad foot or sick?" The man was taken aback, and my father answered for him: "He needs a stick to defend himself against cheeky girls." Katya liked that. My father, like most German men, admired the "spunky little Ukrainian". All the Belgian prisoners were infatuated by her; but her own compatriots showed no interest at all and seemed to prefer German females, except for me… and except for Nicolay, who loved Galya.

I tried hard to make friends and always exchanged a greeting, "*Zdravstvuitye*", but received only polite replies; so I flirted with the Belgians in the fields. Like all students, I was obliged to do a stint of practical work during my holidays, and I enjoyed making that contribution to the war effort conscientiously on our own farm.

Valère Pironnet had fallen seriously ill while I was in Vienna and had been transferred to camp; so I could not avenge his description of me as '*sa prise*', but targeted my retaliation on Lucien Lebrun, who was an easy and pleasant prey. The more I teased him, the more he seemed to admire me, which was gratifying. We loaded the corn together and chatted and joked on top of the loads, enjoying the puzzled looks on the faces of Germans and Russians alike, as none of them understood French.

In the evenings we often met in the Belgians' dining room after the other prisoners had left. Mutti gave me special treats to pass on to Monsieur Lebrun (he always remained 'Monsieur' to me) – biscuits, meringues ('*baisers*' in German), apples, even wild strawberries with cream which we had stolen from our own cow-sheds at night. On Sunday afternoons we met again in that dining room and were joined by Lebrun's friend Armand Claussin, who was working on a small farm in the village of Skirlack. He was by far the most interesting of all the prisoners. A Liberal by political conviction, he greatly admired the British system, which he made sound totally different from my pre-conceived ideas of little boys going up chimneys and asking for more in orphanages, or of women who had to "stitch, stitch, stitch in poverty, hunger and dirt". He did not mention massacres in India; and when I referred to concentration camps in the Boer War, he replied that we had concentration camps in Germany.

"Oh, but they are different. I would hate to be taken to one, but they only indoctrinate people", I said, and Claussin did not contradict me. He said he would like to read Hitler's *Mein Kampf*; I offered to lend him the copy I had bought before my final school examinations, on which I had marked all the important bits, so that he would not need to plod through the lot. To my surprise he seemed to find this statement funny.

Claussin

Most of all, and for totally non-political reasons, Claussin wanted books by Walther von Sanden, who lived at Guya, not very far from Mikalbude. I myself found it quite pleasant to read about birds and deer in these books, but usually felt irritated by the blatantly Christian slant. Nevertheless, I encouraged Claussin to write a fan-letter to von Sanden, and when the author replied with an invitation to spend a Sunday with him, bringing a friend if he wished, he accepted on his own and Lebrun's behalf.

The two prisoners went to Guya in a trap belonging to Claussin's farmer, or the farmer's wife, to be precise: the farmer himself had been missing in Russia for a long time, and the Belgian prisoner was running the place almost single-handed with help from the wife and occasionally seasonal workers. Yet although Claussin had a good room of his own and had never been supervised by a guard, he was longing to go back to Belgium. He knew that people at home were short of food – which he certainly was not, since a small place like the one on which he worked was hardly checked by the authorities – and that they could not make their own wines for lack of sugar. He had no girlfriend waiting for him at home and was enjoying an affair with our secretary; yet he wanted to be free.

I was not sure what an 'affair' was, and when Lebrun suggested that I should love him in the same way as Anni loved Armand, I could only reply that I might, if he came back after the war and thus proved his own feelings. I knew he would not, but I enjoyed being a short-term conqueror, keeping my distance. We were friends and had fun, and whenever I had some spare time I rode to Skirlack to talk to Claussin on horseback.

Our Belgians had acquired a gramophone, and I lent them such records as they liked: "*Bel ami*", "*J'attendrai*" or Zara Leander singing "*Der Wind hat mir ein Lied erzählt*". Sometimes Lebrun brought the gramophone to the prisoners' dining room and we danced. But I never heard the Belgians sing except on that day when Gustot and Pironnet had performed their dances.

The singing of the Russians enhanced our last two summers at home with sad beauty. Always, when people sang from the top of loaded wagons on their evening journey from the fields to the farm, my heart had grown full with a sense of home and belonging. The lengthening of the shadows, the glow of the sinking sun, the voices of men, women and children highlighted by the eerie pathos of Auguste's shaky vibrato rising above our folksongs – it had always been and was forever our home. But when the Russians walked behind, falling in with our melodies by humming four-part harmonies – deep, dark basses and Ivan's tenor – home extended to infinity. Late at night the Russians' own songs reached up from their compound and stretched into space. Then I would sit by my window until the last notes had faded away.

It was jollier on Sundays, when the guard was in a good mood and allowed the prisoners to borrow my accordion. Through the wire fence we watched them dance, and occasionally, when the guard was especially congenial, Katya, Galya and even Marlene and Jutta were allowed to join the rhythmic leaps and acrobatic leg-throwing.

"Savages", said Lebrun, and that summarised the Belgians' attitude to their Soviet allies. We had discussed these problems among students, concluding that the Munich agreement had been signed only because Stalin wanted to fight Hitler then and the Western states would rather be seen dead than allied to Marxists. Moreover, we hypothesized (though some disagreed), Poland would have gone the same way as Czechoslovakia had it not been for the newly-concluded non-aggression pact between the Soviet Union and Germany. We viewed Hitler's invasion of the Soviet Union as his bid to bring France and Britain on to his side – a grave miscalculation, which had ignored the benefit that would accrue to the Western powers if Germany and the Soviet Union bled each other to death. Our theories seemed confirmed when the second front was very slow in coming. Claussin agreed that most of his compatriots rejoiced at the prospect of the Soviet Union being ravaged beyond recovery and believed that the removal of the Marxist danger would eventually benefit the world at large.

Vitya

That summer we received another voucher for two labourers from the East. This time my father sent Heiland, the foreman, to the market, hoping that he would be more practical in his choice than the Inspector had been. But when Heiland returned, we were all dumbfounded at the sight of a small *Panje* cart pulled by a little steppe-pony, with a pot-bellied little boy sitting on top of various bundles. Walking alongside were two men: one clean-shaven, dark-haired and fairly young, the other old and grey with a beard. The younger man wore Western-style clothes, the older one a traditional Russian peasant's shirt.

News of their arrival spread quickly, and people came running to stare. Some touched the child's thin arms as if to test if he were real. And real he was indeed, angrily so: he spat at those who touched him.

"Typical Russian brat", someone murmured. The men stood by diffidently and did not try to stop the child. Then Mutti's dachshund Biene barked and tried to jump up to the cart. The boy's face crinkled all over in a large, affectionate smile. "*Sobashka*", he called and tried to pull Biene up. I helped, and as I put the dog into the child's lap I said in my best possible Russian that it could be his dog. I was sure Mutti would not object.

"Oh, thank you, Mama", the boy looked at me with soft brown eyes. I understood the thanks, but misunderstood the "Mama": only much later did I find out that Russian children address strange women by that name, much as Germans call them Aunty. At that moment I considered myself chosen to take the place of the absent mother.

The boy's name was Vitya; the men were his father Volodya and grandfather Mark Mosin, Vitya's *Dyeda*. They had come from a village near Moscow.

"On that little cart?" I asked in amazement.

Volodya, who spoke some German, smiled and said: "Vitya and sometimes Dyeda on cart, I on foot." As I stared at his German army boots, he smiled again and added: "Many shoes kaput; cow also kaput." Apparently they had set out with a cow as well as a pony. But why had they set out at all? Had they been abducted by the German army? After Katya's and Galya's story anything seemed possible.

Volodya, Vitya and Dyeda

Volodya shook his head. No, it had not been abduction; they certainly were no asset to the German labour market. They had simply drifted along, initially because one German soldier had been kind to them, and then there had not appeared to be any option but to retreat from battles with the army, further and further away from Moscow.

In one short morning Volodya had lost his mother, his wife, four children. That Vitya was with him was a miracle: he had taken him to the forest to collect firewood, and when they came back to their home they found it burnt and all their family killed. They could only guess at the killers – either partisan fighters of their own nation – punishing the family for doing some laundering for the German army, albeit under duress – or German soldiers, because Volodya's wife had

133

told them the previous day that she no longer dared take in their washing, even if the alternative were deportation of their elder daughters. What difference would it make to know? Nothing could resurrect the dead, Volodya remarked, and revenge was a primitive notion.

The Mosin family was allocated a two-room cottage next to the modern one at the eastern side of the workers' complex. Dyeda did the housework, which included looking after poultry and pigs which we had given them. Volodya worked on the farm, and Vitya spent his days very much as I had spent mine at the age of two-and-a-half: in our house, in the yard, playing with children below school age and with those adults who found time for him. He joined his father and grandfather for most meals, but in the evening I often gave him a bath in our house before carrying him down in pyjamas. Then I would say German prayers with him, as Mutti had done with me, and afterwards I listened to Dyeda praying in Russian.

The old man had been a priest in his home village; Volodya had been the schoolmaster. Vitya, who learnt German quickly, understood that his grandfather could not be bothered with a foreign language, and so he always talked to him in Russian – "fluently, like a grown-up", Katya remarked with admiration. To Volodya Vitya spoke in broken, ungrammatical German, even when the boy himself had learnt to speak his second language as we spoke it. Katya often tried to trick him into muddling these three languages, but never succeeded. She was perhaps his best playmate, only too glad to abandon work and take him around on the luggage rack of my bicycle or teach him practical jokes. Occasionally the maids grumbled about Katya's laziness, but on balance it was appreciated that the moody Ukrainian girl had become almost good-tempered.

Prague

For a time I had been half-hearted about a semester in Prague, but an absurd battle with officialdom made me more and more determined to win. Visas for the 'Protectorate' were normally issued to Party members only, and Gerda, who had not managed to slip the Hitler Youth net in Insterburg, had been transferred almost automatically to the Party proper. Unfortunately, when I applied, the Party was temporarily closed to new members. So what could I do?

My father persuaded the *Kreisleiter* to compromise: if I did something of value to the Party, might I not be given a certificate as a promising candidate and a visa for Prague? The man took a few weeks to think about the proposition and then came up with a task for me: I was to recite a poem in front of an assembly in Kowarren!

"Impossible", I said, remembering my agonies at school.

"Rubbish," Mutti replied. "If you borrow Lore's Hitler Youth uniform you won't even know it's yourself standing on the stage. You'll hear your own words as if they were those of a stranger."

It was worth a try, but I just could not quite persuade myself that I was another person on that stage. My heart missed a beat when my arm jerked up and my voice uttered a smart "*Heil Hitler!*" Then my voice – and it really was *my* voice –

134

rambled along the well-memorized and badly understood verses to the full stop of another arm-jerking salute. And I was given my visa!

That had been before Vitya's arrival; now I really did not want to leave Mikalbude. But then something happened that jolted my social conscience. I heard my father shout, "What do you take us for?" and slam down the telephone receiver. Mutti, who had just come through the drawing room with a pile of dirty washing in her arms, asked who had made Väti so angry.

"It was Bagdahn's damn son-in-law, that fat, vulgar Nazi who seems to be in charge of the administration in Bialystock and apparently finds no better place to spend his holidays than at Lenkehlischken with his daughter. Bagdahn himself has cleared off under some pretence, of course."

"And what did that man want from you?"

"Well, as you know, the German army was very surprised to find that so many Jews in Poland were good craftsmen, instead of just bankers, doctors, musicians and lawyers as in Germany; so it seemed fair enough to make use of their skills and let them earn their living, although I always had my doubts about how they were paid. That's why I never ordered riding boots or leather coats when that son-of-a-bitch son-in-law asked before. And now he had the nerve to tell me I should make up my mind quickly, because 'we've already had to *get rid of* the women and children and can't afford to feed the men for much longer.' Yes, those were his precise words!"

At first Mutti did not understand. What did 'get rid of' mean? But before Väti could try to explain, the truth dawned on her and she sobbed loudly: "Now one has to be ashamed of being German!" Handing me the pile of washing, she left the room.

"I'm going to join the Czech resistance", I threatened without having the slightest idea of how one set about such things.

"Grow up, Radish, for God's sake!" Väti groaned.

"Golden Prague of a hundred towers" – a line from a poem I had once read. I had seen *The Golden City*, the first German colour film. It was so beautiful, more beautiful even than Vienna; so what was this weight holding down my joy? It could not be fear, for Edith had written that everything was wonderful – intellectually and socially exciting. Yet why had my parents insisted that I, like Edith, must live in a German students' hostel "for greater safety", whereas Gerda had rented a studio in an ordinary Czech block of flats?

I was going to stay with Gerda for at least the first few days. She had a piece of paper: "Tram No. 1, direction Castle, 3/4-hour journey." We asked passers-by where the tram stop was. Some did not answer at all; others mumbled "Not understand" and hurried past.

"They don't want to understand German", I said miserably, remembering Nicolay. "Let's take the next train home."

Gerda grew angry: "What did you expect? That they would welcome Germans with open arms? You are the one who always believed that universities are for

135

discovering life. This is our chance." She took me by the arm and dragged me towards the first tram stop to read the numbers.

"Perhaps we could ask a policeman...", I wondered.

"Certainly not." Gerda was adamant: "We'll find ways of making friends with Czechs, and such ways are not via the police."

"They are not via anything, not even via love", I thought, remembering that Helmut was jilted by the girl he loved. But I did not reply.

We found the address. It was a large, modern block with a concierge, who handed Gerda a key when she had identified herself. At the end of a long corridor was a long, narrow room with a single window at the far end. Under the window stood a desk, flanked by two divans. At the dark end of the room, near the entrance door, stood a wardrobe and a table with a gas ring for cooking. There was also another small table and several chairs.

Most of the tenants in the block, it seemed, were students; all apart from Gerda and one Egyptian were Czech.

There were no house rules at Gerda's place – a blessing of which I did not become aware until I moved into my student hostel and was handed a large sheet of rules even before being shown my room. Some were amusing, others outrageous. Rule No. 8: "Never disturb other inmates, no loud music, no singing, whistling, banging of doors, loud conversation; absolute silence from 10 p.m.; guests to leave hostel by 9 p.m.; no friends or relatives to stay overnight." Rule No. 10: "Under no circumstances and at no time are male visitors permitted; violation of this rule leads to immediate expulsion without compensation." Rule No. 11: "Light, gas and water must be used economically; possession of private electrical implements strictly forbidden; special permission for the use of a radio may be granted to girls from their second semester onwards upon payment of a fee." Although none of these rules concerned me personally, their very existence was irritating.

But what I disliked most about the hostel was having to share a room with three other girls, one of them an asthmatic. All the best cotton wool stuffed into my ears could not keep out the wheezing and rasping noises of her breathing and the sounds of the oxygen pump, which woke me several times during the night. All my good resolutions to feel sorry for the girl could not alter my dislike of her illness, nor my dislike of myself for disliking her. I hardly dared to look at the girl for fear of triggering off another asthma attack.

Edith was lucky enough to be in a second-semester room, which she shared with Hille and Hetty from the Oldenburg region. I stayed in their room, working on my lap until just before 10 p.m., when I had to sneak to my own bed or escape to Gerda.

Yet I loved Prague, the golden city which turned silver in the snow and moonlight. I could have spent hours just standing by the *Hradčany*, my Holy Grail which I could never simply call 'the Castle'. It was most seductive when viewed from inside the arch of the Old Town Bridge Tower. Silhouettes of saints guarding the sides of the Charles Bridge, dark, squat towers guarding the Malá Strana end, one low, the other higher, "one Romanesque, the other late Gothic",

Gerda explained. "Both just romantic to me", I laughed, and she snorted in good-natured contempt.

Beyond, high above, shone St Vitus's Cathedral. It was a long time before Gerda could persuade me to go up and look at details. She was right to tempt me, not so much for the details as for the experience of walking along terraces and hanging gardens; we ascended wide, cobbled steps, stopping every now and then for the view of the Old Town below, on the other side of the broad Vltava, which we, of course, called the Moldau.

Courtyards, wide vistas, narrow streets, old squares, towers and more towers and churches, breathtaking surprises every time we deviated from a previous route, an agglomerate of the styles of many centuries; and if modern buildings jarred our sensitivities now and then, we learnt to understand that on some future day these too would blend into the picture of a city that grew according to people's needs rather than to an overall plan like the Ringstraße in Vienna. Even if we lived in Prague for years, we would not exhaust its supply of treasures.

But every day presented moments of misery, when only Gerda's determination prevented me from leaving. We were in enemy territory, where the enemy were prisoners and we were victors, whether we liked it or not. At first I tried to smile at people in the streets, but they stared through me as if I did not exist; and if a Czech did smile back, I did not like it either, suspecting him or her of being a collaborator.

Prisoners, perhaps real criminals, were shovelling snow under the supervision of German soldiers with guns and revolvers. I saw one of the prisoners being hit with a rifle butt and wanted to interfere, but Gerda held me back: "Observe, just observe; that is the duty of students."

I did not agree, but restrained myself because I was too afraid to do otherwise. Sometimes, thinking back, it seems that every day in Prague must have been a day of fear or of frenzied entertainment designed to kill that fear. But I know this was not so: there were many moments of blissful emptiness, when time stood still as I looked up to the *Hradčany*, or when I stopped on a hill to stare down at all those bridges across the glittering bend of the river, or when the silhouettes of many towers stood dark and strong against the red evening sky; moments when Prague flowed into me as Vienna had.

But Vienna was dark now, blacked out against air-raids. It was winter, and although many of our summer-semester friends were still studying there, we felt no longer part of the university. Like tourists we spent a weekend roaming familiar haunts in the company of familiar people. We joked and laughed artificially, trying in vain to recapture the past. We all cried a little when we said good-bye to our friends on the platform of Franz-Josef Station. A door had closed just as firmly as it had closed against my village school many years earlier.

Academically Prague compared favourably with Vienna. History seminars, if not completely unbiased, were not provocatively slanted in favour of Prussian militarism, as had been those of Professor Lorenz or even Professor Bauer. We were, of course, made aware of the privilege of being students at the oldest German university, the *Karlsuniversität* or Clementinum, and we accepted the spell of German-ness around us. But propaganda was either absent or so subtle that we did not notice it in our minor subject, newspaper science. It was almost a pity not to have any controversy. Journalists and film-makers seemed to concentrate on the technical aspects of their future trade. I exhausted myself just yawning with boredom during a visit to the Barendov film studios and was grateful when a student called Matzek suggested a long walk home by the river.

French lectures were the most interesting, and Victor Hugo inspired me to look for poor Quasimodos to whom I might be kind. But alas, if there were such people, they hid their insecurity so successfully under cynical humour that I found no opening for emotional attachment except, in a motherly-daughterly way, to Monsieur Pommeret.

I first met the frail little professor in his small corner shop, where I bought my Victor Hugo. His wife was obviously in charge of the book business. She was large in figure and voice. Her polite but categorical statements on what students required were irresistible, and so I bought a Larousse despite her husband's protestations that students could ill afford the purchase of expensive books and could use them in libraries.

"*Seulement le petit*", she replied and handed me the condensed version. As neither Madame nor Monsieur spoke any German, our conversation was entirely in French, and I thought we communicated well. So I was taken by surprise when the formidable lady suggested that I join her husband's conversation classes for beginners at the university. She brusquely wrapped up the textbook for the course and, as I paid, whispered: "Please keep an eye on the little fellow."

I felt curious and persuaded Edith to inscribe for the class with me. We were a few weeks late, but found the language easy enough to follow. It soon became clear why Madame had been so anxious. Two SS men sat at the back of the room, laughing and calling out sarcastic remarks, at which the little professor became nervously disconcerted. At one point I stood up and told them either to shut up or, if they did not want to learn, to leave.

"Oho! But we do want to learn. We are going to Paris next semester and want to cope with the ladies; so we need a different vocabulary from you."

"I am sure you can acquire that kind of vocabulary on the spot", I replied sharply; but seeing fear on the professor's face, I did not continue the argument. I even accepted an invitation to an SS party at the Palais Lobkowitz. Was I too scared, after all, to refuse, or was I simply doing Edith a favour? Perhaps I had already drifted so far into a string of nightly entertainments that I no longer cared where I went.

"Why are you so reserved?" asked the less brash of the two men when we walked in the gardens among the statues. I had no idea what he meant and did not care, but for some reason I remembered the remark.

My Prague diary reads like a noisy, boastful sequence of names, titles of films and plays and men who competed for our company. I no longer remember their faces, nor am I sure if these names were all real or some were nicknames, or if we called some men simply by their surnames.

'Pierre' might have been what the burly SS man called himself in anticipation of the *Parisiennes*. Holler sounds like a surname. One man I called Hannes, because he was from Hamburg and his real name Otto did not fit his face. "Tilde's soldier" took me to students' social events, but I don't know why, nor who Tilde was. There was Achmed A. El-Hamid, a pompous Egyptian who had his own box in the opera house; I ran away from him after a performance and joined Gerda and Fritz in the street. We were telling ghost stories and screaming with pretended fear until we were stopped by some policemen for creating a disturbance. "Felt great to be in trouble with police", my diary boasted.

There were Martin, Gert, Willibald, even "a handsome stranger who invited me to the cinema". Dinners at Kotva's, coffee at Chotek Park restaurants, dances here and there, theatre, concerts, operas. I noted that Millöcker's *Bettelstudent* was fun and that Verdi's *Othello* was too sad. *Madame Butterfly* made me fight to hide my tears, while Gerda sobbed quite unashamedly and, when a soft white curtain waved dramatically across Butterfly's body, howled out loudly: "Oh, the curtain!" The audience looked round at us.

Fritz did not like *Tristan und Isolde* at all and persuaded me to join him for chamber music concerts instead. I agreed, although such concerts made me feel uncomfortably serious.

We saw all the plays which were performed in German, and in my diary I noted that "Hamlet had no right to procrastinate, because he at least had a ghost to give him a sense of direction." Was all my boisterous diary a cry for a sense of direction?

Cinemas were our most common haunts, both for German and for Czech films. All of the cinemas must have been owned by Czechs, because I wrote down ticket prices in *krones* – we paid up to 7 *krones* a seat. Trams too were paid for in Czech currency: 1.50 K. per trip, whatever the distance. I did not record the prices for the opera or theatre, perhaps because we were always invited to these. But poetry readings were paid for in German money: 1 *mark* for a standing place when Fred Liewehr read Rilke's *Cornet* and overwhelmed me with a longing for home. I ran to the station and left.

A soldier sat next to me, on his way back to Poland, he said. He tried to make friends by offering to send me some good, hand-stitched leather shoes. I recalled Bagdahn's son-in-law and tried to control my anger.

My parents were always pleased with surprise visits and asked no questions. I hugged them, kissed them and quickly changed into my riding outfit. My father, taken by surprise, forgot to tell me that Silhouette had not been exercised for a long time. More than anything else I wanted a fast gallop across our fields, and for a few minutes I had just that; then Silhouette threw me and I fell against the frame of a stook that had been left standing in the field. I remember no more, but apparently my horse fell to the ground not far from me. Vet and doctor arrived at the same time, the former treating Silhouette for colic, the latter diagnosing a minor concussion, for which he prescribed a rest.

The accident gave me an excuse to hesitate before I opened Gerda's letters. I knew what she would have to say and that she was right. Prague was more beautiful than even Vienna, so why did I not want to go back to continue my studies? Why could I not bring myself to work for a degree and plan for the future, when deep down I felt sure that I would survive the war?

I got out of bed and prepared to return to the golden-silver city. I sent Gerda a telegram, asking her to meet me in Dresden. She was thrilled, having long wanted us to accept an invitation to stay with Rudi's family for a few days.

The *Zwinger* and the spacious beauty of Dresden's streets and parks impressed us both. The town struck me as a small, dignified version of Vienna. The odd dialect was difficult to understand, but Rudi translated people's remarks into High German. His family's living quarters on the city outskirts were humble and cosy, and the food was homely and tasty. We were treated like royalty and accepted the honour without embarrassment.

Back in Prague I received many letters from the prisoners in Mutti's envelopes. I did not know whom to trust with translating Galya's letters, which might even have been written by Nicolay; perhaps they contained some indiscretions which might bring us into conflict with the non-fraternization rules. Eventually I decided that the Czech assistant at the Slavonic Institute was probably my best bet. He translated the letters orally and handed them back. (I had them translated into English much later.) The lists of books which I was supposed to obtain for Nicolay were not handed back, because the young Czech said it would take him a while to find them.

Encounter with an Artist

Gerda and I treated ourselves to dinner in the Hotel Ambassador on Wenceslas Square, but we had to be patient for service, because two waiters were dancing attendance on the man at the table next to us. He must be an important person, we thought. Quite a young face, perhaps in his mid-thirties, with slightly greying temples. As we watched without staring too openly, the man looked up and asked if we would like to join him for a meal, because food tasted better in company. We nodded consent, and as he rose to offer us our chairs, he bowed politely, saying "Stratil" by way of introduction. We muttered our own names without being sure if that was necessary by the rules of etiquette. It probably wasn't, judging from the way the gentleman ignored our words.

"Enough for three," he said to the waiter, "and this with the fish course," pointing to a Mosel on the wine list.

"Several courses?" I asked timidly. "I am not sure if our coupons...."

"Don't worry about coupons," he laughed. As so often in Prague, we marvelled at the coupon-less gluttony of some people, but had no scruples about joining the feast.

It turned out that Stratil was an artist, and Gerda became very enthusiastic when he suggested that we come to his hotel room to see his work and perhaps be his models. I don't know why the idea scared me, but I quickly declined the invitation on behalf of both of us. Gerda tried not to show how angry she was with me.

Indoor café sketch (Karl Stratil)

We happily accepted an invitation to the cinema, and when Stratil walked us home to Gerda's place, we agreed to meet him again for dinner in a week's time. But alas, just as life was beginning to be interesting, I fell ill with an infection of the middle ear. I had an operation that lasted only a few minutes, but my lopsided swollen and partially bandaged face seemed to last for ages.

Gerda telegraphed for Mutti to come and invited her to stay with me in her own studio while she moved out to other friends. Mutti spent a restless night, scratching herself and itching all over; by the morning she looked as swollen as I was, though more evenly so. She pointed in despair to the numerous black spots on the ceiling, which we had until now thought of as decorations. "They move!" Mutti said, and she was right. So she herself had to move to a hotel for the nights.

Every morning I received a letter from Stratil, and it was flattering to read: "If you knew how much I normally hate writing letters…" Other remarks were very funny: "Gargle every hour. It might not do your ear much good, but it can't do any harm, and I believe in harmless things well done", or: "Wrap a scarf round you and be my model", or: "I could lend you my big grey coat. Should I bring it to you?" Heaven forbid, I thought. Vanity forbade that he see me with my face askew, but as I felt too well to waste the time of Mutti's visit just sitting in a dark bed-bug room, we planned outings which avoided places where Stratil was likely to turn up. So, when he entered the Press Club restaurant in a group of men, I wanted to hide under the table. He tactfully gave me no more than a brief nod and saved me further embarrassment by placing himself with his back to our table. Mutti thought his back looked very impressive.

At home I examined my face in the mirror, wondering if the time had come when I could dare to give Mutti the treat of meeting Stratil. Just then another letter arrived, telling me how pleased he had been to see me look so well again and would I do him the honour of coming for dinner with the lady who must surely be my mother? As always, he ended his letter with best regards to my friend Gerda, whom he found very likeable. We agreed to celebrate Mutti's last night in Prague at the Ambassador with him.

Not many days after Mutti had left, yet another letter arrived, still in the polite '*Sie*' form of address, but calling me by my Christian name. He asked for the chance of one last evening before he had to leave for Italy.

Outdoor café sketch (Karl Stratil)

We sat at his usual table, ate, drank and talked until long after the last tram had gone. We did not talk about art, but about Goethe, particularly Goethe's 'Faust'. I wanted to test how much of a real friend Stratil was, and Goethe was always my yardstick. Of course, since he was older than I was, I could not expect youthful enthusiasm, but I found his diffidence and hints of condescension rather disappointing. When I expressed worries lest our pleasure-drunk students' life was my *Walpurgisnacht*, he laughed out loud: "My dear child, how little you know about orgies! You are leading a normal, harmless students' life which will sadly vanish when you grow up."

"I wonder how I can ever grow up when I have no sense of direction," I sighed.

"Dear child, have patience," he smiled. "A sense of direction will come. Meanwhile the main thing is to survive." And he went on to talk of legitimate double standards which combined inner integrity with outer compromise. It was almost as if he were talking to himself, perhaps somehow trying to excuse his own lifestyle, without expecting me to understand.

I shook my head. All this was not good enough, I had to do something, I could not just opt out of life around me. Stratil put his hand on mine and smiled: "You will find a way, don't hurry."

We walked back to the hostel at dawn. The full moon had not yet given way to the sun and the *Hradčany* looked serene in a blue light. I could hear the cleaner women at work, so I knew I would manage to slip into the building. Mr Stratil kissed my hand.

On the following day I received a parcel – an illustrated volume of poems about Prague by a man called Leo Hans Mally. On the fly-leaf was a handwritten dedication: "To Anneli, Stratil." And inside the pages was a brief letter:

"My dear Anneli, Thank you for everything. I so enjoyed our walk from the hotel that I wanted to walk home in elation, composing poetry. But an early tram came along and it seemed warmer. And the poems have already been written. Good-bye, my dear."

Vienna Opera House (Karl Stratil)

In the afternoon I saw a telegram in my rack: "WILL BURST IF NOT SEE YOU COMMA GERDA".

So I rushed to Gerda's place and she dragged me to an art dealer's shop. The walls were covered with pictures by Stratil, and every one had a 'NOT FOR SALE' label. So now we really knew that he was famous.

Then Mutti sent me a magazine cutting of an article entitled 'In Honour of Stratil's 50th Birthday.' We were amazed to learn his age.

I never heard from him again. The greying temples are all that I remember of his face, but I did not forget that life could be exciting without hectic amusements.

Fraternizing with the Enemy

I still possess two letters I received from Galya. The first was brought by Mutti:

"Letter from Galina Pavloska for favourite people. How do you do, darling Anneli? I am writing to you though I don't know myself if you are able to read Russian, because I cannot write in German. I shall write to you, my sweet Anneli, as I can. I am terribly sorry to find out that you are ill and that your mother had to come. That's why all of us are very sad now – and I was really upset when I found out that you are ill, my sweet Anneli. I remember you every day because you are such a good girl, and everybody thinks of you and asks us if Anneli will come home for holidays. Anneli, I will ask you if you can buy books for me in Russian. I will tell you which, thank you very much, Anneli. Goodbye. Galya."

The other letter was in the envelope with the magazine cutting about Stratil:

"Anneli, you gave me a photo, but I have not got it now: Lebrun took it with him – I did not want to give it to him, but he nevertheless took it with the order 'Make her give it!' And when he found out that you sent a postcard to me, he came to read it and said he would write an answer for you. I asked him what about the woman inspector [i.e. Anni, the secretary] saying he was not allowed to

143

– was he? He answered: 'Let me write the answer', and so he wrote. Anneli, don't be offended with me for this way of writing, because I cannot write otherwise and I shall write as I can. My darling Anneli, write me an answer, because I am missing you very much. My best regards, deep, warm regards from all of us, wishing you all the best in your young life. I want you to live your life in a white world as well as you can. Auf Wiedersehen, I kiss you and give you my right hand to shake with the help of this white paper. Goodbye, Anneli. Galya. I kiss you a thousand times."

When I came home for the Christmas holidays, Vitya rushed towards me, shouting "Mama, Mama!" He no longer called other women by that name, and I made up my mind to marry Volodya after the war, whether he wanted it or not.

Vitya had a special song which haunts me to this day: *"Nochi chyornaya, ya bayatsya, ya bayatsya, pravazhat mnye, o moy slodka..."* I can still hear the ring of his voice. Someone told me that the words meant "The night is dark, I am afraid – accompany me, my sweet..."

Poor little Vitya, and still so full of laughter. We walked on hepatica in the spring. In the far distance we could hear the rumble of battle and occasional sharp claps. Vitya made babyish cooing noises when he stroked the bright blue flower-heads while the dachshund Biene explored interesting holes further inside the forest. "My very own woodland!" Vitya sighed happily and circumscribed the small clearing with his arms.

But Galya left me no time to cuddle Vitya. She tugged at my sleeve, whispering "Urgent!" and came to my room, ostensibly to help me unpack. She told me that the guard and some strangers had searched the Russian prisoners' room and even cut Nicolay's mattress open. They had asked him if he had any books, which he denied. Then they wanted to know if he had connived with a German civilian to get books, which Nicolay also denied. Then, despite my father's protestations that this was illegal, the men had searched Katya's and Galya's room and found Lermontov and Pushkin.

"We said we did not know where we had found the books. We did not betray you," Galya kept saying.

"You need not have said that; there is nothing illegal about me giving books to you and Katya. But thank you, anyhow."

"But they said they would come back when you are at home and question you. I think they did not believe us," Galya replied miserably.

I was glad to have advance warning, but very puzzled indeed. Someone must have complained, most probably about me. I remembered overhearing a conversation between the guard and our foreman long ago, something like: "It just shows what money can do; a lesser person would have been shorn and tarred...", which I had then found a little sinister, even though I did not connect the 'not lesser' person with myself. Now I wondered. It was a pity that Galya had denied my part in getting Lermontov and Pushkin: I would now have to say that I left those books lying about in the kitchen or something like that.

But when the officials arrived, they did not even mention those two books. Instead, they wanted to know about a list of subversive Soviet literature. I could not imagine what they were talking about; then, suddenly, I remembered that I had given a list to the Czech in the Slavonic Institute, that he had commented on the writing being different from Galya's – which, needless to say, I had not even noticed – and that he had never returned the list to me, because he apparently needed time to get them. Did he? My suspicions were awful, but I needed time to think. I asked what was meant by subversive books.

"Don't put it on, any student knows that very well," one of the men replied. "Perhaps you would even like to pretend that you never heard of Gorky?"

"No," I said. I recalled that Aunt Anne had once mentioned that name, but had no intention of involving her. My experience in the Labour Service had at least taught me that much. "But I would not think much of names if someone recommended books for me to learn Russian."

"Ah, now we are getting somewhere. So you did have a list of Russian books!"

"Certainly."

"And who gave it to you?"

"I am not very sure, but I think it was a student at the Slavonic Institute in Prague," I replied.

"Do you remember his name?"

By now I was getting so angry that I grew bold. "I believe it was Nicholas."

Now it was the men's turn to be taken aback by my semi-frankness, and I enjoyed the expressions on their faces. After some hesitation the man whom I took to be the chief interrogator said: "You are of course aware that it is an offence to provide Russians with books?"

"Is that the law?" I asked innocently. I felt I was winning.

"Naturally", was the reply.

"It does not seem very natural to me to force prisoners to ponder mischief, perhaps to harm our country, instead of distracting their minds to concentrate on poetry and novels." I felt great. So often the right words only came to me long after an argument had finished; but now, in my fury, every sentence miraculously came out just the way I wanted it.

The men hm'ed and ha'ed; so I helped them to a face-saving answer, because I was anxious to bring our meeting to an end: "You mean to say that ordinary people like us cannot judge what laws are necessary on a higher level?" If you swallow that, you really are fools, I thought.

"Precisely," the man looked at me with gratitude.

"So I must never leave Russian books lying about carelessly? And always ask for official views before I accept study advice from strangers?"

"So glad you understand, so glad. If you didn't, you might find yourself in serious trouble."

When the men had left, I told Galya that it was all right, but that it had been a close shave, which made it impossible for me to try again to get Russian books. But I would like to learn something about Gorky. After a decent interval of non-fraternization Nicolay gave me a lecture on Soviet literature. But that was during the next holidays, as the Christmas holidays were very short.

Prague Again

On my return to Prague I found Edith in full swing of social excitements. She was in love with an instructor at a cadet school nearby. She called him Göring because of his stature and all the medals on his chest. This man found me a partner for a grand ball at the school, and I later stuck the impressive menu into my diary:

> Crème Ragout
> Italian Eggs
> Grilled Fish and Potato Salad
> Fillet of Beef à la nature, Potatoes, Assorted Vegetables
> Venison with Semmelknödel
> Coffee Mousse with Cream
> Ice Gateaux and Wafers
> Fresh Strawberries
> Coffee

All through the night champagne, three different wines, various liqueurs and nibbles were on offer. Two large orchestras took turns playing waltzes, tangos, and foxtrots. I had hardly time to take sips from my glass between dances.

Once I tripped and felt a sharp pain in my ankle, but a few moments later I was dancing again. It was not until next day, when I tried to get out of bed and my leg gave way, that I noticed the swelling. The pain was real and persistent. I hobbled to Edith's room on one leg and she called a taxi to take us to Vyšehrad hospital, where her brother-in-law worked as a consultant.

I had apparently torn a ligament badly, and my foot was put in plaster. The only shoe I could wear on that foot was a beautiful slipper, which a Russian prisoner had plaited for me in our fields. Thus I hobbled to lectures and seminars, in fine weather, rain or snow. I hobbled to dances in the Press Club, on the island, at the cadet school again.

And I hobbled to riding lessons, because our instructor, Colonel Nehring, said I could ride perfectly well without stirrups. Indeed, any fool could on those well-trained horses of the riding school. They obligingly obeyed commands from the instructor without pressure from our calves, though in order to change from left gallop to right gallop we had to shift the weight of our bodies on the saddle to alternate sides.

"Im Arbeitstempo ga-a-llop," made the animals break into a canter like soldiers reacting to the order of their officer. And they knew that the sharp pronunciation of "Gallop" told them to gallop properly, that the word "T-r-r-r-ab" required a trot… always on thick layers of sawdust to protect us in the unlikely event of a fall. We made jokes about 'circus horses', but deep down I knew that they were good for me, because they gave me confidence, which helped me to ride better than I should ever have dared in the freedom of our farm.

"Arse in, chest out!" Our colonel was deliberately coarse in his language, aiming to create a jovial, matey relationship with his pupils and give us confidence.

Then, while my foot was still in plaster, the colonel really made me proud: he presented his own horse, 'Mikosh', for me to ride. I wrote to Claus for him to share my pride at being a star pupil, albeit in inferior conditions. Claus believed in my abilities, which was really quite funny.

My beautiful, colourful slipper lasted the course, but only just. It began to look sad and scruffy and to feel soggy. Reluctantly I threw it into a rubbish bin when my plaster had come off. But I kept the right slipper in my cupboard towards the day when I might hurt the other foot, or at least as a souvenir to remind me of the Russians after the war.

Real drama and fear came to our hostel in Prague after Easter: the 'knife-stabber' was about. He was prowling somewhere in the vicinity, every night, attacking and wounding girls who came home alone, and he was apparently doing this in spite of increased police surveillance. Girls talked of him in whispers and tears. Warning shots by the Czech resistance? Urging German students to go home to their own country? The stabber did not kill; it was as if he knew how to avoid fatal spots when he slashed his victims.

We were told never to come home alone after dark. But I ignored that order, because, perversely, the knife-stabber gave me hope. *"Aux armes, citoyens,"* I whistled to myself, wishing that Gisela would hear me. Together we would think of something; somehow become part of a group whom some called 'terrorists' and others 'freedom fighters'. The romantic appeal of living with a sense of purpose… That man out there, prowling at night, could be the key to that dream. Perhaps he would understand my whistling?

Not that I actually imagined myself attacking someone with a knife! The idea of blood at close quarters made me feel sick. He would know that and perhaps give me the job of derailing a train, or possibly even throwing grenades at SS men from a distance – something of that sort.

I felt absolutely confident that I would not be stabbed myself, that even in the dark the man would see friendly intent written all over my face. But I told neither Edith nor Gerda, hoping that each of them would believe I was staying at the other's place while I was prowling. They would have called me naïve and tried to stop me.

I dodged the policemen and proved how easy it was to become invisible. But the knife-stabber dodged me, it seemed. It was frustrating, and I found it almost impossible to sustain hope.

Farewell to Prague

I had gone to Gerda's place and was looking forward to a night away from the hostel for a change. Suddenly I heard terrible screams.

"Don't go to the corridor, or else they might take you, too," Gerda whispered.

What was she talking about?

"It has happened before; it always happens at night. This time it must be the pretty little one," Gerda explained.

"How can you! How can you accept that?" I shouted with rage.

Gerda put her hand over my mouth. "Ssh! It's dangerous. How can we not accept? There are many men, I saw them once…"

"You never told me," I murmured, by now thoroughly frightened myself.

"I could not, it's too awful. Willibald knows and he will come with a pudding for breakfast to cheer us up."

"A pudding?" It sounded so absurd that I began to laugh hysterically.

"Ssh, ssh! Please, please!"

It was quiet now in the corridor. We heard a car door slam and the engine start up outside. Then we just sat without talking and were still sitting like that when Willibald arrived. But I simply could not eat the pudding.

Suddenly I remembered Mutti's last letter. She had written quite normally about farm work, about gardening, about Katya and Galya and about how fluent Vitya's German had become. And then, very casually, she had put several addresses at the end of her letter, asking me to keep them safe, "in case we become separated." In my pre-occupation with the knife-stabber I had not taken in those words; now their meaning hit me.

"I am going home," I told Gerda and Willibald, adding dramatically: "I think the curtain has risen on the last act".

"Coward," Gerda replied as so often before, but rather more half-heartedly than on previous occasions.

"You will plunge your mother into a real state of worry," Willibald warned. He had been to Mikalbude at Christmas and knew that Mutti did not need much excuse for panic, though he did not know that she had sent me those addresses. "Besides, we have tickets for Zara Leander in 'The Way to Freedom'", he added. That really made me laugh. Way to Freedom indeed! British convicts going to Australia. But I was going home.

I had to get my passport from the hostel and also took my post office savings book. Edith was not there. She was living in clouds, because she was engaged and spent many nights with her fiancé at her sister's flat in Vyšehrad. I suddenly thought of Edith's baby niece, whose bottom was powdered after every bath, as was the fashion with babies nowadays. Mutti would have been utterly shocked about people blocking the pores of their babies' skins. What would happen to that little mite? Would they all stay in Prague to await events? But there was no time to think if I wanted to catch the last through-train to Königsberg. I scribbled a note to Edith and pushed it under the door of her room: "Going home for good. May or may not return to get my things one day."

I ran through the town. On an impulse I dropped in at M. Pommeret's corner shop. Madame shook hands, dignified as ever, but when the little man said *"Adieu et bonne chance"*, his voice broke and I burst into tears, hugging him. Then I ran on to the station without looking back.

YEAR OF COMPREHENSION: 1944–1945

Home, sweet home, and never as sweet as in that last summer.

Then a terrible commotion disturbed the sweetness. The guard came rushing to the house, shouting at my mother: "I told you so. You would not believe me. You are responsible now: Nicolay has escaped!"

"Perhaps he is sitting on the lavatory," my father suggested.

"I resent that," the guard shouted angrily, because he was nervous: "I have checked everywhere."

"I meant our lavatory. The man might have been in a hurry," Väti said. But needless to say, Nicolay was not there. For some days I had somehow known that this would happen, but had not acknowledged the idea even to myself. Now the army was called in to search the surroundings of the farm until it was too dark to continue. Galya came to my room, shaking with fear.

"For heaven's sake, go to your own room and pull yourself together if you don't want to be suspected of complicity."

"But I can't be calm," she whimpered miserably. "They will see that I know something, I am sure they will."

"Stop that kind of talk at once! Surely, they will notice that you are upset. Who wouldn't be when deserted by a lover – do you understand? DESERTED BY A LOVER!"

Galya smiled under her tears. "You and Nicolay are the same, he told me just the same words."

"Galya, please, don't say such things even to me! Try and persuade yourself, yes, yourself, that Nicolay told you nothing beforehand, that he really has deserted you. And go to your room."

Galya left. The soldiers continued their search on the following day, further afield, right into the forest, but without success.

Then, quite accidentally, old Schwarz, the pigman, shouted with fear from the granary. He had crept in secretly to steal some extra rations for his beloved pigs and had the fright of his life when he found a man caked in sweat and bran lying in the pile.

Nicolay was taken away, we did not know where to. We were afraid for him and just a little relieved that we did not have to witness his punishment. Galya cried for days. The plan had been so good: Nicolay would lie low until the search was called off, hopefully before new rations were weighed in the granary. Galya might have taken him some food, but it was not an essential part of the scheme because Nicolay could survive on grain. Then they would both have left. The Red Army could not be far away. Who could have foreseen old Schwarz's determination?

Nicolay did come back. He looked pale and bruised, but never talked about what had been done to him. His gardening days were over, but Mutti felt that they had been worthwhile despite recent events. Galya now also went to work in the fields where very occasionally they could look at each other, whisper a few words, and let their hands touch when they hoed the same row of beet plants or bound the same ear with a twisted strand of corn.

Sounds of Battle

"Lord: it is time. The summer has been great.
Lay now thy shadow on the sundials
And in the plains release the winds.
Command the last fruits to be full,
Give them yet two more southern days,
Spur them to perfection now and harry
Last sweetness into heavy wine."[*]

Gisela nodded. The spring blossom was not yet fully out, but it felt like autumn. There was a rumbling on the horizon, still far away and intermittent. It came from the north-eastern skies.

"Papa wants Mama to come and live in my flat in Königsberg," Gisela said.

Already? Was there not time for the last fruits to be full, for two more southern days, for one perfect summer? Who knew? It could all end very suddenly, and our sadness was blended with relief.

Ordinary work continued with extraordinary intensity. Sometimes my father came off his horse and grabbed a tool to join the workers.

Gisela went back to her studies. I helped in the fields; I did not have to: officially I was still at university. Physical exertion relieved the tension.

The Belgians joked: "Stocking the barns and cellars for the Red Army?" German workers grinned, grimaced. The Russians did nothing to show their feelings. I did not begrudge them their hopes of going home.

But Katya, who had once been the more optimistic of the two girls, was now strangely sceptical. Why did we not all run away to some hiding place until big people had signed papers to stop the shooting? She wanted to see her Mama soon, not to be killed by things that boomed through day and night. All the prisoners had experienced the sounds of battle before; only we Germans were still innocent.

Even then, when we could already hear the occasional rattle of a machine gun, we were allocated another two slave workers. They were Ukrainians. The young tall man was called Volodya Golubov. He was strong and cheerful, and we called him Big Volodya to establish the difference between him and the now re-named Little Volodya. The fair-haired Marusha gave birth to baby Vera not many weeks after arriving on the farm. It happened at night, in the new granary above the coach house where the couple had settled. Big Volodya proudly informed us in the morning that he was now the father of a girl. My father was so impressed that he gave them a cow as a celebration present.

The military Soviet prisoners were not impressed by the newcomers. They treated them with open contempt, and although no one used the word 'deserter', at least not in front of us, we overheard sarcastic remarks about "able-bodied men arriving without Red Army uniform". It did not matter, anyhow, for though I had a certain irrational aversion to deserters, my reason told me that it made sense to run away from armies, any armies. Besides, Big Volodya was handsome, great fun and, much to Marusha's distress, an unadulterated flirt.

---

[*] Rilke

150

Suitors

Väti wrote to 'Koch's Erben', our wine firm on the Rhine, to ask for an early consignment because of the various regiments that passed and were billeted on the farm. We drank and danced in a gentle, civilized manner.

I suspected that my parents would have liked me to marry Hermann, a lieutenant who stayed in our house for longer than most. At moments I too longed for just that, not because he owned large estates (including a sugar factory near the Dutch border), nor even because he was a "Dr Agr." and presented me with a hard-bound volume of his thesis, though it was probably these things that made him the strong, confident and practical person he was. I felt secure with him, a little too secure for my liking. He did not exploit the mood of 'harrying last sweetness'; a generous, kind and loving gentleman, determined not to extract commitments in times of uncertainty. I often wished he would forget his scruples, but my guardian angel obviously saved me from becoming a rich industrialist-farmer's wife in the post-war years. Edith could not understand our reservations when we both visited her in Prague for two days. I had decided to retrieve my belongings, but had been afraid to go there alone. "Hang on to him," Edith urged me, "he is quite the most impressive man I have ever met."

"You have not met Karl-Heinz," I replied, and she groaned when she heard that my other 'prospect' was a poet. Edith had a hard life with an over-artistic mother and an artist step-father.

Hermann

Karl-Heinz was in the same regiment as Hermann. He was passionate, impetuous, exciting, but not strong, nor sure of what he wanted from life except for wanting me. He did have a sense of humour. Once, as he was sitting next to me on the sofa with his arm round my shoulders, the door opened too quickly for him to remove his arm entirely; so, having it half-way up in the air, he promptly said "*Heil Hitler*" as Väti and Claus entered.

151

Karl-Heinz

There was a certain romantic mystery in Karl-Heinz's life. He might have been illegitimate, or his mother had been divorced, or she was a widow. Karl-Heinz never mentioned a father and I dared not investigate lest the facts destroy my preconceptions. On the basis of such imaginings I developed the idea that I, and I alone, could give the poet a reason for wanting to live. So, when he surprised us all by announcing our engagement, I did not protest. What did it matter now?

As Rilke had written: "Lord! it is time…" The same poem ended:

> *"He who now has no house will never build one;*
> *He who is now alone will long remain so,*
> *Will wake and read and write long letters,*
> *Walk up and down the avenues*
> *Restlessly, with the drifting leaves."*

In 1944 Rilke had replaced Goethe.

The 20th July Plot

No one could now replace Hitler. It was too late.

Nearly ten years earlier two-thirds of our main road had been asphalted, leaving one-third as the 'summer road' in kindness to horses' hooves. We had then been very excited about our *chaussée*, along which the postal bus could run smoothly twice a day. Since those early days the traffic had greatly increased, as military vehicles moved to a distant war, cutting our birch avenue in half between the farm and the farm cemetery on the further hill.

But never before had army transport been as alarmingly numerous as from the 20th of July.

The road led to Hitler's headquarters, somewhere in the Rastenburg region, or maybe near Angerburg, it had long been rumoured. So we knew that something extraordinary had happened even before the radio announced that God had once again preserved the Führer from the bomb of villainous traitors.

"He has the luck of the devil", Gisela muttered. "If only there would come a priest with the power of exorcism!"

We had some immediate worries: there was a reward of a million marks on the head of a distant relative of ours by marriage, Aunt Anne's cousin Dr Karl Goerdeler. I began to scheme in the tradition of all the best detective and spy stories I had read. Surely he would come to us, just because we were not close to him. We had a store-room full of old beds, wardrobes with great-grandparents' clothes, ugly garden statues of plaster-of-Paris, a perfect hiding place. I already saw myself sneaking off to that room with food for the hunted man. For twenty-three days I dreamt dramatic dreams. Then Goerdeler was recognised by a simple, stupid air force girl at Marienwerder station. It was for the sensation rather than the million marks that she betrayed the fugitive; and, according to Aunt Anne, the Goerdeler family harboured no grudge against the girl.

We were too stunned – and too frightened – to talk about the 20th of July plot, least of all to our neighbour, the captain-of-horse in the reserve who had been ominously absent for long periods during the past year. He was a close friend of Carl Goerdeler's brother, the mayor of Königsberg.

Göring had changed the traditional army salute as a mark of allegiance, loyalty and respect for the Führer; and as a consequence of the failed plot, soldiers and officers no longer touched their caps or helmets, but raised an outstretched arm, saying "*Sieg Heil*" – "Hail victory!"

Victory was now in sight; there can have been few who still doubted the identity of the victors, even fewer who did not look forward to the end of the slaughter.

Gisela was pessimistic about survival, but I had no doubt on my own account. It seemed right and proper that I should start a new life, now that I was twenty-one. I romantically visualized beginning from scratch, like a gipsy or a beggar.

But my parents were determined to insure against dependence on charity. Secretly, at intervals, they sent parcels to the West, officially in support of friends who suffered from air raids and were generally worse off than we were: family silver, precious glass and china, registered as "old clothes, salamis, hams, home-made apple-juice", praying that no censor would open the parcels. Such boxes went to Dresden, to Vienna, Celle, Berlin, Hamburg, distributing the risk and favouring Dresden as the safest bet.

I longed for stewed Morello cherries with thick cream, but we no longer dared to steal cream from our dairy. Controls were increasingly rigorous. Besides, cosy family evenings had ceased with the flow of passing regiments and army officers, however pleasant, inhibited the desire for illegal feasts. Until our very last night at home; and then the Morellos tasted sour and the sight of cream turned my stomach, which was heavy and full of nothingness. Only the wine tasted good, and we drank in abundance.

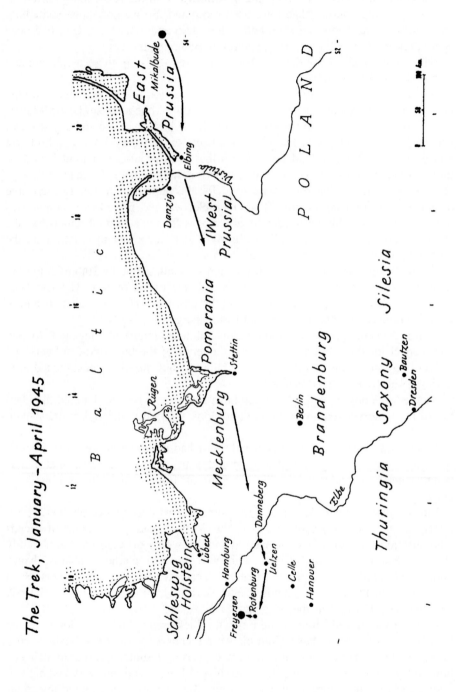

The Trek, January–April 1945

Running Away – But from What?

Karl-Heinz had moved into trenches some weeks before. When I visited him there once I could hear Solveig's Song on a guitar and knew he was expecting me. The music led me to his private bunker, a cheerful underground room with bright blankets and colourful magazine pictures covering the earth walls. His orderly served a meal on a small folding table and wine from real glasses. Cut glass, not crystal, but a luxury which I had not expected.

"We will fight for Mickelau and keep it safe for you," Karl-Heinz said as he raised his glass. It was an absurd statement, considering that the trenches were beyond Kowarren, at least five miles further away from the Russian border than our farm. I replied: "Mikalbude, not Mickelau", which was equally absurd: place-names had been changed and the new names established nearly six years before Karl-Heinz came. I was probably the only one who still remembered the old names and clung to them.

The harvesting had been done and some of the ploughing, but not yet the threshing. The rattle of machine guns had now definitely joined the thuds and booms of heavy artillery, and at night we saw the flares on the eastern horizon coming closer.

When, on 20th October 1944, Karl-Heinz rushed into the yard on his bicycle and told my father that the Russians had broken through the German lines, Väti shrugged his shoulders. It was obvious, was it not?

"But you must leave." Karl-Heinz's voice was urgent.

"Is that a military order?" my father asked the young lieutenant, mocking him.

All day our phone had been ringing at short intervals: to leave or be shot as friends of the enemy; then to stay and seize forks, scythes and hammers or be arrested as deserters. Contradictory orders changed by the hour.

"What the hell are you playing at, don't you know that East Prussia is lost?" Väti had shouted into the phone, and before he had finished listening to the tirade about penalties for defeatist remarks, he slammed down the receiver and ordered the wagons to be loaded for a dawn departure. Karl-Heinz then noticed the progress of the preparations in the yard.

Mutti pushed the uneaten food into the pigs' swill and stacked the dishes in the kitchen. The maids were with their own families; only cook, the Inspector, the *Elève* and Anni helped us. We wanted to leave our home in a tidy state. A dozen or so wine bottles were left on the drawing-room table, together with glasses, some of them containing dregs. I looked round the room, forced a cork into a half-full bottle, re-arranged some glasses, and was satisfied with the casual look of diffident elegance. The Red Army could take up good living in the same orderly manner in which we departed. They would not know about the last-minute pandemonium in the birch avenue.

Väti took the reins of our carriage and cracked the whip. People scrambled on to the other wagons without further argument. Big Volodya sat next to Väti, Marusha and Verushka in the back with Mutti, Marlene and me. Vitya was on the little *Panje* cart with his father and grandfather, and they were the first to jump into the ditch when planes suddenly swooped overhead. We stared up at them in wonder, as we had never seen planes before, except for Gustav Klaudat's belly-flopping machines, of course.

"Get down, lie flat," Little Volodya shouted at us in desperation.

The Golubovs and several other people did as Volodya bid them; others remained on the vehicles, spellbound, watching monstrous big birds doing graceful dives and curves in the air, seemingly weightless, glissading all around us. I saw red stars and I thought I saw a pilot wave at us, but that might have been my imagination. They disappeared as suddenly as they had come, and we went off at a canter until we reached the forest.

The trek begins

We were going south, in the direction of Hitler's headquarters. The idea of Hitler taking the salute of endless columns of miserable refugees had a certain appeal to me; but at Kowarren we turned west, absorbed in a column of other refugees.

When a car wedged itself between our carriage and the refugee cart in front we knew that the telephone threat had not been an empty one. We were also suddenly conscious of my father's redundancy as a farmer and imminent payment for sins which had been overlooked while he was indispensable. But the official charge was 'defeatism'.

"You are in charge now, big daughter, because you can do it," Väti called over his shoulder as the men led him away from us; "and don't forget Rudi."

Dresden, I thought: he wants us to make for Dresden. I sat there, dazed and numb and it was Mutti who took charge. She ran after the men and enquired where we could phone or write to find my father's whereabouts. "The party office in Angerapp," was the reply. We were puzzled, for even as the crow flies Angerapp/Darkehmen was about 12 km. closer to the Soviet Union than our farm. Where did they expect the Red Army to come from?

But perhaps it was not coming at all. After a two-day journey we could no longer hear battle noises. The long refugee trek looked incongruous on peaceful roads, driving along without hurry and almost enjoying the autumn sunshine. We

156

had picnic breaks in daytime and stopped at farms for the nights. Mutti, Marlene and I, clutching Vitya, stalked gingerly across sleeping bodies in large manorial entrance halls. We were allocated special guest-rooms, sometimes because we knew the farmers, sometimes just because Mutti's bearing implied social status.

Sitting by candlelight in our night quarters, we wanted to make use of the picture postcards of the mansion which owners usually put on the desks for their guests. It seemed a little premature to write to Dresden to announce our imminent arrival. So Mutti wrote to Väti, c/o Party Office, Angerapp. I wrote three cards. One was to Gisela in Königsberg, saying *"Carpe diem*, going further south."* On my second card I wrote "In good spirits, unlikely to go as far as the Rhine," and addressed it to Hermann's military post number. On my third card I indulged in romantic wording: "Candle-light, Solveig's Song and you" and did not even sign it. There was no song of any sort anywhere near, but I thought the words sounded just right for Karl-Heinz.

We did not have to write to Omi, because it was still possible to phone her. The sound of her dear voice made me feel warm and sad. I prayed to God that she would not be forced to leave her beloved Alischken. Apparently Uncle Arnold and family had arrived there with their trek from their own farm in the Gumbinnen district. Rumours circulated about a terrible massacre at a place called Nemmersdorf near Gumbinnen and later these were substantiated by newspaper pictures so gruesome that for the first time I became afraid of the Red Army. At the same time the newspapers kindled hopes for return to our homes, reporting eloquently on the way Nemmersdorf had been retaken by the re-grouped German army. There were hints in the newspapers of a new, dreadful weapon which would bring vengeance and German victory. God help us!

Brief Return

By the time we reached the little village of Ebersbach, the Russian October offensive had come to a halt and we were told to travel no further. I was glad: although this south-eastern area was very different from our home, it was still East Prussia, and for as long as we stayed on the eastern side of the Vistula we were still in our country. And the two rooms which farmer Podlech let us have were very cosy.

Mutti discovered that Väti's trial was to be in Trempen; and while she and Marlene went there, I stayed in Ebersbach to look after our people and animals. Väti was found guilty of desertion, but put into the Home Guard on probation instead of prison. I thought it a mean trick, putting him into an army of civilian fighters with Nazi armbands instead of prisoners' clothes, which might have given him a chance of survival after the war; but for my mother it was a relief not to have the stigma of prison in the family. She and Marlene rushed back to us in Ebersbach without exploring if Mikalbude was still accessible.

Nobody was certain of the actual boundaries between the two armies, but since official reports on a Russian retreat were substantiated by unofficial versions, I thought there was a good chance of retrieving some of our belongings from home. At least that was the reason I gave to my family for my journey home.

Trains were said to be running at least as far as Insterburg. The journey took me all day, including a long wait at Königsberg station amid alternating rumours of trains leaving or not leaving for Insterburg. It was night when I reached the once so familiar station of the once so hated town. Now it seemed almost like home despite some bomb damage. I suddenly longed to go and see Omi, but since it was not even possible to phone her, I abandoned the idea and searched for ways of going on to Mikalbude. Fortunately an army truck offered me a lift as far as Trempen.

"It's no-man's-land there," the soldier grinned as I stepped off the truck. I did not know if he was joking, and I could not have cared less. My homing instinct had taken over, and I could not walk fast enough. Farmsteads on the way were familiar, though deserted and strangely quiet and dark in the full moon that lit up the thin covering of snow on the fields.

At first I did not take any notice of certain big humps, but suddenly I saw one close by and realised that it was the bloated corpse of a cow. Of course, I thought, they had been let loose and had died when no one was there to relieve their full udders. Would I find our own yard full of such corpses? Suddenly I longed to be back in Ebersbach, but having come this far and being still a little curious, I walked on, slower now, with a heavy heart.

Mikalbude was so silent, so unlike itself. Even the battle noises were much more distant than they had been for many months. But the third step of the veranda staircase creaked as it always had; it startled me. I did not feel for the candle on the hall table, but groped my way upstairs and went to sleep in my own bed.

I was dreaming lovely dreams: men were feeding animals; the yard pump needed oiling; it sounded awful; it sounded lovely; it sounded real! I jumped out of bed and blew against the frosted window panes. Then, through my little peep-hole, I saw men at the pump. As yet I could not see them clearly, nor could I make out their talk, but it sounded almost like Russian. For one brief moment my heart sank. Then I remembered that our Russian prisoners had stayed behind when we left in October and I rushed out to greet them.

They were less surprised to see me at all than to see me alone. My father had already been to the farm and told them that a threshing party would be sent back from Ebersbach to salvage food for the army. All our remaining Belgian prisoners, Katya, Galya and some German men were already on the way back to Mikalbude when I returned to Ebersbach, laden with food. Some of the farm women had also gone back on the wagons, not in order to stay and do any threshing, but to collect more belongings and food.

All of us spent a last Christmas at home. Even Claus, who had been called up for military training a year earlier, was on leave, and Väti, too, was given time off to join us. Only the Mosins and the Golubovs had no wish to venture east again, and some of the very old people could not face the tedious journey, so they remained in Ebersbach.

The Kowarren telephone exchange was manned over Christmas, and we talked to Omi and Uncle Arnold, making sure that they had all our western addresses. The Kowalewskis had already been evacuated from Insterburg to Saxony and were apparently staying with Annchen Korn, née Klaudat, formerly of Osznagorren. They wrote to our Ebersbach address, offering a home for Marlene so that she could go to school again. My parents agreed that this was a good idea; so, one morning early in January 1945 Mutti set out with Marlene for Bautzen in Saxony.

Trenches

It was intended that I should go back to Mikalbude once more, to collect a last batch of possessions before my mother returned to join us in Ebersbach. 'Getting things' was for me no more than an excuse to enjoy once more the fields and the forest I loved. I would jump on drainage ditches to test the ice, as we had done so many times, or surprise a deer searching for blades of grass in a forest clearing. If the snow was deep, I would wax the skis which stood on our landing and then I would glide and glide, light and peace all around me…

Frau Podlech interrupted my dreams: "You can't go to your farm," she called through the door. "We heard rumours of a new Russian offensive." She did not mention foreign radio, but I knew, and so I believed the 'rumours'. I continued my dreams in the past tense.

It suddenly became very important to me that I should focus on just one memory and implant it firmly in my mind. But I could not single out a special day. Twenty-one years of my life crowded in on me: cuddly St Bernard puppies in a wooden dolls' bath-tub; squelching mud between my toes on the way to the village school; secret shadows in the *pakrausch*, my other home; smells of newly-ploughed fields and freshly mown hay, and of a carriage load of pheasant-eye narcissi for the women's co-operative, warm smells of soups…

The Podlechs were cooking potato soup with pork and onions; they invited Vitya and me for a meal. "The time has come when we no longer have to be secretive," Herr Podlech announced boldly after I had put Vitya to bed. He put the Monopoly board on the table. We arranged our pieces and tried for sixes.

But when we heard footsteps, our bold host was astonishingly quick at gathering board, dice and all in the table-cloth. He had put it under the sofa even before there was a knock at the door.

No respectable German family would have a table without a cloth, but there we were, to all appearances having a social evening sitting round a completely bare table. Gerda's suppressed laughter came out in little snorts; mine went up to the roots of my hair and made them prick.

"*Sieg Heil!*" shouted the man in a brown uniform with a Home Guard armband from the doorway. We too raised our arms in reply, but only Herr Podlech stood up. He apologized for our barely disguised merriment: "young people turning gigglish at the silliest of jokes".

"It's the laughter of youth we are fighting for," the stranger replied with good-natured pomp, triggering a noise in my throat which was the nearest thing to a yodel that I had ever achieved.

But the man had come on a serious errand: he wanted to know how many refugees were living on the Podlech farm and how many spades, shovels and pickaxes were available.

"This girl," Herr Podlech said, pointing to me, "and a child of three living in our house, four adults and a baby in the cottage, ten other adults in the barn."

"Fifteen able-bodied persons," concluded the Home Guard man, scribbling in his notebook. "Tell them all to come to the square at dawn, let's say 7 o'clock, and to bring tools. Of course, the assistance of the other young lady" – he indicated the Podlechs' daughter Gerda – "would also be appreciated, though maybe she could be better employed helping with food at lunch time. A lorry will take the others to a field, to dig trenches." Seeing our astonishment, he added: "just a precaution, of course, in case a temporary tactical withdrawal of our troops is considered necessary."

With that he clicked his heels again smartly, raised his arm and Sieg-Heiled his way out.

Vitya's teeth were chattering when I dressed him early, without first lighting the stove. I told him that he could spend the day with Frau Podlech in the kitchen.

"Why?" he wanted to know.

"Because I am going to dig trenches, and so are your Papa and Dyeda."

"What are trenches?"

"Long holes in the ground."

"For burying people?"

The question made me wince. How much of his tragic past did this child remember? And how right he might be, anyhow… But I told him that the holes were just for hiding.

Vitya loved games of hide-and-seek and pleaded that he might come with me. Our guard did not like the idea of a three-year-old with a trowel, but let it be.

Several uniformed men were staking out the lines. Two metres per person was supposed to be our target for the day, 1.50 metres deep, 1 metre wide. For the men who chopped at the frozen top soil with pick-axes it meant more than twice that length on the surface.

I found the work invigorating and rather enjoyable, except that my fingers were getting cold and stiff, because I simply could not handle a spade with mittens. I was glad when the dixie arrived and I could resurrect my hands around a mug of hot soup.

By the afternoon our seemingly impossible targets were beginning to look within reach. It was too cold to work slowly.

Suddenly an army car arrived and an officer began to shout at our Home Guard supervisors. Apparently the Russians were expected to come from the Baltic and the *Frische Haff*, not from the land side and our trenches were on the wrong slope of the hill. "Have them filled in again and start new ones straight away."

I don't know who started it, but down tools it was, and the troop of diggers burst into song: *"Es pfeift von allen Dächern…"*, a well-known Nazi song about the misery of the 1920s, about whistles blowing from roof-tops to signal the end of work, about hunger and poverty expecting workers at home… each verse ending in a crescendo chorus of "Patience, betrayed brothers, the throne of Judas is on the point of collapse!" Malicious joy, pain and bitter, triumphant anger roared across the hard fields and into the cold, clear evening sky. The men in brown stood in silence, not sure how to react. Their helplessness amused the diggers and stimulated their musical appetite.

I was puzzled by their next choice, but as it was fun to sing in a crowd, I joined in with gusto, *"Brüder in Zechen und Gruben..."* until the person next to me nudged me and whispered: "Not the words, just hum or sing la-la-la." He did not explain that it was originally a Social Democrat song to the words of *"Brüder der Freiheit und Sonne."*

The elation lasted into the night. I could hear singing from many houses when I walked round the sheds for a last check on our horses.

For the first time since Mutti and Marlene had left I felt very much alone. Vitya was fast asleep and the Podlechs were thumping about, busy with I did not know what, up and down their stairs.

There was a knock at my door, and before I replied Big Volodya entered. He smiled his usual half-timid, half-cheeky smile and suddenly seized me in his arms, holding me uncomfortably tight, kissing me furiously and desperately, stammering "I am so lonely" between kisses. Then, just as suddenly, he stood still and hung his head.

"Whatever has happened?" I asked.

"Marusha..." he started and then grinned again helplessly.

"Oh, for crying out loud, how can you take her seriously?" Hysterical outbursts of Volodya's jealous wife had become part of our farm entertainment for the past six months.

We sat down on the bench by the stove, warming our backs, and I had to wait for some time before Volodya replied: "Marusha thinks Red Army will come tomorrow. Marusha has razor blade. Marusha wants me to cut wrists for her and our baby. Marusha serious this time, not jealous."

"But Volodya, they are your own people, they will set you free. How can she be afraid?"

Volodya grinned sheepishly. I guessed the answer to my question, but was still reluctant to accept it. However many times I told myself that desertion was the only way for conscientious objectors in states which made no allowances for conscience, the word 'cowardice' caused me discomfort, particularly since I had a hunch that this strong man objected less to killing than to being killed. Preserving himself for the sake of his tiny baby, I tried to tell myself without conviction. Volodya said nothing.

So I pulled the box of Koch's Erben wine from under the bed and opened a bottle.

"A toast to the future," I said. Our glasses touched and produced a hard, metallic sound.

"Put your hand further down the stem, right to the bottom," I told Volodya.

A beautiful musical chime rang from the crystal, and Volodya gasped "Oh!".

"That's better", I laughed, "And tell Marusha."

The next day was very ordinary. Even the postman came as usual and brought me a card from Gisela, from Königsberg: "Are you still alive? Yours, Gila." That was the last time I heard from her. She must have written it shortly before she was deported to the Soviet Union, where she was killed.

Last Days in Ebersbach

The Podlechs' rooms looked bare except for suitcases, boxes, some furniture and the Monopoly set on the table. We played all day and Vitya threw the die for me. There was no digging; the Home Guard had vanished.

The phone rang. It was for me, Frau Podlech said.

"Big daughter?" asked my father's voice.

"Yes, it's me, where are you?"

"I can't tell you, but listen, quickly. You must leave East Prussia now. You must take my place now. Look after Mutti, Marlene…" The phone went dead.

I kept talking to the phone, telling it that my mother and sister were safe, that we would all meet in Dresden and that our horses were well, too. All sorts of ordinary, cheerful talk, until my voice would obey me no longer. Then I began to pack.

Frau Podlech suggested that I send a telegram to Mutti, to make sure she did not start out on her journey back to us as she had planned.

"Surely she will have more sense," I replied.

"Do you seriously expect German radio to tell her that East Prussia is lost? Or do you expect a law-abiding person like your mother to listen to foreign broadcasts?"

Frau Podlech was right. So I sent a telegram to Saxony.

By morning the official evacuation order had come to the village. Army lorries would take evacuees to the station for the last trains west. We were warned not to try our luck by road.

Our former workers began to unload their belongings from the previously packed farm carts and take them to army vehicles. Most of the horses were already harnessed, and Big Volodya was putting the saddle on Illyrier, our stallion. The horses pawed the ground impatiently.

I saw one of my personal cases being carried by Kowalies, the one-armed man whom the Government had obliged us to employ as a labourer. I tried to focus my thoughts on what he was doing; but it was not until I felt Frau Schalonka's hand grip mine that I was stung into determination.

"Leave my case," I shouted to Kowalies, "I am not abandoning the horses."

"You jolly well are," Frau Schalonka said firmly, and her grip tightened. "I have served your parents before you were born, so you are my baby, too, and I will deliver you safely to your Mutti."

"I am not a baby," I protested, "and I am not coming with you." I sat on the ground, but she did not let go of my hand. Frau Schalonka was a good woman, and she was strong and resolute. She dragged me through the snow and I laughed. Vitya ran along, hoping to join the game.

"All right," I said, "we begin by lifting you on to the lorry, then I will call Papa and Dyeda to join you."

"And then Frau Schalonka will lift you up?"

"Yes", I lied. Frau Schalonka was as delighted as Vitya and let go of my hand. "But first I must untie the horses," I added.

I intended to re-tie most of the animals to the back of our carriage and then make a dash for it on my own. I shouted to the Golubovs and Mosins to make for the lorries and began to unharness the horses by the box wagon, except for their halters, to which I attached the line. I slung this round the bar of the carriage's back seat, emphatically careless and casual, as if it were a provisional arrangement, but secretly tying a firm knot. But before I reached the rack wagon, I saw Big Volodya leading a sobbing wife with baby towards me, followed by an indifferent-looking Little Volodya with Vitya. Foreigners were not permitted to travel on the lorry.

Only then did I notice that Dyeda had been standing by his own cart all the time. The former country priest's faith was firm, mature and childishly superstitious. He believed that God had singled out Vitya for a special purpose when he saved him from the fate of his brothers and sisters, and that the sturdy pony, the humble creature of the steppe which had carried them all the way from Moscow, was part of God's design. They were meant to stay together and would be safe; so would all who looked after them. Dyeda was not surprised to see his son and grandson come back.

The army drivers would not wait, and even Frau Schalonka could not make them. She was calling my name, and the anguish in her voice brought a lump to my throat. I could not find my voice to reply, but as the lorry moved off, I waved to her. I doubt that she saw me. Her husband was holding her tight and the falling snow pulled a curtain between us.

Six Russians, One German: First Day

"Don't follow the lorry," I gave orders to my Russian friends. "Let's take the small road west."

"And how do we tell West?" Little Volodya shouted back through the snowstorm.

"By the sun, of course." We all laughed hysterically.

Marusha, Verushka and Vitya were tucked warmly inside the large sheepskin rugs which were fitted under the back seat of the carriage and extended all the way round their legs, nearly up to their necks. Volodya carefully buttoned down the leather tarpaulin which held the fur in place. I climbed up to the coachman's box to screams from Marusha, who wanted her husband to take the reins and me to ride Illyrier. As if I could control a well-rested horse of that strength! I screamed back at her: "Shut up or be chucked out!" She calmed down when she realised that Big Volodya was riding the stallion very close to our carriage.

In front of us was Little Volodya, driving the foursome harnessed to the rack wagon. He was sitting high on bails of hay, sacks of oats supporting his back, and many more sacks and bags and boxes of bedding, cutlery, saucepans, hams, bacons, cheeses, the entire carcass of a deer which Hermann had shot when he came to visit me briefly in Ebersbach, well refrigerated in sub-zero temperatures, a leg of roast venison insulated from the frost by layers of clothes and blankets – all piled up behind him. All but one of my Goethe volumes were in one box; Volume Two, Goethe's 'Faust', which was the most precious to me, I had sent to the West

163

long ago. Right in front, leading our trek at great speed, was Dyeda in the small cart pulled by Cony, his pony.

There we were, eleven horses, one pony, one German girl and six Russians, all, for reasons I could not understand, escaping from the Red Army. There was no time to think. I listened to the crunch of the wheels and was content.

We travelled inside a diffused cluster of grey whiteness except for the shadowy outlines of tree trunks, which remained dark at the back of the wind.

Big Volodya was the first to notice a human shape staggering towards us. He knew that kind. "A woman," he said. "They go back looking for what they have lost; men run forward when they have lost their heads."

"We have plenty of space; we can offer the poor creature a lift," I replied.

"They don't come. Don't worry, it's all right, they no longer have feelings; they just drop by the wayside."

But I defied Volodya's authority and reined in the horses to wait. Then I heard a lovely familiar voice call cheerfully: "At last I have found you!"

My dear, dear mother. I wanted to jump off the coachman's seat and throw myself close to her. But before I reached her, anger gushed from my stomach to my throat and I drew away from Mutti's outstretched arms.

"How could you?" I shouted. "How could you do this? It was pure chance that we took this track; you might never have met us…"

"But you did take this one, and we did meet," she replied happily.

"Can you imagine what might have happened?" I persevered.

"What is the point of imagining?"

I furiously unbuttoned the tarpaulin and pushed my mother to the back seat, next to Marusha and the children. As I climbed back to the front Mutti pleaded: "Couldn't we just quickly go back to the Podlechs to thank them for their hospitality?" Instead of replying, I hit the horses with my whip, all four in turn.

We soon joined a major road leading to Elbing. It was crowded with refugee treks. Our outrider Volodya kept his nerve against shouts of anger and managed to filter our three vehicles into the stream together.

It had stopped snowing by the time we reached the town. Suddenly there was shouting from behind: "Russian tanks!" Without looking round to check, I cracked my whip hard and pulled our carriage to the left, shouting to Little Volodya and Dyeda to follow as I overtook them and turned into the next side-street. Dyeda just missed a collision with a tank, as he later told us.

For a time we did not pause to talk. Mutti had looked back and knew that the others were behind, as we kept the horses at a gallop. Ridiculous memories of hair-raising carriage-races home after champagne-and-crayfish parties in Darkehmen flashed through my mind. The little steppe-pony proved a match for our Trakehner steeds. We drove into the semblance of a sunset and knew that we were moving in the right direction. The town was well behind when we dared to slow down and relax in the frozen peace around us. Mutti urged me to look for a place of rest and shelter for the horses.

First Night

The small farm by the road was prepared for the reception of either refugees or the Red Army. All the family had moved into one bedroom, leaving two adjoining upstairs rooms with three beds for us. "And if you like, there is a warm shed where the Russian can sleep," the woman of the house told us with a glance at Dyeda. The two Volodyas and Marusha kept their mouths shut, but Mutti said that the old man would be quite all right with us. Vitya chatted happily about food in his broad East Prussian accent.

My mother went out to the carriage and brought some of her parcels to the kitchen, where we were served thick pea soup with chunks of pork. Mutti also produced four candle-stumps and lit them before she handed the packages to Vitya. Dyeda smiled happily and nodded his head; he had not forgotten that it was his grandson's birthday. Volodya and I looked at each other, purple with shame. Vitya himself glowed with excitement, played with new trinkets, some from Marlene, but concentrated most of his attention on eatables. He was still munching apples and singing between bites when he sat on the pillow of the Mosin family bed with Papa and Dyeda snoring on either side of him.

Mutti was impressed by our hosts. "Such ordinary people giving us really clean sheets." I snuggled close to her for a comfort that I had rejected for almost twenty years. By the light of a candle on her bedside table my mother was finishing a letter to Marlene which she had begun on her train journey.

"Were all the Kowalewskis together in Bautzen?" I interrupted Mutti's writing.

"Yes, all of them."

"Even Lore?"

"Yes, of course."

"Then I am really glad I am not there. She is worse than Uncle Egon, if that is possible."

"You should not talk such nonsense while they are so kind to Marlene," Mutti reproached me angrily and went on writing.

"Do you know that Lore once killed a fly, put it into a matchbox and then asked Claus to take it to Walter?"

"Why on earth should she want to do a thing like that? Which Walter, anyway?"

"One of those Hitler Youth boys from Danzig who came to work in 1938, I think. Lore was probably in love with him and wanted to send him a present."

Mutti became angry at that. "Your imagination always runs away with you on the absurdest tracks. Lore was only fourteen then and could not possibly have been in love, quite apart from having the mad idea of a dead fly. You must be very exhausted; you had an awful lot of responsibility today. Go to sleep now and your mind will be clear tomorrow."

She was wrong. The morbid absurdity of that fly had haunted me for years, and Lore gave me the creeps. I should have anticipated my mother's unfair dismissal of my memories, but I sulked. She was either unwilling to accept events and ideas that were outside the range of the tidy, clean, straightforward pattern of her life, or genuinely incapable of seeing them.

Vitya had stopped eating, the men were still snoring, Mutti's pencil made regular scratching noises, and every now and then Verushka gave a little squeal which evoked sleepy soothing mutters from her mother, followed by vigorous suckling and sniffing noises. Then all was quiet for a while.

I wondered what Cossacks would do with Marusha's breasts. Omi had told me that they cut them off women in the First World War to play football with them. It was reassuring to know that mine would barely attract the desires of a ping-pong player. But what was I thinking about? The Cossacks were on Hitler's side now, so there was nothing to fear from the Red Army. Then why were we going west into nowhere? The owners of this little farm meant to stay on. What were we running from and, perhaps more to the point, what were we running towards?

Between dozing and sleeping and dreaming I pondered these questions and alternated my conclusions.

Second Day

We started next day while the stars were still bright, and by the time the sun rose behind us we were again assimilated into a long trek of refugee carts. Big Volodya surveyed the scene on Illyrier's back, as usual. Suddenly he shouted "Adam! Adam!" and trotted ahead a short way. He waved on some vehicles in front of us to overtake two particular rack wagons, from which a familiar grin greeted us.

We could not stop on the congested road and mostly relied on our outrider to carry messages to and fro, and on Katya, who came to join us. Galya must have stayed behind to cook for the Home Guard, but Katya had preferred to escape with the two rack wagons from the threshing party, one led by Adam, the White Russian civilian worker, the other by Fernand, a Belgian prisoner-of-war, who for some reason had been given special treatment by the guard. The other Belgians had been moved somewhere with a military escort. But Fernand had picked up four of his compatriots on the road. They had escaped on foot from wherever they had been during the past few years. I was pleased, expecting a touch of elegance to enter our life with the sound of the French language.

Katya settled on the front seat next to me, and as the coachman's seat raised my lap to the level of her shoulders, she affectionately put her head on my thigh: "How much closer are we now to the Ukraine?" she asked and suddenly added in a frightened whisper, "Or are we driving further away?" So much had happened since those early days, when the same little bewildered girl had pleaded with me to tell her when she would be sent home to her 'Mamaso'; there had been much disappointment, even hatred on Katya's part. But now she again looked to me for reassurance, and I had not the slightest idea of geographical distances. "We are driving towards the end of the war and are rapidly coming closer to it," I replied evasively.

"I want to know in kilometres," Katya hissed.

"We are fifty kilometres closer now than you were in Mickelau," I said firmly, though it hurt me not to speak of Mikalbude by its old name. Katya was satisfied.

By midday the sun was almost warm, and most refugees stopped by the roadside for a rest. We still had many provisions on our vehicles, but the ones from the farm were heavily loaded with food. All that would keep us alive for weeks, I thought.

Belgian POWs and Poles on the trek

Mutti loved gnawing chicken bones, but the thought of chewing meat from a communal joint of venison disgusted her. So we cut off a good chunk for her before we passed the bone around.

My own feelings of delicacy focused on the way people disappeared behind bushes which had no leaves. I decided to hold on till nightfall, and then till morning, because the night was freezing and frightening. Snow fell hard, and a biting wind pushed it into our faces and down our necks, however securely we tried to fix our fur collars. We had to trust the horses to keep in touch with the vehicle in front, because we could not see it. Nor could we distinguish between the road and whatever lay at the sides of it. There was no sign of trees.

"We must be in the marshes of the Nogat-Vistula delta," Mutti shouted at me; "be careful not to let the carriage slip into the bog."

That was easier said than done, I thought, but in this frost the bog would not be dangerous.

"Peat bog – if that's what it is – takes a long time to freeze," Mutti interrupted my thoughts. I wished that my father could hear how his unassuming, gentle wife took charge, while his brash big daughter was scared into a sense of utter helplessness.

My mother called to Big Volodya to make contact with the other vehicles and get them to light their stable lanterns while we lit our coach lamps. But that, too, was easier said than achieved. Katya and I crouched under the tarpaulin and used up at least half a box of matches before we had the candles burning. On the wagons they had even greater difficulties, but eventually we could see flickering lights, off and on, like the will-o'-the-wisps in the peat bog at home on a summer day. It was faintly reassuring, but did not help us to see the edge of what we now assumed to be a dyke. We had completely lost touch with other trekkers.

Big Volodya decided to tie our tired stallion to the back of a wagon and to walk ahead of our convoy on foot, poking the snow at the side with the hard end of the whip. Even so one of the carts slipped over the edge and it took a long time to push and pull it back to level ground. The effort revived my mental energies a little, but not for long.

At moments I seriously considered the possibility of all of us being already dead and simply drifting as ghosts through the blizzard. I must have fallen asleep when Mutti poked me in the back, shouting that she was sure she could see trees.

She must also be dreaming, I thought sleepily, but at the same time I became vaguely aware of sharing her dreams. Soon we saw shadows of houses and numerous flickering lights.

Third Day

We had reached a very large farm. A long line of refugee wagons was standing in the yard, facing the way we came from. They were loaded with bundles and people, but seemed to be waiting for yet more bundles and people. Mutti asked our wagons to wait while we drove up to the mansion in our carriage. Big Volodya stood by the stallion and lightly held the reins of the carriage horses. All our animals were too tired to be difficult.

Mutti wanted me to come with her to look for the owners of the estate. As we walked up the wide marble flight of stairs we clearly recognised the lady of the manor among a number of women coming down from the house. She was astonished to hear that we were hoping to spend the day and possibly a night at this place. "Don't you realize that we are all but completely encircled and that every minute matters if we want to get out alive?" she asked.

"We did not know, nor will that knowledge make any difference," Mutti replied sadly; "our horses are at the end of their tether."

We were told to make ourselves at home, to eat, drink, use anything that was left; and if we had the energy to relieve some cows of their milk and set them free later...; and if we had yet more energy, could we perhaps bury some of the family silver in the hole prepared near the bull's stand?

"Yes, of course we shall, of course." Mutti was overflowing with pity.

"And if by any chance – it is not likely, as he is in the army – but if my husband should turn up, tell him we are aiming for the agreed address near Stettin. He will know... Thank you so much, and good luck to you." At this the lady turned abruptly and climbed into her sleigh. Soon there was no one but our trek and the farm animals.

Adam and Marusha milked the cows, because they were the only ones who knew how. Verushka stayed on her mother's lap for the milking. It was not possible to milk nearly 200 cattle thoroughly, but they tried to take some tension out of all the udders. The Russian men, Fernand and the stray Belgians saw to the horses.

I helped Mutti with the silver, inwardly cursing the stuff. Katya snorted in open contempt and went to relax in a big armchair in the drawing room. "The ungrateful cuss, after all we have done for her, more than was expected of us, more even than we were really allowed to do..." Mutti grumbled, as she had grumbled many times about Katya. My mother really believed that the Ukrainian girl, deported at the age of fifteen, owed us a debt of gratitude, and this time I could not be bothered to argue. I shifted the silver automatically, almost in a trance.

But when Mutti and Marusha began to cook, I woke up and decided to set the table as if for a party. Even the ordinary cutlery of this house shone like real silver in the light of the chandelier, an electric chandelier. Glasses sparkled like crystal, though they were not, Mutti informed me. And what with wine from the cellar and conversation in French at my end of the table, I felt luxuriously light-hearted.

Dyeda sat apart, on a window bench. He had a drink of water, but refused all food. The old priest was beginning to bribe God with a fast.

When I swayed towards him and giggled "*Carpe diem*", he slowly looked up at me and I slowly lowered my raised wine glass under his gaze. His sad, mild disapproval was disconcerting, and I noticed for the first time that the old man's eyes were small and light blue, not at all like the dark round eyes of his grandson.

"Recessive," I commented. Dyeda did not reply.

"I mean your eyes," I persisted. "Now I know that your wife had dark eyes."

"When people have nothing to say, they talk too much," he said quietly. I did not understand that much Russian and looked puzzled. Katya translated with glee, or maybe she made it up because she enjoyed derogatory remarks addressed to me. Anyhow, she had drunk too much, like myself.

Vitya had fallen asleep in a soft armchair, and when we all decided to go to bed, Volodya carried him upstairs.

Mutti made sure that the chandelier was turned off. We were all awe-struck by the electric brightness of this mansion, which made Omi's little generator look dingy in retrospect. Even water seemed to be heated by electricity in this house, and it greatly worried Mutti that so much power should be wasted. So we hunted around for some switch to turn it off, and when one of the Belgians found it, Mutti decided to make use of the already heated water for a bath. My own aspirations for a civilized life concentrated on trying to dream in French, but I did not find time to formulate a dream before I was fast asleep. Only Dyeda stayed up. His faith told him that he had to be vigilant to see the sign which God would give for saving Vitya. And so the old man walked around outside, looking at the sky and at the occasional flares on the horizon which indicated the battle-lines.

Fourth Day

It was good to know that Dyeda kept watch, but I took a dim view of his God-inspired roughness when he shook me awake while it was still dark. "There is a gap in the encirclement," he called, "we have to leave now."

"I like this house," I yawned.

"You let Vitya call you Mama? Come to your senses."

And I did. We all hurried to prepare for departure.

I heard Marusha scream downstairs and Katya came running up, helpless with laughter. "Volodya is beating Marusha hard," she ejaculated between giggles.

"I don't think that is funny," I reproached her.

"But it is funny." Tears of laughter were streaming down Katya's face: "he is beating her because she stole a comb! Just a very small comb!"

"They just like beating each other," Little Volodya commented laconically.

But it was not quite as simple as that. Big Volodya, the atheist, had become scared of God's wrath towards thieves and was seriously concerned that his family might jeopardize their chances of survival for a comb. It was one thing to take food and wine from this house, which had been offered by the owner, but quite another to take a comb which had not. Marusha could use it, but not take it with her.

That being settled, we departed. We heard the rumbling of war, such as we had heard it at home during the summer months, but no worse.

Later that day we saw an isolated inn by the roadside and decided to look for lavatories. The building was deserted. People had left in the same – and probably deliberate – mood as we left places, in the middle of doing ordinary things which could not be finished. There were half-empty glasses on the bar counter and on some tables. On one of them stood a thick, clumsy coffee-cup with bright blue and yellow stripes and the words *"trinkt Kathreiner und ihr bleibt gesund"* printed between the stripes, an advertisement for a cereal-based drink rather like decaffeinated *Ersatz* coffee. Suddenly I badly wanted to possess that cup and, making sure that Big Volodya was not in sight, I put it into my pocket. I left the saucer.

trinkt Kathreiner

On the farm we had been told that we were only 5 kilometres from a place called Tiegenhof, where we could cross the Vistula. We were looking in vain for such a signpost and were soon engulfed in yet another stream of refugee vehicles, some being handcarts pulled by pedestrians. Some wore soldiers' uniforms. One such group shouted greetings to us, raising both their arms high. Then one of them left only his right arm up and laughed: "That's what they taught us, it's the first half of this," and he raised the second arm again in the international sign for surrender. Mutti was a little shocked. We had known from our neighbour that the army resented having to replace their traditional form of salute by the Nazi version, but we had hitherto thought that the resentment had been confined to the officers' class.

A soldier of a different kind approached us later. He did not boast about his desertion, far from it: he jumped on to the step of our carriage, saluted my mother with a brash *"Sieg Heil"* and told her that he was confiscating the riding horse and saddle in the name of the command of the German army. He pointed to Illyrier and my heart sank at the thought of losing this part of home, however unmanageable. But I did not have the courage to object.

"Not so fast," shouted Mutti when the man approached the stallion, "we must have a proper requisitioning receipt."

The man obligingly took a scruffy notebook from his pocket and scribbled on it: "One horse and saddle to the German army", followed by an illegible scribble that was supposed to be his name, rank and unit.

It was not the latter part which Mutti objected to, but the word 'horse'. "Replace that with: '1 pedigree Trakehner stallion'", she insisted. The man then crossed out the offending word and wrote the proper description above it. My mother gave up with a sigh. At least she had preserved her own dignity. When Illyrier started at a gallop that was obviously not a speed of his new rider's choosing, we felt a certain satisfaction, convinced that the soldier would soon be thrown.

On the Banks of the Vistula

The chain of vehicles in front of us stretched a long way ahead, and on this clear, frosty day we could see a very long way ahead. The trek moved slowly and eventually came to a halt. Word spread that we would have to wait for the ferry to be repaired. What ferry? The one across the Vistula, just beyond the horizon. That, at first, was marvellous news: the crossing to take us out of the East Prussian battlefield was close.

"And how much closer to the Ukraine will that be?" Katya kept up her daily question.

"I can't say exactly," I admitted, but she would not have it that way.

"You intelligentsia, yes? You go to university, yes? What for? Make me a map," she demanded.

I drew lines in the snow, something like a right-angled triangle with our home and the Ukraine being the points on the hypotenuse and the Vistula ferry the vertex. Katya measured the distance with her hand and was satisfied that she would be coming closer to her home.

Three, four, five, I thought; $3^2 + 4^2 = 5^2$. How did we prove Pythagoras? I began to work with my fingers in the smooth snow.

"But remember, Katya, that we might not be able to travel in a straight line," indicating the line that equalled 4. "We might have to go like this", and I drew a line parallel to the hypotenuse. Katya nodded indifferently, but I was beginning to enjoy myself with Pythagoras.

"Can you do the proof?" I called to Little Volodya, the ex-schoolmaster.

"Of course," he said and started in the snow next to me. "Well, this is odd, my memory has got stuck somewhere between school and the Vistula dyke," he added after a while. We both laughed and became absorbed, frustrated and determined to solve the problem. Every now and then I looked up anxiously in case the trek would move before we had finished.

Vitya ran along to see what we were doing and accidentally stepped on our drawings.

"Hey, don't destroy my circles," Volodya joked.

"Are those supposed to be circles?" Vitya laughed.

"Triangles, circles… It all seems a bit Greek to me," his father replied.

"What is Greek?" Vitya wanted to know.

Life was beginning to be exciting, and I was torn between Pythagoras and the Trojan Horse. "In a moment I will tell you about the Greeks," I promised Vitya, "some really wonderful stories."

The little boy clapped his hands in anticipation. He did not urge me to tell the stories now: for patient Vitya "in a moment" was good enough.

I loved the cold pastel sunset over the marshland and the clear stars that followed. But the sheepskins could not prevent minus 30 degrees Celsius from making us numb. We had to take runs to stimulate the circulation, "but never further than five minutes' running distance from the carriage," Mutti insisted. At the beginning of our first night on the dyke we thought the trek might start to move any minute. Except for Adam, we were all afraid of being left behind.

The old White Russian wandered off across the marshes towards houses in the distance. He returned dragging a sack of briquettes, matches, newspapers, a paper bag full of dried clover, even a saucepan, because he did not know we had plenty of pans in our luggage. The horses stood still with pieces of sacking covering their backs. There was no need to tie or guard them, and I felt a guilty sense of relief at Illyrier's departure.

On the land below our carriage we sat on bails around Adam's fire. I smoked the first cigarette of my life, Russian fashion – dried clover wrapped in a piece of newspaper.

Katya was cold and said she wanted my fur coat. My father's coat was in the carriage, but no, she wanted mine, a smarter-looking outside fur. I happily changed into my father's heavy, long, inside fur coat. But Mutti could not hide her irritation. Did that girl think we owed her our own luxuries? Did we not? I wondered. Was it, as Mutti now thought – she had not expressed the idea before – Katya's and Galya's own fault that they had heeded the call for able-bodied persons to report to the German Labour Exchange in the Ukraine? Was it just a misunderstanding due to language difficulties that work meant a long journey from home and no chance to inform their families? Was it ever meant to be a short term, to help with one harvest? Was it the fault of the Soviet Union that they were not part of the services of the International Red Cross?

"If Galya were with us, she would not behave like Katya," Mutti said. She was right, of course. The ever-grateful, ever-affectionate and ever so timid Galya would not do anything but try to help us, even here. And I wondered where she might now be, perhaps already repatriated?

Some time earlier Mutti had complained about those awful officials, those over-zealous Nazis who had abducted two young girls much against Hitler's own instructions; I had argued furiously with her. I had told her she was deliberately blind and complacent. But seeing her now with that far-away look in her eyes, all that unspoken worry about the fate of all those she loved so dearly, I had no wish to argue. With numb fingers Mutti was writing letters even here, intending to post them as soon as we had crossed the Vistula.

Adam dished out hot currant juice with a dash of rum. I wrapped more hay round Vitya and told him about the Wooden Horse and about Helen of Troy. Mutti smiled at us.

The Golubovs presented a peaceful nativity scene at the other side of the fire. We dozed while Adam kept the flames burning until he too dozed off.

By morning the fire was out and we were kept warm by blankets of snow which had covered us during the night. It continued to snow all through the day.

Word came that pedestrians could be ferried across the river in small boats, and our stray Belgians set off. Gradually many other people decided to give up hope of crossing by carriages or carts. They unharnessed their horses, loaded themselves with as much as they could carry on foot, and some kindly tipped the vehicles down the dyke so that they would not cause extra congestion. Mutti asked me to make a decision and was relieved to hear that I had no intention of abandoning our horses.

Many men followed Adam's example, and soon a line of fires was burning all along one side of the dyke. Somewhere a cheerful woman sang "Happy is the gipsies' life", which brought tears to Mutti's eyes. It was the first tune I had ever managed to play on the accordion, and I suddenly remembered that my instrument was on the rack wagon.

The trek comes to a halt

Soon our fire became the jolly fire, attracting people singing jolly songs, and sad ones, too. People contributed fuel, drinks, and their voices. We sang of parting and love, of welcoming the harvest home, and of wandering apprentices. More, please, more! And I played until my fingers grew stiff and numb with cold. Then Little Volodya took over. Russian folksongs with melodies which were as nostalgic as ours, sadder still, and wilder in their rhythms. Katya danced solo round the fire until Big Volodya joined her.

"What about you?" Little Volodya called to me, and when I shook my head he added: "Marlene would."

"Of course," I laughed, "she is more acrobatic than I am." I felt so free, much more free than ever before, but not yet free enough to make a fool of myself. Later, maybe...

Were we crying for the real lives we had lost, hardship and all, or for lost dreams? I wanted to cry for Vienna and students' life and balls under the chandeliers of the *Festsaal* in Schönbrunn Castle, which I had never experienced in reality. But the jolly melancholy of the accordion could not transport me to the tender throbs of Viennese violins, and my Strauss and Lehár waltzes did not sound quite genuine. Yet people danced to *The Blue Danube* or to *Gold and Silver*, asking for more and more.

We did not know our new friends by name, but referred to them as "next-door neighbours", or "the family beyond the first vacancy". Over the days the vacancies grew, but at this stage of our trek people did not steal. There was no need for it. Everybody had as much frozen food as any vacant vehicle could offer. Besides, Adam fetched preserved food and drinks from the houses across the marsh.

It would be absurd to pretend that my mother enjoyed our outdoor life, least of all our primitive lavatories. But it amused her to go visiting on foot, to see neighbours, as we had never before been able to do.

One man had binoculars and could see red stars on tanks behind us on the horizon. They had stopped and about a dozen or so people were climbing down and now walking towards us with their bundles while their transport turned back. We ran to meet them, curious to hear their story. They had stayed at home to await the Red Army. One man had retrieved his Communist Party membership card, which he had hidden long ago towards the day when once again it would be legal. But one of the Russian officers just roared with laughter when the man produced the document. "Fine Bolshevik that was!" the man grumbled when he told us this.

Eventually that advance troop of the Red Army had managed to convince the villagers that there was nobody in their army who had not suffered the cruel loss of at least one member of his family, and usually more, during the German occupation. They were bent on revenge, and orders from high command stipulated that the pent-up anger of simple soldiers should be allowed to vent itself. So it was wise to accept a lift out of the war zone while this was possible. Some time back I had heard a similar story of a woman and child caught between opposing armies near Darkehmen. I had not believed it.

We grew accustomed to life on the dyke and lost track of time. Actually, when I later calculated our days and nights there, I discovered that we had spent no more than four days before our trek began to move on.

I had expected my heart to miss a beat when we crossed out of our home province to the safety of the western shore of the Vistula; but in the dark, and crammed between other vehicles, I did not notice the crossing at all and became only aware that it had happened after we had been driving on the other side for some time.

Gdansk

We travelled in the former Free State of Danzig/Gdansk. A terrible smell drifted towards us from the front, such as I had never known before. Big Volodya, who did not believe in God, crossed himself and muttered: "*Bozhe moy!*"

Did he know the stench? "Hunger", he whispered and crossed himself again.

"Say it in Russian, please." I could not believe that he had chosen the right word. I had learnt the Russian for hunger only too well in the last years. Volodya gripped the reins tightly, as if expecting them to support him. His face looked so awful that I offered to take over the driving. He only shook his head and pointed ahead with the whip. Ahead, and to the sides of our road.

I saw the heaps which were human bodies, bloated like the cows I had seen on my walk home from Trempen. They were partly covered by snow, but we could see striped clothing and some stars of Zion in a black material sewn on. But they were frozen and the smell did not come from them. The odours grew stronger and more frightening as we moved ahead.

Staggering on the left side of our road we now saw hundreds, maybe thousands of figures like those corpses, only much thinner and apparently still alive. Men in heavy trench coats pushed those who stumbled with their rifle butts.

The vacant black eyes of a woman reminded me of another one I had seen long ago on a bench in the little park outside our Insterburg school. That other one had a baby on her lap; this one was holding the hand of a stumbling child. That other time I had run in fear and taken the first train home. I had been a coward. This time I felt bravely determined to do something. As if hypnotized, I stared into the woman's eyes while my hands fumbled for bread underneath the sheepskin.

I threw the half-loaf and as the woman stretched out her free hand to catch it, a guard hit her across the back. "Stop begging, you bloody bitch!" he shouted and picked up the bread for himself.

I jumped from the moving carriage, crying with rage: "You bloody, damn bastard, give back the bread! She was not begging. Hit me, if you like and if you dare. I threw it, it was my idea, not hers!"

"Temper, temper," the guard grinned and gave me back my half-loaf. I wanted to spit into his face when I felt myself grabbed from the back and lifted on to the carriage. Volodya quickly jumped back up after me, holding his head low and mumbling in an angry whisper: "Don't you dare do a thing like that again or you will have us all end up like those wretches."

"You mean I will end up with a thrashing from you like Marusha," I hissed back at him. But I felt too shaken even to look again for the woman.

"Shut up, you young idiot," Volodya replied. That really was a bit thick from a youngster like him. Mutti appealed for calm and asked Volodya to take the first turning right, whatever the road.

As in November 1938, I was escaping from the sight of miserable reality.

Away from the congested road we moved fast for a time, even through big snow drifts. The tracks became all but impassable and were very steep. Night was drawing in around us. Forests on either side provided some shelter from the blizzard, but even Dyeda could not tell which tracks led west and which we should take whenever we came to one of the many turning points. Once again we were lost and moved slowly, hoping for a break in the morning.

Suddenly we saw the outlines of buildings. We banged at bolted doors and shuttered windows. We could see dim light through a shutter: there must be people, we were sure, and we shouted: "Please, please, give us some kind of shelter. We are refugees with small children."

At last a woman held a lantern out of an upstairs window. I pushed Marusha with baby Vera into the beam of light, and Vitya next to them. It seemed to work.

When we were allowed in, Vitya made for the direction of children's voices, but one of the women took his hand and led us all to a large room. She began to push furniture to the walls, beckoning to us for help. It was impossible to tell the ages of different women (or girls?), because they all wore long dark garments and pale-coloured headscarves tied under their chins. The stable lanterns barely lit up their features.

While we were coping with the room, other women took the men into a shed for the horses and showed them a pump. They were then to bring bales of straw for our bedding.

Our hosts spoke a strange language. Was it Polish? I asked Little Volodya when the women had left the room. He shrugged his shoulders: "Could be; perhaps a special dialect. Some words are recognisably Polish, but few sound the way I learnt the language at school."

"They think we are thieves," Mutti whispered in such misery that I threw my arms round her neck: "Oh Mamushka, Mamushka!" I had not called her that for years, because it had seemed like an affectation since the Russian prisoners had come to the farm. "Does it matter, Mamushka?"

"That we should have sunk so low?" Mutti had observed how a woman quickly removed a few objects from a sideboard before she left us.

"It's because we don't have a cobbler with us," I tried to joke, flapping the mouth of my right boot in front of her face.

"Oh my God, how long has your sole been like that? Your feet must be soaked, you will catch a cold. Have you no other shoes?"

"There are my patent leather pumps in a box," I laughed.

Volodya said he had once read about some ancient people of Slav origins, or something like that, living in the region of Gdansk.

"Did you hear them turn the key? They have locked us in," Big Volodya suddenly said. "Maybe they will keep us prisoners until…"

"Shut up," I interrupted his speculations.

"How do the shutters open? Could we escape through the windows?"

"I dare say we could, particularly if you don't keep the straw from near the lantern or the stove."

"If they are an ancient tribe, they could have Russian relatives."

"Shut up."

"If you stopped looking at Katya, you might think of something we can do," Marusha screamed at her husband.

Katya sat comfortably in the straw with only a thin petticoat, wriggling her bare feet near the stove. It was really hot in the room, and not only by contrast with those previous nights on the dyke. I too began to strip, starting with my feet to please Mutti. She rubbed them for me, quite unable to accept that they were warm. I liked being mothered for a while.

Only the men stayed as they had slept outside in blizzards, with overcoats, hats and boots. When we turned the wick down to extinguish the lantern, we noticed a feeble light in one corner, on a narrow ledge under a crucifix.

Pomerania

Inasmuch as we had hoped for more organized refugee treks when we entered Pomerania, reality far exceeded our wishes. In no way could we again find ourselves lost in some wilderness, nor deviate from a prescribed route on purpose to find a home with such relatives or friends as were in Mutti's schemes. She was now regularly updating changes of itinerary in letters to Marlene, which she dropped into letterboxes whenever we saw one. What hope there was of the mail being collected, we could not tell.

The inhabitants of Pomerania were beginning to join our treks going west. We could tell the newcomers on the road by the larger piles of luggage on their wagons. Whole pigs, hurriedly slaughtered, hung bundled into sheets from the back of vehicles, well refrigerated in the air. Temperatures were between 20 and 30 degrees minus, we were told.

The ground was too hard to bury those who died on the way. We saw bodies by the roadside, lightly covered with branches. More pious families took their dead along for future burial when spring came. But we met one family whose hopes for a spring funeral were shattered by thieves: their dead grandmother, who had hung in a sheet like other people's pigs, disappeared overnight. Katya collapsed into shameless laughter while I tried more shamefully to hold back an irreverent demonstration of amusement. I almost choked with the effort while Mutti sobbed in deeply felt sympathy. "How can people steal at a time like this?" she stammered, making me feel guilty for my impious sense of humour and for my blue-and-yellow decaffeinated secret.

Hopes of bed-and-breakfast accommodation in Pomerania did not materialize, which worried me on Mutti's account. For myself I found a romantic pleasure in nights spent outdoors, alternating between sheds and stables.

We had officially registered our trek at a road block in one of the first Pomeranian villages: Home base of trek; Number of vehicles; Number of horses, and of persons divided into categories of men, women, children; Name of trek leader, for which Mutti wanted me to put mine.

We were then given a duplicate of the form with spaces for official directions to our next destination and columns for ticks from the supervisors of our night quarters, as well as a column for numbers fed from dixies around noon every day. We were given hot – or nearly hot – boiled swedes, ladled out by women from the *Winterhilfe* organization, who tried to keep us at arm's length and dipped our cups into sterilizing liquid as soon as we had finished the meal. This again made Mutti feel indignant. How could anyone expect us to carry infection! I too found the ladies' attitude upsetting and decided to live up to their expectations by scratching my head vigorously when I awaited my turn at the dixie, sometimes even putting my hand inside the collar to scratch my shoulders. Mutti did not approve of my behaviour, least of all when Katya joined in the fun. But she let us be.

I did not approve of swedes for humans, anyhow. We had used them at home to cut little pieces for lambs in winter. Nevertheless, it was pleasant to feel the warmth of thick soup inside me.

Sometimes we were directed to nothing but a field for the night, or a town square; occasionally we lit a camp fire. But every evening, regardless of whether we were outside, in barns, sheds, schools, there were requests for "the girl with the accordion". It pleased my mother to discover how my fame had spread and to hear how much pleasure I could give to others with my amateurish efforts.

I was much happier than I could possibly have told Mutti. How sad it would have seemed to her that I enjoyed the freedom from no longer being the daughter of the richest tax-payer of the district! To be free from pillars of support! I was now a nobody and very much a somebody at the same time, aware of my responsibilities for the well-being of so many.

One day, when we reached the Baltic coast in our zigzag travels, I ran along the sandy beach and could have shouted with joy. Somewhere, a long way to my right, these waters were touching Cranz, Rossitten and childhood holidays. Straight ahead I could sense Sweden and a wide, mysterious world of foreign travel. The water held a promise of adventure that made my skin tingle with excitement.

"Looking for amber… building sandcastles… coming face-to-face with an elk in a thunderstorm… Do you remember?" Mutti asked with a sigh.

"Oh yes, all that and all the past and so much future, too."

Where were we going? Presumably to the West, but where did the West begin?

"In Belgium," said Fernand.

"In America," said Big Volodya, and Marusha nodded enthusiastically.

"In England," I said, "in a Lord's mansion, with an open fireplace, a bulldog and a butler carrying a plum pudding."

"I thought you did not like English things."

"We weren't discussing what we like, but where the West begins. Do you want to go west, Volodya?" I asked Vitya's father. When he only shrugged his shoulders and smiled, Mutti answered for him with a firm "No!"

But we had no choice. We were twisted along and through Pomerania towards Mecklenburg. "For the time being…"

Berlin was not that far, but almost behind us now. Rumours spoke of the city being bombarded by Russian artillery. We heard no battle noises and saw no planes. Place names had no meaning except for Mutti, who kept a meticulous record and altered itinerary projects according to the latest changes in anticipation of choice. Sometimes she considered leaving our trek and trying rail travel in order to find Marlene, but she could not bring herself to abandon me to all those foreigners in our convoy. Why was it that we never met any of our old friends on the road? They must all be on the way as we were.

Then, one evening when Volodya was playing the accordion near a camp fire, a dumpy man rushed through the crowd and nearly knocked Little Volodya over with a big bear hug. "Misha! Is it really you, Misha?" It was Volodya's cousin, who had been given up for dead when German soldiers had led him away more than three years ago. He had been deported to work for a small farmer in the corner of West Prussia that was on our side of the Vistula. "I am here with them now," he said in Russian and then, having been introduced to us all, he took Mutti and me along to meet "Mama and Papa Seefeldt".

Papa was a short, thin man and Mama an enormously fat woman, whose big bosom heaved as she struggled for breath when Misha pulled her towards us. She was quite unlike any of Mutti's old friends, more like a washerwoman, like Frau Schalonka. But Mutti was genuinely delighted to find such company, and at our next stop we made it official that the Seefeldts were part of our trek.

In name I remained the leader; in practice Frau Seefeldt took charge with great resolution. She would suffer no nonsense, and for a start we all had to celebrate with a bottle of schnapps, which the Seefeldts had originally hidden towards victory celebrations. "To friendship and family reunion," the woman raised her glass. She was so delighted that the two Russian cousins had found each other: it had to be a good omen for us all.

The Seefeldts had become separated from their daughter in a panic situation when Red Army and German refugees had mingled.

Mutti wiped the neck of the bottle before she had a sip, which immediately made her hiccup. "Take a bigger gulp," Frau Seefeldt commanded. Mutti obeyed, and the hiccups stopped.

One night we were offered accommodation in a school. We could feel the heat from the two straw-decked classrooms as we stood in the small entrance hall and decided to pull out the snow from each other's necklines before it had the chance to melt and soak our clothing. Mutti was so ticklish that she giggled like a schoolgirl when I excavated snow from her back.

That done, I opened the classroom door. Dyeda was standing beside me, with Vitya holding on to both of us. Immediately we entered, a tall man sprang up from the straw and yelled at me *"Russenhäuptling raus!"* ("Out with you, Russian chieftain!") I wanted to answer back, but while I was still gasping to recover from the surprise, I felt myself pulled firmly from behind and heard Frau Seefeldt's voice in my ear: "Don't argue; he has a revolver and he means it."

So we all backed into the entrance hall. But that man, who still boldly – or madly? – exhibited the party badge on his lapel, followed us out, shouting "And not into the other classroom; people like you are only fit for the pig-sty."

"Little does he know how sweet a pig-sty is compared with a sheep shed," I tried to joke; but I felt shaken, and my words did not sound natural, though they were true. We had survived a great variety of accommodation, but where sheep excrement combined with the smell of wool we had found it impossible to stay.

Vitya clung to my hand more firmly than ever, but did not ask any questions and I was grateful for that.

We found a cowshed, a narrow gangway between the backs of cows. It was slightly dangerous. One of us had to stay awake to warn the sleepers whenever a cow began to lift her tail. But it was warm, and the night proved uneventful.

In the morning I washed thoroughly in icy water. I did not do this for cleanliness, but because I needed the moral boost of keeping up standards of civilization against the odds. Sometimes we found water in a tap, sometimes it was a pump, more often I made do with snow. Regardless of weather, I stripped to the waist, took my shoes and socks off, rolled up my trouser legs and enjoyed the self-inflicted ritual.

"You're only three and a half weeks away from the Ukraine, and don't you dare to insist on kilometres," I replied to Katya's question, which had become as much her ritual as washing had become mine.

"Then I'll be home for Easter pudding with lots of almonds and sugar, and you will still have boiled swedes," she replied viciously.

And I will forever stay as slim as I've now become while you grow fat and ugly, I thought, but did not say it aloud.

Weeks later we saw 'that man' again, still wearing the party badge and this time trying to confiscate a horse from refugees who had spare ones. But this time we escaped before he could see us. Not that we had many spare horses left; as they weakened, we had had to abandon them one by one at farms en route, crying our farewells while pretending we would come back for them on our way home one day.

(Some months later still, when I was working for the Canadian Military Government, that very man came to the office to claim compensation 'as a victim of Nazi persecution'.)

Mecklenburg

Meanwhile we were coming to Mecklenburg. Our horses were tired and we travelled slowly. The roads were less icy now, snowfalls less frequent, but spring still seemed a long way off. Since we had lost Illyrier, Big Volodya had travelled in the carriage and Katya had joined Little Volodya on the rack wagon. He was kind, almost fatherly to her, but he was not much fun. Whenever we stopped, Katya came to joke with Big Volodya and, yes, she probably flirted with him. I did not take much notice, but Marusha was sure of it.

One day, when we had lit a fire for a midday rest, I found Katya sitting next to it, cross-legged, with little Vera on her lap. She held the baby clumsily and looked slightly frightened even while she giggled: "Oh dear, oh dear, *O bozhe moy*, I have a baby! My Mama will smack my bottom when she sees it." Marusha had dumped her daughter with the words "You take my man, you take my baby, too," and then she had run off to the forest. The baby's father just stood there, looking embarrassed.

Frau Seefeldt took charge: "Don't just stand there, you great big oaf, go and find your wife – at the double!"

Big Volodya did not argue with the formidable woman. Legs apart, and hands on her hips, she had planted herself in front of him. He turned and ran in Marusha's direction.

"That woman is hysterical and likes scenes; she will come back shortly anyhow," I tried to intervene.

"There is always the first time when something really snaps," Frau Seefeldt growled at me, "and you deserve to be lumbered with the child every bit as much as Katya."

I did not think that I had flirted with Volodya, but Katya was quick to catch the remark and pushed Verushka into my arms. The poor baby yelled at the top of her voice.

"A bit of hollering won't harm her. It strengthens the lungs," was Frau Seefeldt's opinion before she distanced herself from the scene. But Verushka did not settle for 'a bit': she just yelled and yelled and must have been heard miles away. Little Volodya well-meaningly added to the row with a lullaby on the accordion. The parents just left us holding the baby while they enjoyed a long reconciliation in some private spot.

Vitya held his ears and ran to Mutti, who was writing a letter in the carriage. I had not told her of rumours that people from Silesia and Saxony had begun to join the exodus.

The Mecklenburgers seemed to enjoy the same abundance of swedes as the Pomeranians and nothing else, until one day, at the outskirts of a small town, word went round that a baker was baking bread. Frau Seefeldt and I ran along with people who seemed to know where they were going, while the vehicles waited in the road. Soon we smelt the aroma of fresh baking, which made my mouth water.

I had our documents with me, and Mutti had by some intuition thrown her purse to me when I set off. The baker was actually selling bread for money, but rationing it according to the number of people on our papers. Frau Seefeldt was just in front of me in the queue, and I blushed with embarrassment when I heard her argue that she was the leader of a trek with fourteen people, including two small children, and that one loaf was not enough, nor could she be expected to run back for the papers with her bad asthma. She puffed and panted so convincingly that I hid in shame and allowed several people to go ahead of me.

For my papers I accepted the one loaf I was given and paid the price the baker asked. Several people grumbled about black market prices, but I could not have cared less, even if I had known the price of bread. Very happy, I clutched the warm loaf and ran back to the trek.

Just then a convoy of American prisoners-of-war was led past on our road.

"Brot, Brot!" they shouted pleadingly.

I threw my loaf without thinking and even as I saw it fly through the air I groaned: "Oh shit, I didn't mean it!" It was too late. For a moment I felt guilty and wretched: that bread had not been mine to give. Suddenly all sorts of things were flying back to me: chocolate, Nescafé, condensed milk, Lucky Strike cigarettes…

Lucky strike indeed! Frau Seefeldt arrived with a number of loaves hidden under her coat. She had joined the queue more than once, each time with a different story. "Fought for and paid for with good money," she said.

We tore chunks off her bread – oh, it was good!

Vitya viewed the chocolate suspiciously and pulled a face when he tasted it, but then memories of the flavour seemed to come back and he enjoyed the rare treat while the men and I lit a Lucky Strike. But we were at a loss as to what we could do with the tins, so we put them under the coachman's seat.

Luck struck again in the evening. We were allocated a field near a farmyard and had permission to light a fire. In an effort to atone for the bread I had thrown away, I went to the farmhouse and asked if we might borrow a tin opener and possibly a kettle with water in return for some real coffee, albeit instant. I told the farmer's wife my story.

She was very kind and offered us the use of their kitchen. She was not afraid of our vermin potential, and all of us were invited. We were given a real meal – by which I mean that it was without swedes – and stewed apple for dessert. Who ever heard of dessert except for birthdays and Sundays?

"It is Sunday today," our hostess laughed. We added the condensed milk to this course. None of us had ever tasted it before, and all of us loved it. Then – oh what bliss to abandon the simple life for one night! – the children had a bath and Vitya had a cot for himself, while the rest of us shared the other five beds we were offered. We sat with the farmer's family long into the night, drinking Nescafé and smoking Lucky Strike.

"When will we ever have such a feast again?" Mutti pondered as we lay in bed.

"Oh that," I replied carelessly. "That was only the hors d'oeuvres before the dinner with the English lord I mentioned."

"More likely to be a Russian commissar," someone joked. "They are beginning to cut us off at the Elbe, I was told."

"What utter rubbish," I said firmly before Marusha had the chance to scream.

But was it really rubbish? And if not, where would we find Marlene if we made it to the other side? Through our Belgian friends, of course, and all would be well even if the entire former Germany were renamed and turned into some republic of the Soviet Union. What did names matter, after all?

Goebbels thought otherwise, or at least he said other things. We heard his voice blaring across the market place of the little town where we spent the night outdoors a few days later. Was it someone's idea of a joke to turn those loudspeakers on us? To mock us with a final insult? Or did Goebbels mean to comfort us as we huddled under sheepskins, trying to get some sleep?

There must have been about a hundred refugees, wagons crammed side by side, tired horses munching hay on the ground, men standing around, smoking dried clover, and every now and then a child whimpering, unaware of Goebbels.

"… Our gallant troops…" – I remembered the soldiers on the dyke, those who lifted their arms, and the one who took Illyrier. "Final victory… the new V2 weapons about to devastate those capitalist countries supporting the Bolsheviks… the Bolsheviks themselves already in disarray, demoralized, desperate… great Russian plains opening up to the spirit and energies of German enterprise and civilization…" On and on came the voice on the radio waves from some safe distance.

Safe from the explosive tensions here on the market place, anyhow. But really safe? And yet, even here, amid hard laughter and sarcastic snorts I could hear some cheerful exclamations: "That means we will be going home soon."

"Why isn't it Hitler talking to us today? Has he lost his voice by now?" someone shouted across the square. Perhaps Goebbels's words might have been more effective from the mouth of the Führer himself, but for the first time it now occurred to me that the most hypnotic voice is nothing without a Minister of Propaganda to get the packaging right. Karla had expressed ideas to that effect in the Labour Service, and I had not believed her then. I wondered how she had been punished.

The terrifying power of the propaganda machine was still at work. I remembered the professor of newspaper science who had spoken of "those who own radio waves and newspapers". It was the same all through history, he said, long before the word 'propaganda' was invented to describe the process; it applied in democracies as much as in dictatorships, or almost as much. It depended on the availability of finance, for that was what controlled our minds.

I was no longer listening to Goebbels, nor to his audience, but was inventing essays in preparation for my return to university. A lovely dream of the future; but that, alas, was one thing that certainly was controlled by finance. My newly-won freedom from property began to taste a little bitter. Perhaps Mutti's nostalgia for the past had more solid foundations than my hopes for the future?

The two national anthems screamed at us from the loudspeakers. Goebbels appeared to have finished. Then I saw many people standing up inside their wagons and lifting their right arms; and I was certain that nostalgia for the past was misplaced, whatever the future. Other refugees also knew it and remained seated or lying down during the anthems.

"What would Uncle Egon say now?" Mutti wondered.

When we were directed further south at our next stop, the authorities were confronted with rebellion. Not from us, because Marlene lived in a southerly part, nor from several other refugees who simply did not care. But many East Prussians longed for a countryside similar to the one they had left behind, and they had been led to expect such a country in Schleswig-Holstein. So they whipped their tired horses to canter northward from the prescribed route.

We saw a sign marked Hanover, and even my limited knowledge grasped a certain geographical context.

West of the Elbe

We crossed the River Elbe at Dannenberg, but once again an important crossing failed to rouse my emotions to the dramatic climax I had anticipated.

We suddenly heard a loud, eerie noise, a mechanized cross between a scream, a groan and a squeak.

"Air-raid sirens," someone shouted.

Big Volodya jumped from his seat and threw his cap into the air. "Hooray, hooray! We must be in the West!"

But Dyeda urged us to lie down flat in a roadside ditch and await events.

That was it: the Elbe had made a clean, clear incision between East and West, between past and future. We drifted in limbo, detached from the old life and unable to imagine a new existence in the dense mists ahead, somewhere beyond dreams.

We joked, of course, of hunting gentlemen in England and of philosophers in France, of Hollywood-style life in the New World, or life among the sheep of Australia. But we did not aspire to any of these, nor indeed to anything else.

"How far are we now from the Ukraine?" Katya was beginning to irritate me, and I replied with malice: "Hundreds and hundreds of kilometres away."

If I had expected her to burst into tears, I was mistaken. Her question was no longer more than a daily ritual, and even when Little Volodya tried to comfort her, she only shrugged her shoulders with a snort. Whether it was days, weeks or months before she would hug her mother in Odessa or Kiev was no longer im-

183

portant, and she knew that neither of the other former citizens of the Soviet Union cared in the least. Neither of them wanted to go back to the scenes of their traumatic past, and Katya was alone. But I admired the fire of hope and of revenge in her eyes.

Our trek drifted the way we were told to go until we saw a road sign to Uelzen. Mutti came to life and shouted for us to turn in that direction.

"You can't," said the official by the crossroads, "you are going to Rotenburg an der Wümme."

"Maybe we will later," Mutti replied firmly, "but first we are going to see my son, who is a soldier in Celle."

To my surprise the man allowed us to turn. My heart was beating under my chin. It had been more than eight weeks since we had last heard from Claus, and I tried to warn Mutti that he might well have been sent to the front by now.

"Don't be absurd," Mutti reprimanded me with conviction, "they don't send young boys into battle when they have just begun their training."

She was right, and Claus was delighted to see us. He fondled the surviving horses, cursed the soldier who had stolen Illyrier, but did not dwell on the sad circumstances of our reunion. Nor did he tell us that he had orders to join a fighting battalion on the following day. We had a celebration meal together and slept in real beds in a hotel.

Freyersen

Next day we set forth in a northward direction again, but when we reached Rotenburg we found the small town full to capacity and were told to move still further north. Mutti pointed out one of the wonders of the Third Reich when we crossed the Hamburg-Bremen autobahn. I wondered if such a wide motorway would ever be full of traffic. Our own road was still very crowded, albeit less so than a few weeks ago. I was driving our carriage in front of the other vehicles, following instructions which were given at various crossroads.

It was already dark when two huge barn doors opened and swallowed us up. I had not been able to see much of the village, whose name was Freyersen; but inside this barn or whatever it was two stable lanterns were suspended from the ceiling. I could see that several farm carts stood in the centre where we had stopped. On our left were the backs of a number of cows, on our right two horses, and I heard a man say that the space next to them was for our four. While Big Volodya unharnessed the horses and tied them to their places, the rest of us were given long, emotional hugs by a big, friendly woman who introduced herself as Mimi Brinkmann. She was full of pity, particularly for our little ones, Vitya and Verushka. I vaguely wondered where the rest of our trek had disappeared, but there was no time to ask questions for a while.

Mimi – whom we all preferred to call 'Frau Brinkmann' – showed us the pump behind a partition. There were a number of buckets and brooms, a large wash tub and a small bowl on a stool. It was the family washroom. We were told we could use the family soap that evening to give us time to unpack in peace next day. We smiled at the illusions this woman seemed to have with regard to our provisions for hygiene, but did not enlighten her.

She opened a small door which led to the large kitchen. We were told that we could use a spare pot-hole on their range, though we would also find an iron stove in our room, which we might not want to heat in summer.

From the kitchen we went to the spacious entrance hall. The Golubovs' room was on the left. It was just big enough for one double bed and a bedside table squeezed in next to it, a single chair at the other end.

Opposite was the farmers' 'best room', now furnished with a bed as well as the sofa, table and chairs that must have been there before refugees were expected. As we opened the door, we saw several mice scampering out of sight. An involuntary squeak escaped from Mutti's mouth. The farmer's wife smiled and apologized for the shock. She patted Mutti's shoulders in a reassuring way: "You will get used to mice. Unfortunately there is nothing we can do to stop them coming in; we have to leave a gap along the floorboards for ventilation to stop dry rot."

"Of course, of course," our brave, ladylike mother replied, "I quite understand. It was only the unexpected movement that made me jump." I did not dare look round for Volodya, who seemed to be having a coughing fit.

Mutti's dignified self-control amazed me. When she went on to express admiration for the layout of the farm, I was not at all sure if she really meant it. She sounded absolutely sincere. Perhaps it was a good idea to have everything under one roof, animals, barn, hayloft, granary, all except for pigs and the family lavatory, which were in a building joined to the main one at right-angles near the washroom door.

There was one other, totally detached amenity, standing opposite our windows, half-way between the farms of the Brinkmann and Heinz families. It was the bread oven shared by the two families, about three yards long and a yard in height, made of brick with a rounded roof and a small chimney-pipe.

Later that evening we discovered that the Seefeldts, their Misha and the two Mosins had been billeted next door. I asked Little Volodya where Vitya should stay and was glad when he replied that the best place was with his Mama.

Mutti's politeness was tested to the limit when we were invited to share our farmer's family supper. We were introduced to the rest of the family, four boys, one of them about Vitya's age, and one cheerful, neatly dressed girl called Marianne. They all sat round a refectory table by the kitchen windows. There was a communal stew bowl at either end and we each had our own spoons to dip in and satisfy our appetites. Volodya glanced at me, and I quickly looked away so that I could stifle my laughter at my mother's gallant attempts to suppress her disgust. I more than made up for her lack of appetite, and Frau Brinkmann patted me with approval.

"Thank God we can cook for ourselves tomorrow," Mutti said when we were alone in our room, "I could taste other people's spit with every spoonful." The delicious smells of the Brinkmanns' cooking never made her feel envious.

With slight reservations about mice and the difficulties of keeping our few clothes and meagre rations safe from their greed, I was grateful for a benevolent fate that had led us to Freyersen.

The village was no more than a small hamlet, separated from the larger Weertzen by a stream, heathland and forest. All but one of the farms were built under one roof, like the Brinkmanns', though two families had erected two-room cottages for later retirement. Now these were occupied by refugees.

In one of these lived a bombed-out couple from Hamburg, a divorced young woman and her artist brother. They were the villagers' contact to the Hamburg black market. We had no food for barter, of course, but were sometimes on the receiving end, because the two young people seemed to like me and often invited me to their Bohemian parties. I found their eccentric sophistication vaguely interesting and the tasty gifts I was allowed to take back to Mutti and Vitya rather more so.

The inhabitants of the other retirement cottage – at the far end of the village, inside the forest – came to our notice on the day after our arrival. It was 'that man', Katya reported. I was taking no chances, even though Katya swore that he no longer wore his party badge. So he too was expecting the arrival of the Allied troops. I hoped and prayed that we would not have to wait long.

Mutti met the wife when she was collecting ration cards and accepted an invitation for coffee – but not before Marlene reached Freyersen, when she would feel more relaxed.

Mutti travelled to Rotenburg post office every day for news from my little sister. At last there came a letter, poste-restante, saying that they had all managed to leave Bautzen before the Soviet troops arrived and were now at a Thuringian address. It seemed quite possible that their particular area would also be occupied by the Red Army soon, so there was no time to be lost. Mutti set out straight away on a long journey, struggling with train delays and air-raids at stations, but persevering until she brought Marlene to Freyersen.

During my mother's absence I visited my Labour Service friend Rita for a day in Hamburg. Vitya came with me and could not comprehend the throng of people on trains and platforms. "So many people! So many people!" he kept shouting, and people looked round and smiled at "that sweet little East Prussian refugee". Had he lost his Russian looks?

Rita did not think so. She found Vitya far more beautiful than any German child and took us round to various friends who were likely to have cast-off clothes for the little boy; but not before she had made me look respectable in one of her old dresses and proper sandals!

Rita's father was keen to practise his amateur photography on Vitya in new clothes. He provided an array of toys to absorb the little boy's attention while the camera clicked and clicked.

Meanwhile Rita's mother produced an equally absorbing meal. All the ingredients came from the father's patients, because he practised his homeopathy for payments in food, which were more realistic than money. Between bites, with his mouth full of tasty food, Vitya kept singing his favourite song: "Butter, butter, butter, butter..." to the tunes of German and Russian nursery rhymes in turns.

We did not risk an air-raid night in Hamburg, nor would I consent to games of hide-and-seek among precariously leaning ruins. But there were large areas of totally flattened houses on the way to the station, where Vitya could jump from big stones and duck behind piles of rubble.

On my return to the village Frau Brinkmann hardly gave me time to put Vitya to bed before she wanted an urgent talk. The grocer's wife in the big village – a rival of one of Frau Brinkmann's sisters, who owned the second grocery shop – was the leader of the local Nazi Women's League. "Make no mistake, she is a fanatic," Frau Brinkmann explained. "She prays every morning and every night on her knees in front of Hitler's picture! So now you know how dangerous she is."

This woman had been complaining to people in her shop about me and a Russian boy, saying that something would have to be done about it. She had written to her superiors.

"So what can I do now?" I asked.

"Well, we don't want to push the poor little mite out of the house, but I don't quite see how to avoid serious trouble. Could we say that he was staying with Marusha and Volodya? Would they lie with us?"

I was sure that they would, far less sure that Vitya would, or even should. Having kept up certain standards in adversity, we must not now succumb to teaching a four-year-old to lie.

"You can easily deny that you knew where Vitya was sleeping. You've never seen him in bed, have you? As for me, I'll just have to hope for the best..." And pray for the arrival of the Allies, I thought. I was not as brave as I tried to sound.

Where were the British, or the Americans? We heard of bridgeheads here and there, but our geography was becoming more confused every day. Hurry up, come and make an end to this war, whoever you are! I copied Claussin's Belgian address on several pieces of paper and distributed them to various drawers and pockets of clothes in the big wardrobe in the entrance hall.

The Last Month

April 1945, and still no sign of the occupation army.

It was Vamir, the Brazilian, who came first. He and Rita had walked from Hamburg and knocked at our window at dawn. Why now of all times? I had not met Vamir before, but Rita had told me about her boyfriend, a Brazilian student at the university. Since his country had declared war on Germany the young man had naturally lost contact with his family and that had been his only restriction. There was no internment scheme in Germany, or at least there had not been.

"But now Himmler is in charge of Hamburg and foreigners are in danger," Rita explained. "We must hide Vamir."

"How do you propose to do that?"

"In your room?"

"But Rita, people keep coming without even knocking at the door during daytime. And if Vamir lay flat under the sofa Vitya would consider it a good game of hide-and-seek. I can just hear him shout cheerfully: 'There he is!' when an outsider enters the room."

"We could pretend he is an ethnic German", Mutti suggested.

"With his Hispanic looks?" I wondered, but it seemed the only chance, provided the Allies arrived soon... and provided that nobody came to do something about my relationship with a Russian child, of course. I had not told Mutti or Marlene about that particular threat.

Again I was in a situation where it seemed as well to be hanged for a sheep as for a lamb. Rita was my friend.

Fortunately our farmers swallowed the ethnic bit, so the first hurdle was overcome. The second proved more difficult and dangerous. Every newcomer – visitor, evacuee or refugee – had to register with the local mayor after the first three days. Those days went by, at once too fast and too slowly. We waited in vain for a foreign army to rescue us.

Rita and Vamir slept under the table in our room. At first Marlene and I had generously offered to sleep in the hayloft. After all, we were used to mice by now, hardly taking any notice when they scampered across our eiderdowns. So we climbed the ladder, lay down in the hay, listened and talked to frighten the creatures away from our bodies. We talked and talked, too frightened to fall asleep all night. The things running about in the hayloft sounded heavier than mice; their squeaks were louder. Marlene and I humbly withdrew the offer of space in our refugee quarters.

Luckily the mayor lived at the far end of the big village, close to the forest and a small footbridge across the stream. So we rambled along woodland-and-heathland paths on our way to Rita's and Vamir's registration. As a matter of fact we knew the mayor in person and could have trusted him, but we did not want to involve him in risks at this stage of the war. So Vamir conveniently disappeared in the thicket while I accompanied Rita to the edge of the stream. Then she registered herself as our visitor, duration of visit to be decided according to the air-raid situation in Hamburg.

We behaved as if Vamir had done the same and listened more anxiously than ever for signs of battle. We listened in vain and were totally taken by surprise when British tanks appeared on the muddy main street of our village.

Vamir immediately reported to the commanding officer – and was arrested. It seemed to the British inconceivable that an alien could have lived freely and unmolested unless he was a collaborator. However, it did not take them long to sort out the true facts. Vamir and his fiancée Rita were given permission to remain in our refugee room while we had to move to the Dietmars' chicken house: Mutti, Marlene, Vitya, myself – and Volodya and Dyeda as well.

It was hilarious. Even Mutti had to giggle when we made up our beds on drop trays, three abreast, with feet overlapping in the middle. The chicken house changed our perspective. We had tunnel vision through holes where the knots of the wood had fallen out, and recognised friend or foe by the shape of legs passing our floor-level windows; later, when my house-building instincts produced curtains from scraps of old chequered pillow-cases, we were reduced to recognizing people by the size of their feet.

The weather was fine, and we enjoyed meals on an open fire by our door. Katya, much to Mutti's annoyance, strutted about in the fur coat I had given her during our stay on the dyke of the Vistula. "Lent, not given," Mutti was at pains to explain to me, but Katya obviously thought otherwise and I had mentally written off the coat. The young Ukrainian girl looked very attractive when her plaits jumped and her eyes sparkled, but for some strange reason few British soldiers were taking any notice.

Rita, on the other hand, was a great success with the troops, particularly for her knowledge of so many English and American pop songs. We could hear them on my accordion, spreading through the quiet night air of the village. Vitya tried to make his "Butter, butter" fit the tunes, not very successfully.

We stayed in the chicken house for only a week, but it seemed to us like many months. A Dutch officer serving in the British army came to see us. He felt embarrassed, almost personally responsible for the way we were living and said that we deserved better.

"Why?" I wanted to know.

"Because you have adopted a Russian child." His answer shocked me. Was he implying that there should be different standards for different nationalities even among civilians? He understood my point and apologized. But would we at least accept some army rations of corned beef, chocolate and coffee?

Yes, we would, and thanked him for the treasures.

I wondered why he talked to me in English when his German was perfect, certainly more perfect than my almost non-existent English.

"Long things in woods with leaves," was my description of trees when I could not remember the word. The Dutchman roared with laughter and asked if I would like to try for a job as interpreter.

"Oh yes," I grinned.

But he was serious. The military government was desperately short of interpreters who were politically sound, and it was unlikely that I should fail the denazification test.

"But what about a language test?"

"You'll do," he replied. "I have tested you."

With my permission he wrote a letter to the military governor at Bremervörde.

We moved back into our room when the troops left the village and Vamir went with them. Rita provided a bottle of whisky for a celebration; others celebrated with illegally brewed alcohol.

Volodya told me he had noticed smells of secret home-slaughter on the farm opposite. He had knocked at their kitchen door, which was not normally locked. "Coffee and cigarettes," he had called through the door.

"Ssh!" warned the farmer's wife when she opened a slit, "the refugees next door will hear you."

"Never mind them," Volodya replied. "I don't want meat, only beets, and the refugees have already given me quite a lot."

"How can they? They have no fields, no beets..."

"Can you denounce them for theft?" Volodya had grinned to them and they had given him all the beets he required to make his schnapps. The Red Cross now provided ex-prisoners and slave workers alike with food, coffee and cigarettes, but not with alcoholic drinks.

"*Na zdorovye!*" Volodya said when he offered us a glass. The stuff tasted awful.

"Good luck", he said when he made me drink a second glass. That morning I had received a letter from the military government's representative in Zeven, saying that in addition to the report by the Dutch officer he had found my name among party documents denouncing me for un-German activities. Could I present myself at his office next morning?

The letter had been delivered by a soldier in a private car.

8th May 1945

Hitler had died in Berlin, "killed in action at the side of his soldiers", German radio had announced; "suicide", the British explained. To me it did not matter which version was true, as long as it speeded the day of German surrender. I had often joked that the war would end on my birthday, and it seemed a good omen that my appointment with the military government should be on the very day I was twenty-two years old – May 8th.

There was still no news of an official end to hostilities in the morning, but Rita and I left for Zeven in an optimistic mood. We had a long sunny day ahead of us, and the best news would come before night – I was convinced of it. Rita waited for me outside the office while I went in.

The white-haired man behind the desk had the brightest blue eyes I had ever seen, or maybe it was the way they smiled that made me think so. He rose to offer me a seat. I noticed that he was tall and thin and that his uniform hung loosely round his body. His skin was sallow, his teeth were yellow, but all that faded into insignificance behind the brightness of his eyes and the reassuring softness of his voice. If only his enunciation had been more intelligible!

"My English is not good," I explained, "I can't understand you."

"It's my accent: I am a Canadian," he said very slowly and smiled at me. "I shall try and talk slowly, and you will soon get used to it. Can you give me your precise address, so that I can pick you up for work tomorrow?"

Was I dreaming? He had spoken so carefully that I could not have misunderstood.

"Really?"

He nodded as he rose to shake hands and open the door for me.

"Oh Rita, Rita, Rita!" We danced in the street with joy. But five miles are quite a distance on a hot day when we had already walked them earlier on. I was impatient for my birthday lunch and eager to tell Mutti my good news. So we tried to attract the attention of passing military vehicles, not exactly by waving them down, but alternating sexy perkiness with an appeal to pity for weary walkers.

I do not know which tactic succeeded in making a lorry stop. The driver's mate came to the back to sit with us and interrogate us about our present life and future aspirations. When I mentioned my journalistic ambitions, he said that he had just been to Lübeck to inspect newspaper offices and printing works with a view to a possible move for his army newspaper, currently produced in Bonn. The arrangements might take a few months, but eventually he would like to employ some German reporters. Could I give him my name and address?

Rita and I looked at each other. Neither of us believed a word of what the soldier said, but what harm could it do to give him what he asked for? After the miraculous interview at the military government's office just about anything seemed possible. I added Edith's address near Bonn for good measure.

190

The soldiers turned off the main road and took us right to our doorstep. So we invited them in for a cup of *Ersatz* coffee. When my little Russian Vitya ran towards me and called me "Mama", the man who had talked to us was absurdly impressed.

He explained that he was a member of the British Communist Party and greatly admired not only Stalin but also Rosa Luxemburg. Mutti cringed at that name, but kept her ladylike composure while I burst out laughing. If he was trying to compare me with that woman just because I had become involved with a little Russian child, he could think again. The man was hurt and began a heated argument which could have been as much fun as such disputes had been with M. Claussin, except that this soldier appeared to have his undoubted intelligence impaired by irrational, immature and almost Dostoyevsky-like obsessions.

Long after the journalist-soldiers had left, I was still waiting for my best birthday present. There were rumours of a surrender, but not until late in the evening did official confirmation come. We went outside to celebrate. In the distance we saw flares like fireworks: the German army was exploding its last ammunition. War in Europe had ended at last. Now we could plan for the future.

Little Volodya and I ignored the curfew rules and walked in the heath. We sat down near a juniper bush and he kissed me very gently and carefully. I replied in the same gingerly manner.

Vitya would decide where we should live.

Vitya

191

Die Krähen schrei'n
Und ziehen schwirren Flugs zur Stadt:
Bald wir es schnei'n –
Weh dem, der keine Heimat hat!

Whirring to the town,
Crows screech as they roam:
Soon snow will fall down –
Pity those with no home!

Nietzsche

APPENDIX I: A Letter from Anna

One of the people to whom I often wrote letters from Prague was my friend Anna, a Polish deportee working on Omi's farm at Alischken. Judging by her replies, I must have written a great deal of pompous nonsense in my eagerness to cheer her up. I have translated one of her long letters, originally written in almost perfect German:

"Yesterday I received your letter. How pleased I was! I wanted to jump, laugh, cry, sing, but fortunately I am old enough to know better. To be serious: singing and laughing is still possible, but jumping would be a bit odd for a 26-year old, particularly with Herr Herzberg [Omi's Inspector] watching. He does not know that you have written to me, nor does Gerda [the village forester's daughter], and you can rest assured that no one will read your dear letters. I read this one many times and afterwards I thought a great deal about it. Anneli, perhaps you are right, perhaps I should not say that fortune is blind, as you say. I am not quite as pessimistic as when I last wrote to you. At that time I was eaten up with longing for my home – such great longing that I was almost going mad.

"I don't know if it has something to do with not having worked at home, except academically, and never having had employment. But those changes are not as bad for me as homesickness. The longing comes suddenly, and then I see the world all grey; the sun darkens; before my eyes I see poor villages, grey houses, but all so much dearer than the most beautiful castles. It does not last long, perhaps a day, or only for a few hours' walk, and then I am calm again. My old professor used to say: 'Anna is like a bird, always gay, always friendly,' and that is so. Deep inside my heart is a battle; blood rises high to my head, but eyes and mouth laugh and they all think: 'Anna is cheerful and happy.' They don't know that being cheerful does not mean being happy.

"Now it is already spring. In the park, in the garden. Thousands of flowers, sweet little violets, white anemones and others. Here and there the trees show a little young green. The park is so beautiful, I must not moan that the world is grey. Oh no! Anneli, in Omi's – Frau Hahn's – garden, or rather in the park, I have discovered a wonderful little corner and in the evenings, when the sun goes to sleep, and when I have to cover the forcing frames for the night, I always go to my corner. There I sit for a long time, like in a dream. How happy I am during those hours, or maybe minutes! The world is beautiful! In the air is the scent of spring; silence, calm. The River Droje murmurs quietly to me, the trees whisper some fantastic news, of suffering, suffering. A scream cuts the evening silence, perhaps an unknown bird. I am far away with my thoughts and perhaps I am not thinking at all? My heart is full of happiness. Without desire, without worry, without longing, I look round and my mouth whispers: 'How beautiful is this world!' At those moments there is no home, no parents, only the beauty of the evening's realm.

"But then I have to go back. 'Anna, where are you?' How sharp the sound of a human voice. I walk back slowly and I probably look serious, because Gerda asks: 'Anna, what are you thinking about? Of your fiancé?' Ha, hm, hm, hm, ridiculous Gerda, a good, but very naïve girl; I have to laugh. She asks so many questions, and I give so many stupid answers... Now I am glad that we shall soon have to do more work in the garden instead of in the kitchen.

"With every day I discover more love for your Omi. Anneli, how grateful I am, she is so good, she never does anything that might hurt my feelings...

"You say that life is only just beginning. Yes, but sometimes I am afraid of this day and of the days to come. This fear is not fear for my person. No! I only want to be a human being, a good human being, to work for old people, to help my people, to be wherever hard work is required. Anneli, Anneli, I feel so strong, I would like to start now to serve my country! I used to think of a profession, of quiet days and hours. I used to think of a simple, calm life. But at other times I dream of being a poor girl – in materialistic terms – leading a hard life like a soldier. How wonderful it must be to fight for every crumb of bread, how wonderful must be the taste of such bread!

"You must know, Anneli, it is now too late for me to start studying philosophy. But there are other meaningful careers. Perhaps I will be a librarian, perhaps a teacher. I don't yet know, but I certainly will never be a good housewife!

"You write that suffering ennobles people. Yes, you are right. As the Latin philosopher said, 'Per aspera ad astra'. Yes, it is true. Every person grows by hard experience, even the earth is fresher and more beautiful after a thunderstorm. Man is like a tree, and sometimes a tree is broken by the wind because it is not strong enough. We too are not strong enough, we have not enough strength, nor enough courage, which is worse. Anneli, I am so excited today, I don't know why. I want to write to you about everything.

"I am a bad girl. Perhaps you don't believe it? Ask your Omi! Sometimes I am so moody, I have to be super-merry and then I am right down and look into myself and cry like a little child. I am not happy, Anneli: not counting those evening hours, I can't be really happy. Perhaps my personal happiness is not so distant from me; but, for heaven's sake, don't think of a man! Yet I see my people, so lost, so poor, and my heart aches... You understand that, don't you? But we must hope for the best. Perhaps we shall again live quietly, our villages full of people, and the houses clean, the children healthy. I keep thinking that all will be well, that the German people will help us. What do you think, Anneli? Then I would be really happy. Anneli, today I can't say I am unhappy. No! How many people must suffer, suffer so much, that my life is bright by comparison with those poor ones. My compatriot in the village here has a hard life. She no longer believes that one could be lucky, be happy. She stands quite alone in this big world. Her parents are dead and she has no sister. She had sad days even as a child. She is never cheerful, she does not know how to laugh. What would I give to make her happy, just for one hour! But how?

"I wanted to write so much to you, but I must stop before I say more and more stupid things. Last year your Omi said that May 8 (or is it 9?) is Anneli's birthday. And that is soon, soon. I want to wish you happy hours, health and all good things you wish for yourself. Between these pages you will find a violet picked in Alischken garden; not a big present; it must be like that; other things I cannot send. The little flower from home, that's it.

"Dear, good Anneli! Be happy, as happy as in childhood, as happy as I am in the silence of the evenings under the big fir tree in Omi's park. You are worthy of great happiness. And don't laugh about that, I don't like compliments, I only say what I think, and sometimes such openness is not good... Must I always write such crazy letters? I wanted to pull myself together....

"A thousand greetings from your Anna.

"P.S.: Please tell me how many mistakes I have made and don't laugh about my letter."

APPENDIX II: Place Names Changed since 1938

As mentioned on page 85, many names of farms, villages and even towns were changed by the Nazi authorities in 1938. Maps issued in 1939, of course, showed only the new names. Those most relevant to this book are listed below and shown on the map on page 5. After the war the names were changed again, this time by the Soviet authorities. No large-scale maps of the area were available in the West between 1939 and the advent of glasnost in the late 1980s, but satellite imagery and online mapping services have now made it much easier to pinpoint place names both old and new. There are also quite comprehensive lists online now, for example at gov.genealogy.net and www.kalte-heimat.de.

Old Prussian	New German	New Russian	Romanized
Alischken	Walddorf	Карпово	Karpovo
Angerapp	Klein-Angerapp	Рапа	Rapa
Aussicht	–	Октябрьское	Oktyabr'skoe
Beynuhnen	Beinuhnen	Чернышевка	Chernyshevka
Darkehmen	Angerapp	Озёрск	Ozyorsk
Gumbinnen	–	Гусев	Gusev
Insterburg	–	Черняховск	Chernyakhovsk
Königsberg	–	Калининград	Kaliningrad
Kowarren	Friedeck	Заозёрное	Zaozyornoe
Lenkehlischken	Gutbergen	Гоголевское	Gogolyevskoe
Mikalbude	Mickelau	Сучково	Suchkovo
Osznagorren	Adlermark	Отпор	Otpor
Rossitten	–	Рыбачий	Rybachy
Skirlack	–	Опоченское	Opochenskoe
Trempen	–	Новостроево	Novostroevo

APPENDIX III: Karl Stratil

Stratil's name (see "Encounter with an Artist", p. 145) features in a number of reference works on the history of German art. Born in the Moravian town of Olmütz (Olomouc, in what is now Czechoslovakia) in 1894, he was forced to give up studying architecture in Vienna by the outbreak of World War I. He fought against the Bolsheviks, was taken prisoner, somehow reached China and eventually found his way back to Leipzig, where he entered the Academy of Art in 1920. He soon made a name for himself as a lithographer, etcher and wood-engraver, earning his living mainly by illustrating books and magazines. After the Second World War he also published some watercolours. He died in Leipzig in 1958. His daughter Dorothée, born in Leipzig in 1931, likewise became an artist.

The books illustrated by Stratil included works by Hartmann von der Aue, Emil Karl Berndt, John Cleland, Charles de Coster, Wolfgang Fikentscher, Gustav Freytag, Arthur Comte de Gobineau, Nikolai Gogol, Ricarda Huch, Erwin Kolbenheyer, Louize Labé, Rainer Maria Rilke, Heinz Rusch, Rosemarie Schuder, Robert Louis Stevenson, Adalbert Stifter, Karl Toth, Aleksei Nikolaevich Tolstoy, and Viktor Wendel.

Collections of his work include:
Erinnerungen an China (6 wood-engravings, 1924)
Prag (20 drawings, 1943)
Mensch und Werk (16 wood-engravings and lithographs, 1950/52)
Berühmte Funde aus der Wikingerzeit (wood-engravings)
Ostseebilder – Der Mensch und die Landschaft (20 watercolours, Berlin 1953)

APPENDIX IV: Further Reading

Works in English (including translations from German):

Skating at the Edge of the Wood
Marlene Yeo (née Wiemer)
Private printing, 2006

Before the Storm: Memories of My Youth in Old Prussia
Marion Countess Dönhoff, translated by Jean Steinberg
Alfred Knopf 1990 (ISBN 978-0394582559)

The Past is Myself
Christabel Bielenberg
Corgi 1988 (ISBN 978-0552990653)

When I Was a German: An Englishwoman in Nazi Germany 1934-1945
Christabel Bielenberg
University of Nebraska Press 1998 (ISBN 978-0803261518)

East Prussian Diary – a journal of faith, 1945-1947
Count Hans von Lehndorff
Wolff 1963 (Amazon ASIN B0000CLPTH)

From East Prussia to North Yorkshire
Hans-Dieter Hundsdoerfer
Old Hall Publishing 2006 (ISBN 978-0955271205)

Ursula – my other life
Pat Skinner
Malvern 1986 (ISBN 978-0947993139)

Flight of the East Prussian Horses
Daphne Machin Goodall
David & Charles PLC 1973 (ISBN 978-0715360613)

Forgotten Land: Journeys Among the Ghosts of East Prussia
Max Egremont
Picador 2011 (ISBN 978-0330456593)

Works in German:

Adlig Gut Alischken
ed. Wulf Dietrich Wagner
Supplement to "Ostpreussisches Bauen", August 1994, Karlsruhe

Namen Die Keiner Mehr Nennt
Marion Gräfin Dönhoff
Diederichs Eugen 2004 (ISBN 978-3896314413)

Weit ist der Weg nach Westen
Tatjana Gräfin Dönhoff
Nicolai'sche Verlagsbuchhandlung 2004 (ISBN 978-3894792152)

Menschen, Pferde, weites Land
Hans Graf von Lehndorff
Beck C. H. 2001 (ISBN 978-3406481222)

Kindheitserinnerungen aus Ostpreußen
Bettina von Arnim
Husum Druck 1987 (ISBN 978-3880423527)

In langer Reihe über das Haff
Patricia Clough
Deutsche Verlags-Anstalt 2004 (ISBN 978-3421051295)

Als die Deutschen weg waren
Adrian von Arburg, Wlodzimierz Borodziej, Jurij Kostjaschow
Rowohlt Taschenbuch 2007 (ISBN 978-3499622045)

Ein Land so weit
Petra Reski
List Taschenbuch 2002 (ISBN 978-3548601540)

Die grosse Flucht: Das Schicksal der Vertriebenen
Guido Knopp
Econ 2002 (ISBN 978-3430155052)

Im Galopp nach Ostpreußen
Heidi Sämann film about rebirth of the Weedern Trakehner stud

OTHER PUBLICATIONS FROM ŌZARU BOOKS

Carpe Diem

This sequel to "Reflections in an Oval Mirror" details Anneli's post-war life. The scene changes from life in Northern 'West Germany' as a refugee, reporter and military interpreter, to parties with the Russian Authorities in Berlin, boating in the Lake District with the original 'Swallows and Amazons', weekends with the Astors at Cliveden, then the beginnings of a new family in the small Kentish village of St Nicholas-at-Wade. Finally, after the fall of the Iron Curtain, Anneli is able to revisit her first home once more

Publication planned for 2012

Ichigensan
– The Newcomer –
David Zoppetti

Translated from the Japanese by Takuma Sminkey

Ichigensan is a novel which can be enjoyed on many levels – as a delicate, sensual love story, as a depiction of the refined society in Japan's cultural capital Kyoto, and as an exploration of the themes of alienation and prejudice common to many environments, regardless of the boundaries of time and place.

Unusually, it shows Japan from the eyes of both an outsider and an 'internal' outcast, and even more unusually, it originally achieved this through sensuous prose carefully crafted by a non-native speaker of Japanese. The fact that this best-selling novella then won the Subaru Prize, one of Japan's top literary awards, and was also nominated for the Akutagawa Prize is a testament to its unique narrative power.

The story is by no means chained to Japan, however, and this new translation by Takuma Sminkey will allow readers world-wide to enjoy the multitude of sensations engendered by life and love in an alien culture.

ISBN: 978-0-9559219-4-0

Travels in Taiwan
Exploring Ilha Formosa
Gary Heath

For many Westerners, Taiwan is either a source of cheap electronics or an ongoing political problem. It is seldom highlighted as a tourist destination, and even those that do visit rarely venture far beyond the well-trod paths of the major cities and resorts.

Yet true to its 16th century Portuguese name, the 'beautiful island' has some of the highest mountains in East Asia, many unique species of flora and fauna, and several distinct indigenous peoples (fourteen at the last count).

On six separate and arduous trips, Gary Heath deliberately headed for the areas neglected by other travel journalists, armed with several notebooks... and a copy of War and Peace for the days when typhoons confined him to his tent. The fascinating land he discovered is revealed here.

ISBN: 978-0-9559219-1-9 (Royal Octavo)
ISBN: 978-0-9559219-8-8 (Half Letter)

West of Arabia
A Journey Home
Gary Heath

Faced with the need to travel from Saudi Arabia to the UK, Gary Heath made the unusual decision to take the overland route. His three principles were to stay on the ground, avoid back-tracking, and do minimal sightseeing.

The ever-changing situation in the Middle East meant that the rules had to be bent on occasion, yet as he travelled across Eritrea, Sudan, Egypt, Libya, Tunisia and Morocco, he succeeded in beating his own path around the tourist traps, gaining unique insights into Arabic culture as he went.

Written just a few months before the Arab Spring of 2011, this book reveals many of the underlying tensions that were to explode onto the world stage just shortly afterwards, and has been updated to reflect the recent changes.

ISBN: 978-0-9559219-6-4

Turner's Margate Through Contemporary Eyes
The Viney Letters
Stephen Channing

Margate in the early 19th Century was an exciting town, where smugglers and 'preventive men' fought to outwit each other, while artists such as JMW Turner came to paint the glorious sunsets. One young man decided to set out for Australia to make his fortune in the Bendigo gold rush.

Half a century later, having become a pillar of the community, he began writing a series of articles for Keble's Gazette, in which he described Margate with great familiarity (and tremendous powers of recall), while introducing his English readers to the "latitudinarian democracy" of a new, "young Britain".

Viney's interests covered a huge range of topics, from Thanet folk customs such as Hoodening, through diatribes on the perils of assigning intelligence to dogs, to geological theories including suggestions for the removal of sandbanks off the coast "in obedience to the sovereign will and intelligence of man".

His writing is clearly that of a well-educated man, albeit with certain Victorian prejudices about the colonies that may make those with modern sensibilities wince a little. Yet above all, it is interesting because of the light it throws on life in a British seaside town some 180 years ago.

This book also contains numerous contemporary illustrations.

ISBN: 978-0-9559219-2-6

The Margate Tales
Stephen Channing

Chaucer's Canterbury Tales is without doubt one of the best ways of getting a feel for what the people of England in the Middle Ages were like. In the modern world, one might instead try to learn how different people behave and think from television or the internet.

However, to get a feel for Margate as it gradually changed from a small fishing village into one of Britain's most popular holiday resorts, one needs to investigate contemporary sources such as newspaper reports and journals.

Stephen Channing has saved us this work, by trawling through thousands of such documents to select illuminating and entertaining accounts of Thanet in the 18th and 19th centuries. With content ranging from furious battles to hilarious pastiches, witty poems and astonishing factual reports, illustrated with over 70 drawings, The Margate Tales brings their society to life, and as Chaucer, demonstrates how in many areas, surprisingly little has changed.

ISBN: 978-0-9559219-5-7

A Victorian Cyclist: Rambling through Kent in 1886
Stephen & Shirley Channing

Bicycles are so much a part of everyday life nowadays, it can be surprising to realize that for the late Victorians these "velocipedes" were a novelty disparaged as being unhealthy and unsafe – and that indeed tricycles were for a time seen as the format more likely to succeed.

Some people however adopted the newfangled devices with alacrity, embarking on adventurous tours throughout the countryside. One of them documented his 'rambles' around East Kent in such detail that it is still possible to follow his routes on modern cycles, and compare the fauna and flora (and pubs!) with those he vividly described.

In addition to providing today's cyclists with new historical routes to explore, and both naturalists and social historians with plenty of material for research, this fascinating book contains a special chapter on Lady Cyclists in the era before female emancipation, and an unintentionally humorous section instructing young gentlemen how to make their cycle and then ride it.

It features over 200 illustrations, and is complemented by a website.

ISBN: 978-0-9559219-7-1

Sunflowers
– Le Soleil –
Shimako Murai

A play in one act
Translated from the Japanese by Ben Jones

Hiroshima is synonymous with the first hostile use of an atomic bomb. Many people think of this occurrence as one terrible event in the past, which is studied from history books.

Shimako Murai and other 'Women of Hiroshima' believe otherwise: for them, the bomb had after-effects which affected countless people for decades, effects that were all the more menacing for their unpredictability – and often, invisibility.

This is a tale of two such people: on the surface successful modern women, yet each bearing underneath hidden scars as horrific as the keloids that disfigured Hibakusha on the days following the bomb.

ISBN: 978-0-9559219-3-3

Lightning Source UK Ltd.
Milton Keynes UK
UKOW020921041111

181475UK00001B/29/P